HONORING NATIVE
WARRIORS

A Tribute to American Indian Service
in the United States Armed Forces

GARY ROBINSON

Honoring Native Warriors
©2024 Tribal Eye Productions

Tribal Eye Productions
P.O. Box 1123
Santa Ynez, CA 93460
TribalEyePro@gmail.com
www.tribaleyeproductions.com

Paperback ISBN: 979-89887862-07
Hardcover ISBN: 979-8-9887862-5-2

FOREWORD

Since America's beginning, whenever the call of duty has come, Indigenous American peoples have stepped forward to proudly defend and serve the United States in both peacetime and in war. Yet, outside their own local communities, many American Indian veterans have not received the recognition they deeply deserve nor, in many cases, have they obtained all the benefits and services they rightfully earned.

This book is another chapter in the ongoing story of unique contributions made to the democracy, freedom, and cultural diversity of America. And, as revealed in these pages, it provides another example of delayed or overlooked recognition experienced by American Indian veterans.

For far too long, American Indian warriors have been this nation's forgotten veterans. Important issues that affect indigenous American veterans include a lack of adequate housing and the inability to receive proper representation to obtain health care, earned compensation, pension, and burial benefits for their families.

Historically, American Indians have served in the armed forces at the highest rate of any ethnic group in the United States, and Indian people have a proud legacy of defending our homeland. These facts must be acknowledged by national Veterans Affairs policies and translated into actions that support our people.

There has long been the need for one effective, representative body that speaks for the American Indian, Alaska Native, Native Samoan and Native Hawaiian Veteran. That's why the non-profit **National American Indian Veterans** organization, or N.A.I.V., was created.

N.A.I.V. is devoted to representing and supporting American Indian and other indigenous veterans and advocating for the improvement of their quality of life, and that of their families. It is the heart, soul, and voice of the indigenous American veteran.

The United States Department of Veteran Affairs recognizes N.A.I.V. as the one national organization to represent the unique needs, concerns, and issues of indigenous veterans to Congress and the Veterans Administration. NAIV has also been recognized as the voice of the American Indian Veteran by the National Congress of American Indians (NCAI) as well as the National Association of States Directors of Veteran Affairs (NASDVA).

Our Federal Charter was introduced in Congress many years ago, and, at long last, has finally been passed and signed into law. This bill is important to Indigenous American Veterans in gaining full recognition of their needs and concerns.

As National Commander of NAIV, I invite you to increase your knowledge and awareness of the important part played by American Indians in the history of our great nation. I also invite you to join us in making a positive difference in the lives of American Indian veterans and their families. For more information call our headquarters at (605) 770-7106, or contact Frank Ramirez in northern California at (916) 224-8049. Thank you.

Don Loudner (Sioux)
National Commander
National American Indian Veterans, Inc.

INTRODUCTION

This book represents years and decades of the work I've done to bring greater awareness of the courage and sacrifice exhibited by Native American men and women who've answered to call of military duty. In these pages, you'll find the text of two entire books I'd previously written and published along with links to video and television documentaries I've help produced about Native American military service and Native American veterans.

I am not a veteran, and I hope that my efforts prove acceptable as part of my "thank you" to those who have served, often in the face of prejudice and distrust aired by mainstream American society.

--the author

ACKNOWLEDGMENTS

Much of the information for this book was rigorously researched, beginning in the 1990s, with the intention of producing a documentary television series for national broadcast. Native American Public Telecommunications (now Vision Maker Media) provided initial funding to conduct the research and create the scripts, for which I am grateful.

However, when it came time to raise the several thousand dollars needed to produce the series, no funding agencies were interested. It seems this project was ahead of its time. My production partner, Phil Lucas, and I spent many years attempting to procure financing, and the project went through several permutations in efforts to provide the various proposal formats required by various funding agencies.

It wasn't until my dear friend, partner, and mentor of twenty-five years, Phil, passed away in 2007 that the idea of converting the material into book form came into being. Phil was a Choctaw filmmaker and teacher who dedicated his life to telling true stories about Native Americans through films and television documentaries.

I miss him and will be indebted to him for the rest of my life.

I also want to acknowledge the financial support provided by the United Indians of All Tribes Foundation, headquartered in Seattle, for their support of the initial publication of *From Warriors to Soldiers*, included here in its entirety within these pages.

Last, but not least, I want to thank generations of Native American men and women who served in all branches of the US armed forces for their sacrifice and service. I particularly want to thank those who willingly participated in the creation of this work, including the multiple original sources (videos, feature stories, etc.) by sitting for interviews, both on and off camera, which is the heart of the story.

CONTENTS

PROLOGUE: I AM THE WARRIOR

"I AM THE WARRIOR"

Gary Robinson c. 2008

HOMELAND SECURITY

Homeland Security is nothing new for Native American people, who have fought to defend their tribal homelands for thousands of years. The names of many legendary native warriors have been noted in America's history books.

Later generations of American Indians continued in the proud warrior tradition by serving in every branch of the United States military as soldiers, sailors, pilots, and paratroopers, fighting alongside their fellow Americans. These are not so well documented in the history books.

So, in these pages, we take space and time to express our thanks for their service, and to honor our American Indian veterans and active-duty soldiers: Honoring Native Warriors.

As we go forward into the future, let us work together for peace and continue to remember them in our thoughts, prayers, and national consciousness.

I AM THE WARRIOR

(This is the transcript of the author's documentary short film "I Am the Warrior."-It won Third Place in the national video competition hosted by the Smithsonian's National Museum of the American Indian, which focused on Native American service in the U.S. military.)

"I was, I am, and I always will be The Warrior. Not as some have portrayed me: the bloodthirsty savage who kills for the sake of killing. But as the guardian, the defender: protecting my family, my people, my homeland. It is my way.

In the ancient days of my people, I learned to become a hunter and warrior by watching and imitating the creatures of nature. The animals taught us and the medicine protected us.

At America's beginning, I was there… to teach the wilderness way of warfare, and thus were the British defeated. When America was divided – blue against gray – I was there as the white man pitted Redman against Redman.

And when America sought to conquer the plains, my scouting instincts were put to use. And so it continued.

In World War One, I went to France and fought for freedom, even though I wasn't allowed to be an American citizen. When hope of winning that war was almost gone, the language of my Choctaw brothers became the code that won that war. But it was soon forgotten.

And during World War Two, twenty-five-thousand of us, more per capita than any other race, left our homes to fight against our common enemies across the seas.

Before Congress in 1945, one of my brothers testified: "As the original Americans, this war really and truly means something to us. Because we are Indians doesn't mean that we do not have as much at stake in the land as you do. Our stake may not mean so much in dollars, but in respect and feeling, it means as much and probably more, because our religion is about the land…"

And so it is today.

Why do I fight on the side of a nation that sought to displace and exterminate me? *That is the question.*

I say: no matter who governs these lands, or by what name they are called, they <u>are</u> my native lands, the lands where my ancestors are buried…. Forever.

And I am still the guardian of these lands, a defender of the blood and bone of my ancestors.

Proudly I serve, and proudly I carry on that ancient tradition. I was, I am, and always will be… The Warrior."

--The Spirit of the American Indian Warrior

FROM WARRIORS TO SOLDIERS

A History of American Indian Service in the United States Military

GARY ROBINSON & PHIL LUCAS

Original Copyright 2008
TRIBAL EYE PRODUCTIONS
Santa Ynez, California

Tribal Eye Productions
P.O. Box 1123
Santa Ynez, CA 93460
www.tribaleyeproductions.com
tribaleyepro@gmail.com
805-245-9630

Initial publication of *From Warriors to Soldiers*
was made possible in part through the financial
support of the *United Indians of All Tribes
Foundation*, Seattle, Washington.
For more information, go to www.unitedindians.org.

To my father, Don Robinson,
a veteran of World War II and the finest
role model any son could have.

Gary Robinson

24

Contents

Dear Readers, Friends, and Relatives,

On behalf of United Indians of All Tribes Foundation (UIATF), I would like to extend our great appreciation and heartfelt thanksgiving to our very dear brother, the late Phil Lucas, and to Gary Robinson for all the great love, energy, dedication, sensitivity, and caring they displayed in the creation of *From Warriors to Soldiers,* which poignantly reflects the voices and dedicated service of our Native American warriors and soldiers.

UIATF was honored to contribute funding to support the publication of this long-overdue book, and we look forward to continuing our support by developing a complementary Web site that will provide an opportunity for our warriors, veterans, and their friends and relatives to relate the heartfelt stories of military service and sacrifice reflected in *From Warriors to Soldiers*.

As always, it is our prayer that you and your beloved ones are in the very best of health and happiness.

With warm, respectful, and loving greetings,

Phil Lane Jr.
Chief Executive Officer
United Indians of All Tribes Foundation
Seattle, Washington

FROM WARRIORS TO SOLDIERS INTRODUCTION

"What does it mean to be a warrior in the traditional Native American cultural sense? It means doing what's right, even when it's difficult and requires sacrifice."

—Native American Vietnam War Veteran

There's an American military cemetery and memorial in France that few Americans are aware of. It is located twenty-six miles north of Verdun at a place called Meuse-Argonne, and it contains the remains of more than fourteen thousand American military personnel. There you will find row upon row of identical gravestones bearing the name of American soldiers killed during World War I. You might be surprised to read the names on some of the gravestones. Mixed in with the "typical" GI Joe names are those of Native Americans, names like "Joe Standing Bear" and "Leon Little Wolf." These men, these Native American soldiers, most of them volunteers, lie here—so far from the sacred land of their fathers.

Some seventeen thousand American Indians volunteered for military service during World War I, even though they weren't allowed to become citizens of the United States until 1924, seven years after that war ended.

The truth is that from the American Revolution up until today, Native American people have served the United States unfailingly in battle and have sacrificed their lives and resources for a nation that was once their enemy. Today, Native American men and women continue to enlist and serve with distinction in all branches of the armed services at rates that far exceed other ethnic groups, and their tribal communities carry on proud traditions that include the honoring of those who've participated in the defense of their homeland.

This book tells the untold story of those brave heroes, and it is written in honor of all Native American veterans of all tribes to bring much- deserved attention to the dedication and sacrifice offered up by Native Americans of all tribes in all parts of the United States.

PART ONE
Native Warriors:
Myth and Reality

The Warrior—*The Chiricahua Apache who became known as Geronimo was the epitome of the Indian warrior. Though originally a peaceful farmer and family man, he led the resistance against white encroachment of Indian lands after his family was killed by U.S. soldiers. (National Archives Photo)*

A True Warrior—*Typical of most tribal leaders, Nez Perce Chief Joseph avoided warfare whenever possible. However, when the United States took his tribal lands, he led his people on a cross-country retreat that managed to elude the army's best military commanders beyond all expectations. His maneuvers were studied and later taught to cadets at West Point. (National Archives Photo)*

PART ONE—NATIVE WARRIORS: MYTH AND REALITY

Native American powwows—you can find dozens of these colorful, social events during spring and summer months in major cities or on any of the three hundred or so Indian reservations in the United States. Based on ancient Plains Indian traditions, modern powwows began springing up around the United States after World War II as a way for the growing urban Indian populations to maintain cultural connections within what was to them an alien environment.

A powwow is a bountiful blend of tribal singing, dancing, eating, camping, and visiting among family and friends that attracts dancers, drummers, vendors, indigenous craftspeople, and spectators from far and wide. They all come for one reason: to participate in something uniquely Native American, something that preserves and honors the best aspects of native cultures.

Dancers often compete for prize money in a variety of native dance categories, including the Jingle Dress, Ladies Buckskin, Men's Traditional, and Men's Fancy Dance, to name a few. Each dance category is known for its own style of movement and regalia, while each dancer within a category expresses his or her own individuality through variations in dance style and clothing.

Every dance session of a powwow begins with the Grand Entry, the procession that brings all the dancers into the arena. At the front of the line, moving to the beat of the drum and bringing in the American flag, state flag, and traditional Eagle Staff, are Native American veterans. They may be dressed in dance regalia, street clothes, or sometimes their military uniforms, proudly carrying the colors and leading all the dancers into the arena.

And the crowds of onlookers stand, doff their hats, and watch attentively as the flags and the veterans circle the arena. To many, this is more than pomp and circumstance; it is part of a sacred culture. It is one of the more public ways that native people honor their veterans and acknowledge their sacrifice and service for the good of the nation.

Why have American Indians served, and why do they continue to serve, a government that has betrayed and broken promises to native peoples for multiple generations? Why do so many American Indians take pride in military service?

Native American men and women who have served their country's military with pride may be able to help answer such questions. They often gather to share experiences and insights during powwow weekends, as a dozen or so did at a 4th of July powwow a few years ago. They begin by talking about the reasons for Native American service.

The Powwow: A place of honor for Native American veterans

At Native American powwows, it is traditional for veterans to be honored for their sacrifice and service by bringing in the colors during the Grand Entry, which begins each session of dancing. Photo taken by the author at the Oneida Powwow, July 1992.

Among the flags carried by the veterans is the tribe's Eagle Staff, featuring a row of eagle feathers, each feather representing a tribal member who has served. Photo by the author.

Menomonee Vietnam Veteran Apesanahkwat proudly displays his military service in this unique display of quill work on his powwow dance regalia. Photos taken circa 1992.

"Most American Indians don't view their military service as something simply patriotic," stated Northern Cheyenne Vietnam veteran Windy Shoulderblade. "It's something deeper than that, passed down from generation to generation. It was our fathers—it was our grandfathers. The warrior status was always an achievement for Indian men. They have always gone to face the enemy when it was their turn."

"Members of my tribe, the Oneida, have served the United States in every conflict since the Revolutionary War," Amos Christjohn offered. "We helped out General Washington back then and taught the American colonials how to fight the Indian way."

"Native Americans have a great deal of respect for the Supreme Being, the Creator," stated Douglas Long, a Korean vet of the Winnebago tribe. "The eagle is the one who can fly the highest, and the elders have taught us to respect this bird. We hold the eagle feather to be very sacred. Each one of the tribes has an Eagle Staff, and the only way that another feather can be added to that staff is through experiences of defending their territory. And so that tradition continues even today."

The reasons for Native American participation in the U.S. military are as complex and unique as their ways of fighting. Historically, the unique style of native warfare was noticed by British American colonists and military personnel in the 1700s.

"Indians are the only match for Indians, and without them [on our side] we shall ever fight on unequal terms," stated then Colonel George Washington in 1756 during the French and Indian War, an extended war fought between the British and the French from 1754 to 1763.[1] Caught in the middle of an essentially European-based war, American Indians fought on both sides of that conflict.

British General John Forbes, writing of his experiences during the same war, attested to the natives' prowess at what would come to be called "guerilla warfare tactics," a term coined many generations later. In a letter from the battlefield to his superiors in Philadelphia, he told of the "howling out in the forest" that came from Native American warriors who flitted from one tree trunk to another. Forbes watched in horror as British soldier after British soldier fell to snipers' bullets, though the sources for the mortal rounds could not be located.

General George Washington remembered well his previous first-hand experiences with the effectiveness of Indian warriors, and after the Revolutionary War got under way, he convinced the Continental Congress to allow him to employ Indians in his colonial army. He knew they'd be of excellent use mixed with his regular army as scout and light troops.

Oneida veteran Amos Christjohn offered additional insights regarding native warfare techniques. "We learned a lot about conducting warfare from watching our four-legged brothers, the animals, and we have always respected the strength of their powers," he said.

Differentiating between Euro-American warfare tactics and Native American techniques, Windy shared something he learned from his tribe. "The Cheyenne rule was for each member of a warrior band not to wait for orders or try to do like the rest," Windy explained. "He could retreat if he wanted to, but he would be criticized by many who watched the battle. White Elk and the others used to say the white men have a poor way of fighting. They all listen to one man say 'shoot,' and sometimes the warriors could come up behind them before they had time to turn around."

Anthropologist and author Jack Weatherford has studied and written about the accomplishments of Native Americans, including American Indian warfare techniques. His book *Native Roots* includes a chapter on this topic.

According to Weatherford, Indians did not line up in formation and march onto a large field, as did European armies. They fought the same way they hunted, using stealth, camouflage, and familiarity with the forest to their advantage. Indians also used traps, lures, decoys, and calls effectively in warfare, as in hunting. As noted earlier, the American colonists learned how valuable this kind of fighting was long before the Revolution and began adopting these techniques, as well.[2]

During the 1700s and 1800s, the accepted view among Americans and Europeans was that Native Americans were inferior, war-loving savages. As will be discussed later, early explorers purposefully created and disseminated this image of Indians to justify the wholesale displacement and genocide of indigenous peoples. This myth, however, experienced some revisionism after the Second World War, due in part to the well-publicized heroism of Indian soldiers in both the Pacific and European war theaters. For some unknown reason, President Harry Truman took a particular interest in Indian affairs and Indian leaders.

His thoughts on the subject are found in the papers kept in the Harry S. Truman Library.

They weren't an inferior race at all, of course. They were wonderfully wise people, and there were Indian setups that were almost ideal systems of government, almost paral- lel with the government of the United States under the Constitution. The Indians had some very great leaders of the Indian tribes, men like Pontiac in Michigan, Tecumseh of the Shawnee, Geronimo down in the Southwest, Black Kettle of the Cheyenne, Sitting Bull and Crazy Horse of the Sioux and Chief Joseph of the Nez Perce, who performed one of the greatest military maneuvers in the history of the world.

He took his whole tribe—something like eight hundred men, women and children—and outmaneuvered practically the whole cavalry of the United States, including one of the great strategists of the Civil War, General Howard, mov- ing his people over a thousand miles up toward Canada—a record that has never been equaled. Howard's outfit and another force of soldiers were miles apart, and neither general knew where the other was, but Chief Joseph knew where both of them were, and he got his people out. Finally, after the cavalry kept chasing him and killed off many of his people, he surrendered, but old Joseph out-marched them all— they never did catch up with him, not really.[3]

It is ironic that Chief Joseph was not a War Chief at all. Like Sitting Bull of the Lakota and Apache leader Geronimo, Joseph was the spiritual leader of his tribal nation who rose to the occasion of fighting to save the lives of his people.

According to Dee Brown in his respected history, *Bury My Heart at Wounded Knee,* one of the greatest so-called Indian warriors was the Lakota (Sioux) War Chief Tashunka Witco, known to the white man as Crazy Horse. According to Lakota tradition, Crazy Horse's father was an Oglala medicine man who gave his son "strong powers." Crazy Horse first went to war at the age of twelve in response to the slash-and-burn attacks used by U.S. Army General Harney during his punitive 1855 expedition against the Sioux.

As a young man, Crazy Horse meditated regularly and had visions. According to oral traditions, he had a powerful vision of a young rider in a storm with long, unbraided hair with the feather of a red hawk in it, a smooth stone behind one ear, and lightning zigzags painted on one cheek and hail dotted all over him. (Lightning and hail were recognized by the Lakota as powerful natural phenomena.) People gathered around him and clung to him. Soon the storm lifted, and a red hawk flew over the rider's head.

When he awoke from the vision, Crazy Horse recognized that he'd received an important message, and from that time forward, when he dressed for battle, he painted his shield and his body with lightning and hail symbols in the way of the warrior in his dream.

Amazingly, Crazy Horse led his warriors into battle off and on for twenty years—against Generals Crook, Miles, and Custer—without being wounded. He was finally killed by a soldier's bayonet in 1877 after he surrendered and was already in the army's custody.[4]

According to Dee Brown's Sioux sources, Crazy Horse is said to have "dreamed himself" into the real world in 1876, and he showed his people many strategies and techniques to use when fighting the white man's soldiers. For example, when General Crook sent his pony soldiers in mounted charges against the Sioux, instead of rushing forward into the fire of their carbines, Crazy Horse had his men fade off to their flanks to strike weak places in their lines. Also, he kept his warriors mounted and moving from one place to another. By the time the sun was directly overhead, he had the soldiers mixed up in three separate fights. Thus, the Sioux were able to keep the soldiers apart and on the defensive.

As demonstrated by Crazy Horse, Native American warfare practices extended beyond simple technique. The warriors also called upon "powers" from other sources. It's often repeated in Native American ceremonies and prayers: "The bear is stronger, the deer swifter, the eagle more far seeing than us. We are without power; have pity on us." So native people find the power somewhere else: in "medicine," a name for power that comes from mystical sources.

Every tribe has its own way of preparing for war, finding power, and receiving good medicine as protection in battle. Very often, these quests involved visiting physical places, which were considered sacred—places with natural power or a connection to the creator.

The Apache and the Navajo had their sacred mountain where they went to fast and pray, or a river could be a place to find powerful medicine. Objects such as bones and claws that came from animals with respected abilities could also provide medicine in battle. The Cheyenne warrior Brave Wolf was given a mounted hawk after fasting and prayer, which he wore on his head when going into battle. On a charge, the bird seemed to come to life, and Brave Wolf would plunge right into the middle of the enemy, knowing the bird was helping and protecting him.

In the days before the gun came to Indians, shields made of stretched buffalo hide offered some physical protection in war. But the protection with which these shields were endowed went far beyond the physical buffalo hide. The shield was believed to possess mystical powers, and not just anybody could make one. After much fasting and spiritual questing, a warrior was spiritually shown what designs and patterns to use on his shield.

Sioux shields carried images of lightning to capture its destructive powers and often included images of swift, powerful, and respected animals—buffalo, bear, elks, and horses.

Kiowa writer N. Scott Momaday recalled a legendary shield belonging to one of his Kiowa ancestors. In the summer of 1992, Momaday Arrived in Oklahoma just after Sitting Bear's shield was returned to his people. Sitting Bear was one of the Qkoie-Tsain-Gah, the ten bravest of the Kiowa warrior societies, who lived from 1800 to 1871. He had been a great chief and a brave warrior.

After much success in battle during the 1860s, Sitting Bear was captured by the army and taken in chains to Fort Sill, Oklahoma. His shield was taken from him when he was captured. Later, he was to be removed from Fort Sill with three other Kiowa warriors, and they all were loaded into the back of a wagon.

As they rode in the wagon, Sitting Bear began to sing the death song of the warrior society, which upset the other warriors. They said he should not sing the song, because the white men would hear. Historically, Native Americans often tried to keep their sacred practices from the prying eyes and ears of outsiders for fear that the outsider might steal a person's power by duplicating his words or actions, or, in this case, singing his death song. Sitting Bear told them he was singing the song because he was going to die soon, when the wagon reached a large tree up ahead.

When they reached the tree, Sitting Bear grabbed the wagon driver's hunting knife with his shackled hands and plunged it into the man's leg. Accompanying soldiers shot him dead, and he is buried close to Fort Sill, near that tree. Sitting Bear's shield was taken to New Jersey and kept by the family of the cavalry officer who had taken Sitting Bear captive, until that summer of 1992, when the officer's family returned it to the tribe.

Tribal legend said the shield possessed much supernatural power, so much so the women gathered around it when it arrived, fearing the men would either withdraw its great power or be harmed by it. That shield is said to now be in a safe place where its power cannot fall into the wrong hands.

(Author's note: I can attest to the "power" of the shields referred to in these paragraphs. When researching material for this book, I traveled to the Heye Foundation Museum of the American Indian, located in New York City, and was granted access to their Plains Indian collection. I entered the large room that housed thousands of Native American cultural items collected by George Gustav Heye in his travels near the end of the nineteenth century. In drawers and on a large set of shelves in the center of the room

were century-old Plains Indian war shields, bows, arrows, medicine bundles, and other items. When I opened the first drawer to peek at the items held within, a palpable, yet invisible, force emanating from the objects hit me squarely in the chest. I stepped back. It was as if the objects themselves were warning me not to handle them, for my own sake. Each time I opened a drawer, I felt the same force projecting out, and each time I only looked, but did not touch.)

Back at the 4th of July powwow, one of the drum groups pounded out another song for the dancers as our circle of Indian veterans turned their attention to the women.

"Speaking of women," commented Nathan Hart, an Oklahoma Cheyenne veteran, "they have always been a great motivator for warriors. In traditional Indian societies, it was hard to court a girl unless you had proven yourself in battle. A girl's mother would ask a young man what acts of courage he had done. The women would sing songs about a man whose courage had failed him: 'If you are afraid when you charge, and you turn back, the women will eat you'—meaning the women would talk about you so badly it would have been better to die! John Stands-In-Timber's grandfather, a Cheyenne leader of the 1800s, used to tell him that the possibility of having the women sing about you that way made the men ready to do anything," Nathan concluded.

"My mother was half Cheyenne, half Sioux, from Pine Ridge," said Carol Red Cherries, a Northern Cheyenne vet. "According to the stories that my mother and grandmother told me about the old days on the plains, the women were always very protected, and we had a very strict moral code. Traditionally, during warfare women could move the camp at a moment's notice—take down a tepee in about three minutes.

"During the time I was growing up in the 1970s," she continued, "it was still not proper for women to be in positions of leadership, and some of my relations didn't feel right about me joining the military. But I heard about two Cheyenne women that served during World War II, and that's where I got the idea to join up."

"Some of that might be the white man's influence," Nathan replied, smiling. "But Cheyenne women sometimes rode into war with the warriors. There's the story of Chief Comes-In-Sight in the late 1800s, who was rescued by his sister in the battle against General Crook at Rosebud.

"Some of the bravest Cheyenne warriors were riding back and forth in front of the cavalry volley, letting the soldiers shoot at them. Most of the bullets missed them, but Comes-In-Sight's horse was shot when he was halfway across an open area.

"He landed on his feet, zigzagging to dodge the barrage of fire. His sister was riding with the warriors that day, and she saw the soldier scouts start down the hill to kill him. She came on the run, right into the firing—he jumped on her pony behind her and got away. To this day, the Cheyenne call the battle Where the Girl Saved Her Brother."

Ruth Williams, a Navajo veteran of the Gulf War, sat down in the circle. "Then, of course, there is Lozen, the Apache warrior woman," she said. "My tribe, the Navajo, have long been close allies of the Apache—we're related way back. Lozen was a medicine woman and sister of the famous Warm Springs Apache leader Victorio, who evaded the cavalry for many years. He said she was as strong as a man and braver than most. He called her a 'shield to her people.' She wore ammunition belts and fought alongside the men, just like some of the women in Desert Shield or Iraq."

World War II Choctaw veteran Schlict Billy remarked, "The Choctaw always held women in very high regard. They were part of the councils and had equal freedom with the men. But we always tried to avoid warfare with neighboring tribes in the past.

"Our ancestors set up these inter-tribal stick ball games—it was real serious playing, but it kept us from fighting and killing each other. In fact, we called the stick ball game 'the little brother of war,' and we settled our differences that way whenever we could. But there wasn't a whole lot to fight over in those days; there was plenty of fields for growing corn, good fishing in the rivers, and lots of open hunting ground—so we played hard in the games to get out any resentments."

The Pueblo Indians of New Mexico also preferred to avoid war whenever possible. Made up of Tiwa, Tewa, Towa, and Keres tribes, the Pueblo people tended to stay in their own villages and mind their own business, according to Pueblo historian and anthropologist Alfonso Ortiz. Their

War Captains were more concerned with keeping the religious rules of the community than going to war.

Of course, they defended themselves against raids by the Navajo, Comanche, and Apache, who made a regular practice of attacking the sedentary Pueblo people, but by and large, they were concerned with growing their corn and raising their children. After the Spanish conquistadors arrived at the end of the sixteenth century, however, pueblo life would never be the same.

The Spaniards had steel, gunpowder, and horses, making them formidably equipped invaders. They destroyed Pueblo religious ceremonials, which they considered devil worship, burned their spiritual leaders at the stake in the plaza of Santa Fe, and took their women and children into slavery. In Pueblo belief, a person cannot perpetrate such evil without suffering the consequences, and sure enough, a terrible drought ensued that affected both Pueblo and Spaniard alike.

The Spanish took whatever corn the Indians were able to produce from the parched soil, leaving the people weak and starving. But the Pueblos are patient people, and, thinking that the Spaniards surely must see what was happening, Pueblo leaders waited for the wrongdoers to come to their senses. When it looked like that wasn't going to happen, they finally took up arms and fought.

A spiritual man named Popé from San Juan Pueblo planned a complex strategy from the Kiva (religious center) at Taos Pueblo. Although representatives of the four Pueblo tribes in attendance at Popé's planning meeting did not speak the same language, he devised a system of communication that employed knots tied in ropes and long-distance Pueblo runners. Once the decision to go to war had been made, Popé gave each of four runners a rope tied with the same number of knots. The knots marked the number of days until all the Pueblos were to simultaneously attack their oppressors.

On the appointed day—and with little other than bows and arrows, clubs, and a few captured guns—the Pueblo people surprised the Spanish and successfully evicted them from Pueblo lands. The year was 1680, and it could be considered the first American Revolution. The Pueblo people were fighting for freedom of religion and self-determination.

When speaking of American Indian war practices, the subject often turns to scalping, because this issue looms large in the public perception of Indian warfare. There are many opposing views of the origins of scalping among American Indians. The conventional view is that it was a gruesome practice unique to American Indians, but forms of beheading and scalping have been practiced by societies all over the world.

Some scholars claim that scalping on the American continent was actually introduced by the Europeans, referring to notices published in the 1600s by the Dutch and British colonial authorities advertising a bounty to be paid for Indian scalps. Whatever its origin, the taking of heads or "human pelts" certainly seems to have arrived late on the North American continent, because archaeological sites reveal little evidence of the practice before the 1600s.

As early as 1637, the English colonists of Connecticut offered the Mohegan Indians a bounty for every Pequot Indian head delivered to them, capitalizing on an inter-tribal dispute that had turned violent. The plan also happened to aid the English in their competition with the Dutch for regional natural resources.

Later, in 1675, authorities in the colony of Massachusetts were offering colonists a bounty for what they called Indian "head skins," later also called "redskins." The French got into the scalp trade as well in colonial times.

In the next century, in the American Southwest, the Mexican Army offered high bounties on Apache scalps—women and children alike. One general collected the ears of Apache warriors on a string in his office.

As if the practice of scalping wasn't bad enough, the mutilation of defeated enemies and the collection of "human war trophies" also came into popular practice. However, in the 1800s, members of the U.S. cavalry seemed to take particular pride in this activity, cutting out Indian women's private parts and displaying them like military regalia.

Whether scalping was originally an American Indian practice or not, evidence suggests that it was taken to excess after, and probably as a result of, European contact. Also, it was odd that what became known as the Indian practice of scalping should be met with such horror by the British—who for centuries beheaded political prisoners and stuck their heads on pikes over London Bridge until they rotted off—and by the French, whose republicans made great show of weaving souvenirs of locks of hair from the basket of aristocratic heads severed by the guillotine. The truth of the matter is that most of the world's cultures have exhibited barbaric practices at one time or another.

A war-related practice that does come from Native American tradition is known as "counting coup." The term is of French origin from the verb *couper*, which means literally to hit or strike. The heart of this practice calls for a warrior to touch an enemy warrior during battle without killing him or being killed.

Barney Old Coyote, a member of the Crow tribe, described the practice. "The Crows spent a lot of time on the warpath, but we weren't interested in killing everybody," he said. "In fact, like a lot of Plains tribes, the bravest thing a warrior could do was 'count coup' on the enemy—touch him without his killing you.

"There were four specific acts you had to perform to be eligible for chieftainship with the Crow Tribe. The first was to count coup. The second was to take an enemy's weapon. The third was to take his horse, and the fourth was to lead a successful war party.

"The white people—they thought we Indians were just dirty horse thieves, but to my way of thinking, stealing horses or sneaking up on an enemy without killing anybody is a better way to make war than to slaughter everybody in sight, which is what the cavalry did. Before the white man came, things were different among the tribes."

Carson Walks-On-Ice, another Crow vet, confirmed Barney's words. "Crows have always fought for this land," he said. "We were raised with traditional stories of counting coup and performing deeds to become a chief. Old Crow guys would come to visit my grandfather, and they'd talk all about the coup they had counted in the old days before they settled on the reservation. In our time, Joe Medicine Crow was the only living Crow to do all four deeds to become a chief during World War Two, but that's a story for later.

"Traditionally," Carson went on, "the Crow went on the warpath only for revenge for an enemy raid or to gain honor. It was never to gain territory or wealth or power. When a warrior came back from a war party, he had to give away most of what he had captured. The more you gave away, the more honor you had. We still do that today."

What Carson is referring to is the continued practice of the "give-away," in which a family that has been honored or blessed in some way gives large quantities of goods to other Indian families in their community. This is sometimes done at powwows, when the dancing stops and the honored family takes over the arena, calling up people who may have helped them in some way during the past year. Hundreds of items, including Indian blankets, shawls, dining flatware, food, and clothing may be distributed during the give-away.

Wrapping up their first round of discussions, our circle of veterans started to disperse as another powwow dance session came to a close.

Before departing, Winnebago veteran Doug Long said, "My grandfather was a veteran of the First World War. My older brother is a veteran of the Second World War. My other brother and I are veterans of the Korean conflict, and I have seven grandsons that were in Desert Storm. That meant my grandsons were now Winnebago warriors. In our tribe, every time you get a new warrior, you add a new eagle feather to the tribe's Eagle Staff. So we added seven more feathers to our Eagle Staff.

"I remember that ceremony. It followed our Winnebago tradition. I offered tobacco, as we were taught by our ancestors, blessed the feathers, and prayed to each of the four directions, so that that good feeling could be shared by everyone who is out there in those directions.

"I'm sure I speak for most Native American veterans when I say I was proud to serve, and I'd serve again."

PART TWO

From Freedom Fighters to Rough Riders

Revolutionary War—*Peace medals such as this one, which depicts George Washington and an American Indian, were often pre- sented to tribal leaders who had sworn allegiance to the United States. (National Museum of the American Indian)*

Civil War—*This hand-written ledger page, on display at the Oneida Tribal Museum proudly lists the names of Oneida veterans who served in the Union Army during the Civil War, such a James Otter and Martin Doxtator. (photo by Gary Robinson)*

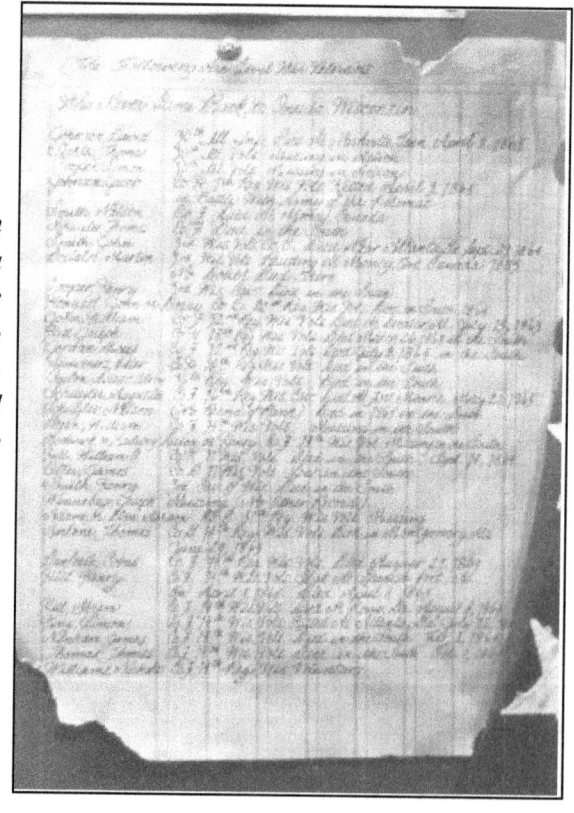

Civil War—*Cherokee Stand Watie served as a brigadier general for the Confederacy. (National Archives)*

Civil War—*Seneca Chief Do-ne-ho-ga-wa, known as Ely S. Parker among the whites, served as General Grant's adj tant (secretary) and drew up the terms of General Lee's surrender at Appomattox. (Smithsonian Institution National Anthropological Archives)*

Indian Wars—*This Crow Indian Scout named Curley served in General George Armstrong Custer's 7th Cavalry but survived the Battle of the Little Bighorn. (National Archives)*

Army Scouts— *Apache Scout William Major posed for this photo with an offi- cer of the 25th Infantry in the 1930s. Though the Army Scouts saw most of their ser- vice in the 1800s, the unit was revived for WWI ser- vice under General Pershing. (U.S. Army Photo)*

PART TWO—FROM FREEDOM FIGHTERS TO ROUGH RIDERS

The Oneida Tribal Museum, located a few miles west of Green Bay, Wisconsin, is filled with wartime memorabilia, letters, and photographs collected from Oneida tribal vets and their families, who want people to know of their proud military service.

Oneida tribal members living today are proud of the fact that members of their tribe have served in every war America has fought from the Revolutionary War until modern times. That's a remarkable accomplishment when you consider what this and other tribes suffered at the hands of the American government and its citizens.

Members of tribes all across the United States are proud of their veterans and their past and present military service. Every veteran has his memories, and every war has its stories.

The Revolutionary War

It's a fact that most of the tribes in the Northeast sided with the British during the Revolutionary War. The reasons for this are clear.

The colonists were increasingly encroaching on Indian territory, breaking agreements that protected Indian lands. Many tribes had long-standing treaties with the British Crown, which included trading treaties on which the tribes had become dependent. To all the tribes, treaties were not just contracts that could be forgotten or broken—they were sacred promises.

There were, however, many instances in which tribes fought with and supported the colonists. The colonists' pleas for freedom against oppression moved some Native Americans to offer help and support, since many of the tribes in New England had themselves been oppressed by France, Britain, and other European powers.

In other cases, friendships and intermarriage had forged deep ties between settler and Indian, which was true for several Northeastern tribes who had been dubbed "praying Indians" by colonists because of their conversion to Christianity.

There were actually several Native American Minutemen, and there were thirteen Delaware Indians in one colonial military company. It is also a matter of U.S. military record that George Washington's aide-de-camp, Simeon Simon, was an Indian, though his tribe is not mentioned.

And then there were the Oneida, a whole tribe that came to the rescue of the colonial rebels at times of dire need.

The Oneida were part of the League of Six Nations of the Iroquois, a confederacy that predated the thirteen colonies by some three hundred years. In fact, that's where the colonies got the idea of a union of states. In 1751, during one of many meetings called to form the union of colonies, Benjamin Franklin told James Parker, "It would be a very strange thing if Six Nations of 'ignorant savages' should be capable of forming a scheme for such a union [the League of Six Nations] and be able to execute it in such a manner, as that it has subsisted ages, and appears indissoluble, and yet a like union should be impracticable for ten or a dozen English colonies."[1]

Officially, the Six Nations had elected to remain neutral during the colonists' Revolutionary War, but all of that soon changed. In January of 1776, Colonial General Schuyler led a raid into Mohawk territory to capture suspected British loyalists. A prominent and well-respected member of that community was taken prisoner, which sent most of the Six Nations over to the side of the British. But the Oneida were closely tied to the settlers in upper New York State, and they stayed neutral—that is, until the British attacked.

Not far from upstate New York's Fort Stanwix were both an Oneida camp and a colonial settlement. In August, 1777, military personnel at the fort got word that the British Army was coming down from Canada to attack. The British plan under General Burgoyne was to converge in Albany and cut the colonies in half.

Both the Oneida and the colonists gathered inside the fort for protection just as the British forces approached. The fort commander, Colonel Peter Gansevoort, refused the terms of surrender offered by the British, and the siege commenced. According to documents in the Oneida Museum, the Oneida men and women at Fort Stanwix aided in driving off the British and their Indian allies who were trying to undermine and blow up the fort. When they learned of the nearby British invasion, American volunteers of the Mohawk Valley rushed west to relieve their besieged comrades at Fort Stanwix. On August 6, 1777, they blundered into an ambush set by the British around a small ravine two miles from the Oneida village of Oriska. A tremendous slaughter of Americans occurred during the opening minutes of the engagement. The survivors, including several Oneidas, gathered around their commander, Nicholas Herkimer, on a plateau west of the ambush ravine. In the ensuing battle, they and their Oneida allies fought the British and Tory Indians to a stalemate.

Of particular interest in this conflict, known as the Battle of Oriska, were the elderly Oneida war chief Hanyery and his wife. Probably in his fifties, Hanyery was said to be "too old for the service." Yet he and other Oneidas fought side-by-side with their American allies on the main plateau of the battlefield.

After the battle, it was reported that Hanyery, who was on horseback, was shot through the right wrist so as to disable him from loading his gun. Subsequently, his wife repeatedly loaded it for him, and he managed to continue firing. His wife also had a gun, which she used in the fight.

The details of this battle were confirmed by a local newspaper, which noted that Chief Hanyery and his wife "distinguished themselves remarkably on the occasion. The Indian killed nine of the enemy, when having received a ball through his wrist that disabled him from using his gun, he then fought with his tomahawk. His son killed two, and his wife on horseback fought by his side with pistols during the whole action, which lasted six hours."[2]

The Oneida immediately moved on to Fort Saratoga, where they helped defeat the British in the battle that is considered the turning point of the Revolutionary War. By that time, the Oneidas had officially been enlisted into George Washington's Continental Army.

According to Oneida records, the then leader of the Oneidas, Chief Shenandoah, sent hundreds of bushels of dried corn to feed George Washington's army during the terrible winter of 1777–78 at Valley Forge. An Oneida woman, Polly Cooper, even showed the soldiers how to cook the corn. Martha Washington gave her a shawl as thanks. That shawl resides in the Oneida Tribal Museum to this day, alongside a letter from George Washington in which he writes that his soldiers would have died of starvation if it hadn't been for the Indians' corn.

One of Washington's surgeons at Valley Forge, a Dr. Waldo, wrote in one of his reports, "I was called to relieve a soldier thought to be dying. He expired before I reached the hut. He was an Indian, an excellent soldier, and had fought for the very people who disinherited his forefathers."[3]

When, many years after that winter at Valley Forge, Washington was concerned about the British advancing position, he turned for help to his French aide, Marquis de Lafayette, a French citizen who'd come of his own volition to aid the Americans in their fight for freedom. Washington sent Lafayette across the Delaware River with some of his troops, including a whole contingent of Oneidas.

As the British forces approached, Lafayette found himself and his forces surrounded, with their backs to the river. There was one chance to cross at a low place in the river, so LaFayette sent 150 Oneidas to hold off the British, while the rest of his troops crossed the river to safety. When the British Cavalry arrived in the vanguard, the Oneidas let out blood-curdling war whoops, which spooked the horses, and they threw all the officers.

The British infantry coming behind didn't know what was going on, and chaos ensued long enough for Lafayette's men to get across and the Oneida to escape without a scratch, as well.

The Colonists always promised the Oneidas would participate equally in all the good things that would come after the war, including land, food, money, and integration into American society. General Philip Schuyler even wrote to the Oneida people, "Sooner would a mother forget her child than we shall forget you."

But when the war was over, the colonials left the Oneidas with nothing, blaming all Indians for the fact that many had fought on the side of the British. Oneida villages and fields and all they owned had been destroyed during the war, and they lived as refugees on the banks of the Mohawk River, their crops burned, the game killed or scared off, and with no relief from the fledgling U.S. government.

White squatters, settlers, and speculators began pouring into Oneida country by the thousands at war's end, and instead of assisting their former allies, the New York state government moved quickly to dispossess the Oneidas of their territory. The state claimed these lands for several reasons. Some Indian tracts had been promised to veterans as bounties in place of pay, and the state's plan for economic recovery was largely based on income from the sale of Indian lands.

But most importantly, the government of New York wanted a population of non-Indian farmers who would be expected to expand and defend the borders of the state while taming wilderness and paying taxes. New York acquired most of the Oneidas' land in a series of forced land cessions beginning in 1785.

It took the Oneida another ten years of petitioning the U.S. government before they were able to sign a treaty that included an official "thank-you" for their service in the war, small compensation for lost land and the promise that they could keep their remaining lands forever. As a result of this treaty, the Oneidas have fought for the United States in every major war since then.

Red Sticks and the War of 1812

When the British and Americans went to war again in 1812, the Muscogee (Creek) Nation, occupying large portions of Alabama and Georgia, decided to remain neutral. This resolve changed, however, when American settlers began aggressively moving in on their tribal lands in violation of existing treaties.

The British played some heavy politics and convinced the Creeks that it was in their interest to fight with the British against the Americans.

When the Creeks held a War Council and decided to go to war, it was their custom to send a bundle of sticks painted red to nearby villages to mark the number of days until warfare would begin. Thus, these Indians were dubbed the Red Sticks.

The tribesmen hoped the British might honor their treaties better than the Americans had, and offered their allegiance. But promises were made on the other side too. Pro-American Creeks and members of other tribes, including some six hundred Cherokee, were recruited to fight under General Andrew Jackson, later to become president, declaring that they were "all fighting under one cause." Jackson attempted to wipe out the Red Sticks first by using only the Indian soldiers, but wholesale slaughter was not the Indian way to make war. Jackson finally brought in his white troops. By the battle's end, only seventy of the nine hundred Red Sticks were left alive. Half of Jackson's casualties were his Indian auxiliaries.

Jackson revealed his true feelings for his Indian troops to Thomas Pinckney, then fighting as a general alongside Jackson. He told Pinckney that he'd rid himself of the Indians at the earliest possible opportunity. Jackson made his feelings public when, after his inauguration as president in 1829, he announced that he had no intention of honoring treaty obligations to the tribes. Jackson pushed his Indian Removal Act through Congress in 1830, in which the majority of the tribes of the Southeast—including the Cherokee who had fought and died under his command—would be removed from their ancestral lands to territory west of the Mississippi.

The Choctaw were the first to be driven on the long trek from their ancestral homelands in Alabama and Georgia to a place called "Indian Territory" (now Oklahoma). Under guard of U.S. Army troops, they were forced to walk through blizzards and freezing weather. Many of the Choctaw were barefoot and starving. The Creek Indians were next, many of them in chains. Nearly half the Creek Nation died. The Cherokee were next, losing a quarter of their numbers to sickness and exposure. Still others were to follow. The path that each of these tribes took became known as the Trail of Tears.

"We never had a thought of exchanging our land for any other … it being the land of our forefathers.… Fearing the consequences may be similar to transplanting an old tree, which would wither and die away, and we are fearful we would come to the same," said Levi Colbert, a Chickasaw.[4]

The Civil War

Though most tribes tried to remain neutral during America's War Between the States, many natives, including entire Indian regiments, ended up fighting on both sides.

The U.S. War Department, as well as a number of individual career officers, initially opposed the enlistment of Indian troops. Aside from considering Indians the enemy, they feared that Indians would "revert to savagery" in battle.

But as the war continued, and realizing the stronghold the Confederates were gaining with the tribes in Indian Territory, the War Department began to soften its position. For many Indians, the Union government was still the enemy. It had, after all, removed them from their ancestral lands and placed them on reservations. So when the Union leaders asked the tribes to become allies, most were unresponsive. The first inclination among the majority of tribal leaders was to stay out of the white man's war.

However, several minority splinter groups within some of the Southeastern tribes (Cherokees, Choctaws, and Creeks) considered the possibility that the Confederate government might be more honorable than the one they currently had to deal with, and this swayed the loyalties of some Indian people.

The Trail of Tears had created rifts and factions among many of the eastern tribes, which were now in Indian Territory (Oklahoma). There were those who would rather die than leave their land, and they stayed behind, often hiding out in the mountains or forests to escape capture. Others, who felt that a sacred agreement must never be broken, no matter how the other party behaved, had agreed to be relocated.

The Confederates offered the tribes new treaties and promised that the Indian regiments would be mobilized only if there was action in Indian Territory. And, for the first time, several Indians were offered commissions as officers in the Army—the Confederate Army.

The Union, on the other hand, only offered the tribes a wartime reduction in the already meager rations that had been promised at the time of removal. Some tribes, nonetheless, chose to honor the treaties in place with the federal government and agreed to form Indian regiments within the Union Army, with white officers in command.

So the rosters of Confederate Indian forces grew, with outfits called the Creek Mounted Rifles, the 1st and 2nd Cherokee, the Seminole Battalion, and others. Even the Kiowa and the Comanche, still roaming the plains of Oklahoma and Texas, agreed to participate in the Confederate Army, looking for opportunities to attack a now well-established foe.

The Union armed its Indian regiments badly, the Confederates far worse. Often, the soldiers resorted to bow and arrow and tomahawk rather than the old, useless flintlocks they had been issued. Of greatest irony, they were drilled in the organized style of warfare practiced by the Euro-American forces the Indians had been so successful in defeating in previous wars. But they stood their ground, and the Cherokee, Creek, and Seminole took losses proportionately higher than any state, North or South.

Among those who remained loyal to the Union was Opothleyahola, an eighty-year-old chief of a band of Creek Indians. Because of his refusal to take up the Confederate cause, his band was attacked by Colonel Cooper and his regiment of Confederate soldiers and driven from their homes in Oklahoma. The old Creek chief led his people out of Indian Territory to sanctuary in Union-controlled Kansas. Four thousand, mostly women and children, began the long trek eastward. They were repeatedly attacked in their flight by Colonel Cooper's troops and fought them off successfully with their rearguard defense.

Cooper then ordered the first Cherokee Mounted Rifles to attack the Union Loyalists. But attacking a retreating band of men, women, and children who were simply honoring their treaty agreements was not an order the Cherokee could, with honor, carry out. They deserted en masse and eventually joined Opothleyohola as he struggled toward Kansas.

Through the rest of the blood-drenched Civil War, the Indian regiments would gain honors in battle on both sides, and Indian officers earned the highest of medals and promotions, some achieving the rank of brigadier general. This did not, however, stop the popular press from characterizing them as the "Aboriginal Corps of Tomahawkers and Scalpers."[5]

A young white Union soldier, James Newton, wrote from the battlefield, "I was on picket duty one night about three quarters of a mile from camp. I had two Company F Indians. One, a new recruit, couldn't talk or understand our language, and the other had to give him his orders. He was posted in front across the road from the house. When I went to relieve him, he was gone. He had gone into the woods, where he could get out of sight as it was open ground where I had posted him. The Indians were good skirmishers, but didn't like the open country or pitched battle."[6]

Probably the most well-known and most written-about Indian who fought for the Confederacy was Cherokee General Stand Watie who commanded the 1st Indian Brigade. This brigade was composed of Colonel R. C. Park's 1st Cherokee Regiment, Colonel W. P. Adair's 2nd Cherokee Regiment, Major J. A. Scales's Cherokee Battalion, Colonel D. N. McIntosh's 1st Creek Regiment, Colonel Chilly McIntosh's 2nd Creek Regiment, Captain R. Kenard's Creek Squadron, Major Broken Arm's 1st Osage Battalion, and Lt. Colonel John Jumper's 1st Seminole Battalion.

Military reports indicated that whatever the Indian units lacked in military training, weapons, and uniforms they more than made up for in the courage and devotion they showed their cause, whether Blue or Gray. The reports do also show, however, that they disliked the repetitive training and military ceremonies, which for them held no cultural or practical significance. [7]

In a Virginia farmhouse owned by Wilmer McLean in the town of Appomattox Court House, Confederate General Robert E. Lee surrendered to Ulysses S. Grant at the war's end. Grant's adjutant was a Seneca

Indian named Do-ne-ho-ga-wa, better known among whites by his English name, Ely Parker.

Parker had studied law in New York but had been denied admission to the Bar because he was Indian and not a citizen. He then studied engineering and later volunteered for the Union Army but was rebuffed. He wrote, "I had, through the Hon. Wm. H. Seward, personally tendered my services for the non-slaveholding interest. Mr. Seward replied: 'The fight must be made by white men alone. Go home, we will settle our troubles without any Indian aid.'

"But the quarrel of the whites," continued Parker, "was not a wrangle of boys, but a struggle of giants and the country was being wracked to its very foundations. Then came to me in my forest home a paper bearing the great red seal of the War Department. It was an officer's commission in the Army of the United States."[8]

This reversal was due to the intervention of Parker's lifelong friend Ulysses S. Grant. Ely Parker's distinguished service, education, and skill made him such a valuable asset that he was promoted to brigadier general in later years, after the war.

At Appomattox, Parker was at Grant's side, drafting the terms of surrender. Parker remembered, "After Lee had stared at me a moment, he extended his hand and said: 'I am glad to see one real American here.'"[9]

At the end of the Civil War, Indian soldiers and officers of both sides returned to find what little they had devastated. Regardless of how many of a tribe's warriors had fought for, been decorated by, and died for the Union cause, any involvement by *any* tribal members with the Confederates resulted in the whole tribe's subjection to the punitive measures of reconstruction. Tribal lands and property were seized and often sold to the highest bidder. And the great Oklahoma Land Rush of 1895 was made possible through the seizure of Indian lands at the end of the Civil War.

Indian Wars and Indian Scouts

The desire to survive as a people was a basic part of Native American existence in the eighteenth century. It flowed in the veins of native warriors as it had for generations. As a result, Native Americans were not easily ushered from their homelands.

The "Indian Wars" is the name generally used in the United States to describe a long series of conflicts between the U.S. Army and Native Americans from about 1825 to 1890. Much of this action took place in the plains region as white settlers spread out and took control of more and more Indian lands. When the Indian Wars started, the U.S. Army set up forts to defend the white settlers and in the process, took over thousands of acres of Indian territory.

All the Indian people had ever fought for was the right to keep their lands and their ways of life. In essence, they were fighting for homeland security, as Americans do today.

As in Revolutionary War times, some U.S. military personnel realized that if the country was to win the war for more land, it would be necessary to enlist Indian warriors on their side. So on July 28, 1866, an act of Congress established the Indian Scout service to provide "in the territories and Indian country, a force of Indians not to exceed one thousand, to act as Scouts, who shall receive the pay and allowances of cavalry soldiers."[10]

General John Schofield, Secretary of the War Department, wrote that the practice of recruiting Indian scouts for the army "will move these men from the rank of savage enemies to the ranks of friends and practically civilized allies—from the life and character of savage warriors to those of civilized husbandmen."[11]

So, army representatives went to meet with tribal leaders of the various Plains tribes and request that tribal members be allowed to serve in the U.S. Army. Tribal response was mixed. Among the Cheyenne, for example, there was a long deliberation on this request, for there were many related issues to be discussed. Two factors played a part in the final decision to allow young Cheyenne men to serve. Firstly, said Little Chief and Dull Knife, two Cheyenne leaders, of that time, their people must learn a new way of life—leave the old way behind, build schools for the children. They recognized that the Cheyenne would no longer be able to live the way they had once lived.

Secondly, their warriors were among the most feared of the plains at that time. A small remnant had held off several thousand U.S. troops. They were willing to continue fighting and would have, but they saw a more pressing need to preserve life for their children and give the elders an opportunity to live out their last days with their grandchildren.

These same warriors laid down their weapons so that their young people and their elders could receive food, clothing, and other aid. Thus, a large number of Cheyenne enlisted and were used as scouts to track down Chief Joseph of the Nez Perce during his well-known flight toward Canada.

But there were also dissenting warriors who fired their guns in the air and called Dull Knife "a white man's woman" when he made the decision to cooperate with the army. These warriors were among those who prolonged the Indian Wars into the 1890s.

Many warriors from the Cheyenne, Crow, and other Plains tribes served honorably as Army Scouts. By 1867, there were four hundred seventy four Indian Scouts, and twenty years later, they reached their peak number of six hundred.

For the first thirty years of the scouts' existence, their enlistment was for only six months at a time, as is evident from the following facts recorded in military discharge papers: "Know ye, that Run-All-Over-the-Ground, a Private of the 5th U.S. Mounted Infantry of Enlisted Indian Scouts, who was enrolled on the First day of August one thousand eight hundred and eighty to serve six months is hereby discharged from the service of the U.S. Army. Character: Excellent. Paid in full $25.68 at Ft. Keogh, Montana, February 15, 1881."[12]

During the Nez Perce War of the mid-1860s, Lieutenant Hugh Scott commanded thirty-five Northern Cheyenne Scouts, men who had recently surrendered to the army. Some of Scott's colleagues warned him of the Indians' capacity for treachery. Scott emphatically differed.

He said, "These Scouts are keen athletic young men, real specimens of manhood—more than any body of men I have ever seen before or since. They just knew what to do in every emergency and when to do it, without any confusion or lost motion. I watched their every move and learned lessons from them that later saved my life."[13]

While on duty, Indian Scouts wore the same uniforms as regular soldiers, except for their footwear, which were the Apache-style buckskin moccasins that extended above the calf with hard soles turned up at the toe. For a period of time, the scouts were distinguished by a patch on the front of their hats made up of the letters U.S.S. (United States Scouts) above a pair of crossed arrows. Often, however, before going into battle, they would strip down to loincloths and cover their heads with bandanas to differentiate themselves from the hostile Indians on the field.

Indian Scouts were so immensely useful to the army because of their experience and mastery of hunting and warfare techniques. They were the fastest runners, the toughest riders, and the most quick-witted, and they were honored for being so.

Of the Indian Scouts, one army field captain wrote, "A few such men as the Delawares, attached to a company of troops upon the Indian frontier would, by their knowledge of Indian character and habits, and their wonderful powers of judging the country, following tracks (which soldiers cannot be taught), enable us to operate to much better advantage.... [They are] intelligent, brave, reliable and in every aspect well qualified."[14]

As stated earlier, the hiring of Indian scouts by the army to hunt down and often kill members of those tribes and factions of tribes who resisted confinement to reservations was a source of some controversy. Even now it is hard for many people to understand how the descendants of Apache Army Scouts, for instance, take pride that their ancestors helped capture Geronimo.

In order to understand this, you have to understand a little of the Indian way of thinking, the Indian idea of honor. Native American culture has tremendous respect for the rights of the individual, even though the societies are close knit and built around extended family units. If a man, or woman, follows an individual vision—the path that person sees as the only one he can take, with integrity and a moral commitment—then that choice must be honored. If he finds that path is not the right one and he has been mistaken, like the Confederate Cherokee units in the Civil War, then he is free to come back to the community, be cleansed, and be welcomed back into the circle.

With few exceptions, traditional Indian peoples are deeply devout. The acknowledgment of a higher power is a profoundly rooted part of native cultures. Life is a balancing act, every action has consequences, and those consequences might require spiritually mandated, follow-up actions aimed at reestablishing the balance.

For example, the taking of a life, human or animal, friend or foe, red or white, is an act that carries with it grave responsibilities and the need for forgiveness. Treaties, therefore, were not just political documents to be manipulated or forgotten when they proved inconvenient. A sacred promise must be kept or the consequences were grave—even if that agreement meant a person must go out to fight his or her own brother.

There is a strong tradition, particularly among the Plains Indians, of the "honorable" enemy—an opposing tribe or band so brave and strong that they make one a stronger warrior, with greater honor, by fighting them. Sometimes, the army was considered an honorable enemy.

General George Crook, in command of Arizona's army forces in the early 1880s, confided in later years that, often, the Indians he had to fight went to war only when pushed beyond normal human endurance by government agencies and white settlers. He said that his men had to fight *against* the Indians when their sympathies were often *with* the Indians.

However, General Crook's views were not shared by the War Department or many of his fellow officers. He was replaced by General Nelson A. Miles, to whom Geronimo finally surrendered.

All of Geronimo's people, the Chiricahua Apache—including the scouts who had served the army—were removed from their Arizona desert to a dank prison in Florida, where disease and confinement brought more death and suffering than the army ever could.

Between 1872 and 1890, sixteen Indian scouts were awarded the Medal of Honor, the highest military decoration of the United States government, for bravery in action during the Indian Wars.

Historians generally consider that the Indian Wars ended with what's known as the Pine Ridge campaign of 1890, culminating in the Wounded Knee Massacre, in which 146 Lakota men, women, and children were killed by the Seventh Cavalry on the Pine Ridge Reservation.[15]

The end of the Indian Wars meant there was less need for scouts in general and brought a dramatic reduction in the number of Indian Scouts. By 1891, there were only twenty-three still on active duty. However, they were temporarily reactivated the following year to serve with General Pershing's punitive expedition into Mexico in pursuit of Mexican revolutionary general Pancho Villa.

In May of 1916, the Indian Scouts fought in their last official bat- tle, which was against Pancho Villa's men at Ojos Azules Ranch, located about three hundred miles inside Mexico.

The last of the Indian Scouts, who were kept in service after Pershing's expedition, were stationed at Fort Huachuca, Arizona, until the unit was disbanded in 1947.

Troop L—An Experiment

The success of the scouts prompted several army officers to recommend, in the 1890s, the creation of all-Indian regular army units similar to units of East Indian soldiers created by the British Army in India.

At the time, there was no general agreement among military leaders as to the fitness of Indians for regular service. As the *New York Times* reported in a story published on December 27, 1893, "It is remarkable how widely officers of experience differ on this matter." The same story went on to quote a report from Army General Schofield, stating that the army service of Indians "has been quite satisfactory—the young Indians become obedient, subordinate and contented soldiers, instead of restless and dangerous elements within their tribes."[16]

Similarly, Army Inspector General Breckingridge, quoted in the same newspaper story, found that Indians under his command were "amenable to discipline, generally of good habits, proud of their occupation, and of great attitude for military service."

However, other high-ranking officers, including General Philip Sheridan and Adjutant General Williams, believed that Indians should only be allowed to serve as scouts and nothing more. Over the objections of General Sheridan and others, the U.S. Army did create a few experimental all-Indian companies. One was known as Troop L, commanded by Lieutenant Hugh L. Scott of the Seventh Cavalry. Scott was known for his understanding of Indians, Indian ways, and even Plains Indian sign language.

According to reports collected by the *New York Times*, Scott's Troop L was praised for "their rapid progress in drill and discipline," and the Indians in that troop were expected to become "among the very best soldiers in the army."

However, in the long run, Indian soldiers did not take well to the regimen and regulation of life in the barracks and became bored with this lifestyle, so alien to their own style of life and warfare. Their hair was chopped off, they slept in barracks and marched in neat rows in constricting uniforms and boots. In contrast, the Indian Scouts were still living and fighting like warriors—and they were paid more.

And so the experiment failed—but the final deathblow for Indian companies was really the refusal of white officers to lead them.

The Rough Riders

The "Rough Riders" was a nickname coined by the American press to refer to the 1st United States Volunteer Cavalry Regiment, formed to fight Spain during the Spanish-American War of 1898. At the outbreak of this war, Theodore Roosevelt was serving as assistant secretary of the Navy. He resigned that position specifically to form this regiment, which began recruiting men in several states, including Oklahoma.

Despite the overt prejudice they faced, a number of Oklahoma Indian men enlisted in this regiment. Mr. Roosevelt had been known to express some fairly harsh views of Native Americans, but of his Rough Riders he remarked, "We have a number of Indians who are excellent riders and seem to be pretty good fellows."[17]

Roosevelt claimed they lived on the same terms as the white soldiers. They served with him in Cuba, in the Philippines, and later, during the Boxer Rebellion, in China. This service seemed to confirm a nation-wide movement known as "assimilation" that sought to bring Native Americans into the social mainstream as soon as possible.

But that was a debate yet to be resolved.

PART THREE

Doughboys and Leathernecks

World War I—*First World War Native American veterans Cecil Gallamore, Rabbit Boney and Ray McDonald stand at attention for this photo. (Mathers Museum of World Cultures, Indiana University.)*

World War II— *The Comanche codetalkers used in Europe are not as well known as their Navajo counterparts but proved to be just as effective in preventing enemy code-breaking. These codetalkers were part of the U.S. Army's 4th Signal Company. (U.S. Army Photo)*

World War II—*Pima Indian Ira Hayes is probably the most publicized American Indian soldier in U.S. history. After participating in the famous flag-raising on Iwo Jima, he and the other men in this photo, toured the United States promoting war bonds. Tragically, Hayes was found dead in a ditch on his reservation shortly after the war. (U.S. Marine Corp Archival Photo)*

PART THREE—DOUGHBOYS AND LEATHERNECKS

During the opening years of the twentieth century, America was engaged in a national debate concerning the fate of Native Americans. The assimilationists, mostly educated whites living on the East Coast, believed that Indians should continue to be mainstreamed in all aspects of life, including clothing, customs, hairstyles, housing, employment, religion, and education. Separatists tended to believe that Indians were incapable of full integration into American society due to their "inferior" nature.

American Indians, it seems, were seldom consulted regarding these issues. Many were eager to prove themselves within the national arena in all walks of life while firmly maintaining their preference for practicing traditional native ways. To indigenous people, the two are not mutually exclusive.

Into this debate stepped retired minister and self-proclaimed academic doctor Joseph K. Dixon, who had been hired as a lecturer for the Wanamaker Department Stores, located in New York and Philadelphia, in 1907. Dixon, whose research and lectures increasingly focused on Native Americans, convinced his employer to finance a series of expeditions into Indian Country to gather educational information on what he believed to be a "vanishing race."

During his expeditions, Dixon discovered the degree of prejudice to which Indians across the country were being subjected. In 1913, he conceived of the idea of creating "The Declaration of Allegiance of American Indians to the United States." With permission from the newly elected President Woodrow Wilson, Dixon traveled to eighty-nine Indian reservations to perform signing ceremonies, in which he obtained 900 signatures representing 189 tribes.

World War I

With America's entry into World War I in 1917, several Indian tribes declared war on Germany independently of the United States, and thousands of Native American men and women volunteered for military service. Initially, they were rejected because they did not speak or read English. However, the efforts of Dixon and others in the Department of the Interior may have influenced the War Department to reconsider.

In the early 1900s, the Department of the Interior operated about twenty-five Indian boarding schools around the country, and, with War Department approval, the schools quickly became recruiting sta- tions. At Virginia's Hampton Institute, one Lakota student, Charles Roy Morsea, gave a patriotic speech to his fellow students encouraging their enlistment. He explained that his father had served earlier, in the Spanish-American War, and was already fighting in France with General Pershing.

Despite a variety of racial, social, and linguistic barriers, more than seventeen thousand Indians saw active service in the army and navy during the First World War. Some two-thirds were volunteers, even though Indians as a whole weren't allowed to become citizens until after the war.

Ironically, the federal policy of assimilation mandated that, with few exceptions, soldiers of the American Indian race were not designated as such, resulting in little official recognition of the accomplishments of this group during the war. But, thankfully, they did not go entirely unnoticed.

To the surprise of many of the commanding officers, Indian sol- diers proved adept at learning to use complex equipment and speak other languages. However, their methods were not always orthodox. For example, two Comanche soldiers in a unit, endangered by not knowing the German strategy, devised an unusual plan. They waited until nightfall, stripped down, and covered their bodies completely in whitewash. Under the cover of darkness, they crept out into "No Man's Land" and waited near the enemy lines until daylight. There, they stood absolutely still next to white-washed fence posts, eavesdropping on the enemy communications. They were able to sneak back to their unit and report what they'd heard.

Also, Winnebago vet Douglas Long remembered stories he'd heard growing up of a WWI Winnebago soldier, Henry Decora, and his father, Foster, who had enlisted in the army. Their division took on the Germans on August 3, 1918, and Foster was killed. The unit then crossed the Hendenburgh Line and went on to push the Germans across the Marne River. There, Henry was gassed. He never received any veteran's disability coverage, although he had to have an eye operation as a result of the gassing. When he came back to Minneapolis, he went into a bar for a celebratory drink, but they wouldn't serve him because he was an Indian.

Personal accounts of Native American heroism like these are numerous. There were the daring exploits of Lieutenant Sylvester Long Lance, who took part in many wartime maneuvers and was reported dead four times. Francis Lequier, a Chippewa, was wounded eleven times during the process of capturing a machine gun nest. And a northern California Indian named Philip Jim was noted for leading charges against the enemy thirty times.

The least known and most underappreciated aspect of Native American service during WWI was probably the use made of a tribal language to send coded messages that the Germans never broke. According to a report filed by Army Field Commanding Officer Colonel A. W. Bloor, the Germans were masters at listening in and decoding all U.S. Army field communications during the war in Europe. Every planned battle or maneuver was effectively thwarted by German forces, who obviously knew what was coming. America was losing the war.

It was in 1918 that a group of Choctaw soldiers presented the idea of using their so-called "obsolete" tribal language as a code. Having exhausted every other means of transmitting coded information, military commanders felt it was worth trying. One Choctaw was placed at each of the Allied field camps to send and receive messages in the Choctaw language. The first use of this system came in October of that year, when a delicate withdrawal of two American infantry companies was ordered. When the movement was completed without mishap or injury, Army Command knew it was on to something.

The Indians were used repeatedly throughout the rest of the war, and according to Colonel Bloor's report, "within 24 hours after the Choctaw language was pressed into service, the tide of the battle turned, and in less than 72 hours the Allies were on the full attack."[1] A captured German officer confessed that his intelligence personnel were completely "confused by the Indian language and gained no benefit whatsoever from their wiretaps."[2]

According to tribal records, nineteen Choctaws served in the communication corps as what became known as "codetalkers," though they've never been officially recognized for their contribution by the U.S. government. They were, however, honored by the French government in 1989.[3]

Back home on the reservations, despite the fact that federal money promised for Indian health and education programs was diverted to the war effort, native people went all out to support the war effort, volunteering for the Red Cross and buying Liberty Bonds, even though they were not considered American Citizens.

It was largely due to the military service of American Indians that they were at last deemed worthy of American citizenship on a national scale, with passage of the Indian Citizenship Act, in 1924.

World War II

Of course, America's official entry into WWII came with Japan's attack on Pearl Harbor on December 7, 1942. It was rumored that many Native Americans reported to their nearby induction centers the following day, bearing their own rifles and ready to go to war. This was in spite of the fact that Indians still didn't have the right to vote in six states.

Whether or not that is true, within six months of the Pearl Harbor attack, seventy-five hundred American Indians had enlisted in the military, and the numbers grew steadily throughout the war.

Indians fought in every theater of the war, often assigned to the most dangerous operations or duties. They became bomber pilots, scouts, communications experts, gunners, commandos, and even brigadier generals, as we shall see. By war's end, at least twenty-five thousand Indian men and women had served in the armed forces, far outstripping the numbers, per capita, of those who served from other ethnic groups.

The Office of Indian Affairs, within the Department of the Interior, was very eager during the war years of 1941–45 to document and publicize the efforts and accomplishments of American Indians. As a result, the department's periodical "Indians At Work," which had been covering progressive developments in Indian Country for several years, featured multiple articles and photos about Indians in the military, as well as wartime activities back home on the reservations. The stories always seemed to support the theme that the Indian had indeed become a valuable American citizen, standing shoulder to shoulder with his white brother.

The wartime media, in general, capitalized on the well-accepted, stereotyped images of the American Indian. Newsreels bombarded American audiences with such news stories as "Heap Big Launching"—about the launching of a wartime freighter, which featured Indian dances and the presentation of a Plains Indian war bonnet to Eleanor Roosevelt—and "Dragons Get Heap Big Medicine," documenting the presentation of Laguna Pueblo dances to Chinese Nationalist pilots training at Kirkland Air Force Base in Albuquerque.

To many Indian people, these stereotyped portrayals were often puzzling, sometimes offensive. Seldom did reporters or media purveyors take time to actually research and portray Indians as they really were, rather relying on concepts and images already accepted by mainstream America.

However, both on the front line and on the home front, Indian people *did* throw their meager resources wholeheartedly into supporting the war effort. Tribes and individual Indians purchased U.S. War Bonds in the millions of dollars. Tribal industries were adapted to wartime production, as portrayed in newsreels seen in theaters all across America. One such segment featured women on the Navajo reservation who had applied their sewing talents to the production of insignia patches.

Even tribal lands were turned over outright or leased to the government for military purposes. For example, the Sioux of the Pine Ridge

Reservation in South Dakota openly received a representative of the War Department in 1942 who asked to lease a portion of their lands for use as a gunnery practice range. The tribe was happy to contribute to the war effort and accepted a three-cent-per-acre fee, far below market value, with the promise that the land would be returned at war's end. A portion of the land was finally released back to the tribe some twenty- five years later.

Service with Distinction

From Sicily and Germany to the South Pacific, Native Americans of all tribes served in WWII with distinction, fighting in greater proportionate numbers than any other race and garnering an impressive number of Silver and Bronze Star Medals and Purple Hearts.

Thomas Yallup, a Yakama Indian delegate presenting testimony before Congress in 1945, stated, "As Americans, in fact the original Americans, this war really and truly means something to us. Our young men have gone forth to war and have been cited for bravery just as in 1918. Because we are Indians doesn't mean that we do not have as much at stake in the land as you do. Our stake may not mean so much in dollars, but in respect and feeling it means as much and probably more, because of our religion about the land and its resources."[4]

Crow Indian veteran Joe Medicine Crow surprised himself with his own actions during the Second World War. In retelling the events that had transpired during the war, he realized that he had unconsciously performed all four deeds traditionally required for a Crow warrior to become a chief.

His wartime deeds included running on foot under heavy fire into an enemy camp to perform a military objective (leading a successful war party), stealing an enemy's weapon, capturing several enemy horses, and touching an enemy warrior without harming him or being harmed. This series of military actions earned him the title of chief, according to traditional Crow culture. His full story is recorded in the book *Native American Testimony*, edited by Peter Nabokov.

Codetalkers in WWII

Once again, as in World War I, native languages were used to trans- mit coded messages that were never broken by the enemy. The Army recruited approximately fifty Native Americans for special native language communication assignments in Europe, and the Marines recruited more than three hundred Navajos for communication duty in the Pacific region.5

In Europe, the Army Signal Corps first used a cadre of Comanches to send secret telephone messages up and down the line. But because Hitler had learned of America's use of Indian languages in WWI, he had sent a team of German anthropologists to learn native tongues before the outbreak of WWII. However, the task proved daunting, due to the existence of some three hundred Native American languages. The army safely used the Comanche communicators during their D-Day assault on the beaches of Normandy and in other instances.

As a matter of fact, Indians from nineteen different tribes were used in some capacity for sending and receiving tribally based coded messages during WWI and WWII. The best known and most publicized codetalkers were the Navajo, used in the Pacific against the Japanese. The 2002 motion picture *Windtalkers*, starring Nicolas Cage and Adam Beach, brought aspects of this story to the big screen.

Philip Johnston, who had grown up on the Navajo reservation as the son of a non-Indian missionary, introduced to the Marines the idea of using the Navajo language shortly after the beginning of the war. A civil engineer who'd served in the Army Corps of Engineers during WWI, Johnston read about the use of Comanches in Europe and thought the Navajo language could be put to similar use.

Impressed by a demonstration of Navajo code-talking capabilities arranged by Johnston, the Marine Corps authorized a pilot program using thirty Navajo men. After their successful deployment to various battlefront locations in the Pacific, the Marine Corps officially instituted the codetalker program. Throughout the war, the Navajo codetalkers repeatedly baffled the Japanese during numerous battles. Of the thirty-six hundred or so Navajos who served in all branches of service, about four hundred Navajo Marines served as codetalkers.

Nowhere did the codetalkers shine more brightly than during the famous Battle of Iwo Jima. The United States desperately needed a midway location for a bomber base that would allow for strategic attacks on Japanese military targets. Iwo Jima, a small, desolate island covered with volcanic ash, was that place.

In February, 1945, the U.S. Marines began their invasion of Iwo Jima. Japanese forces were entrenched in almost impenetrable underground bunkers overlooking marine landing sites. During the four-day battle, six Navajo codetalkers transmitted and received more than eight hundred messages without a single error, immeasurably aiding in the final capture of the island.[6]

Almost fifty years later, Navajo codetalker Harold Foster reflected on Navajo history and his years of military service in an interview with the author. "For hundreds of years," he said, "the Navajo lived in our homelands. These lands provided good grazing for our animals and good hunting. In the 1800s, when the Anglos and the army moved in, the Navajo were pushed north, to more arid land. Still, our leaders wished to keep the peace, and the Navajo came to the fort to trade and to race horses with the soldiers.

"Some years later, the government arrived at our villages and took our children away to boarding schools where they could learn to be like white people. When we put our children in those schools it was like giving our hearts up, and when the Superintendent abused our children it hurt us very much. When Navajo children spoke their language in school, they were punished.

"My older brother was at Normandy, and my oldest brother was a codetalker, too," Foster continued. "After I arrived at boot camp, I sat and thought to myself, 'Why, why did I join up?' Then I remembered— I joined because I wanted to defend my people, my parents, my relatives, my reservation, my state, and my country, the United States. That's why most of the Navajo's veterans went into service, to defend their homeland."

After the War

When they returned home, Indian veterans were hailed as heroes and used by military-sponsored P.R. campaigns to strengthen support for the war on the home front.

A classic case of home-front P.R. involving an Indian soldier is the case of Ira Hayes, a Pima Indian born in a one-room adobe house and educated at an Indian boarding school. He joined the marines and became a paratrooper, earning two Bronze Star Medals for gallantry in the South Pacific. On February 23, 1945, Hayes, four other marines, and a navy corpsman raised the Stars and Stripes atop Mount Suribachi on Iwo Jima, and the famous photograph of that event was widely distributed back in the States.

As portrayed in the Clint Eastwood movie *Flags of Our Fathers*, Hayes and the others became celebrities back home and were reassigned to sell U.S. War Bonds stateside. "I want to go back to the Pacific," Hayes told his superiors—combat was easier for him than P.R., and he often said that he didn't feel like a hero. His request to return to active duty was denied, and he turned to the bottle to drown his inner conflict. After discharge, he returned to the reservation to find no jobs and nothing but despair.

On Veterans Day 1954, Hayes was brought to Washington with the two other survivors pictured in that famous photograph of the flag-raising on Iwo Jima. The occasion was the dedication of a 750-foot bronze statue of the photograph. Two months after the dedication, Hayes's body was found in a roadside ditch near his reservation home. He had died from alcoholism and exposure. He was just thirty-two years old.

Many Native American veterans of WWII suffered similar, though less tragic, experiences after the war's end. While they might have been viewed as heroes in their own tribal communities, the American society at large viewed them once again as merely Indians—which was the equivalent of second-class citizens.

Nothing dramatized the postwar experience of unassimilated Indians so pointedly as the crisis that hit the Navajo Nation in the winter of 1947–48. The New Mexico Association of Indian Affairs reported that the "poor economic situation of the Navajo nation is beyond belief—two-thirds of the tribe's total income had been lost." The Navajo returned to a subsistence economy, and the average male was earning less than one hundred dollars a year. The tribes' infant mortality rate was seven times the United States average, and only one in five children of school age could be accommodated by the overcrowded Bureau of Indian Affairs–run school system.

After the war, Indian veterans and war workers alike faced uncertain futures. Thousands had been accepted into white mainstream society, relocating to cities to go to work or serving side by side with Anglo men and women in the military. Many found new stature and respect back in their home communities and reservations. Others found that they no longer seem to fit in among their traditional counterparts and so migrated to the nearest cities looking for work. Whatever the case, World War II had forever changed the way Indian peoples interacted with one another and the larger, non-Indian society.

The rapid integration of Indian citizens into white America became the official goal of federal Indian policy. "Termination" of tribal status became the legislative strategy in the postwar years from 1947–53, and liquidation of tribally owned property a major goal. Meanwhile, individual Indian people were simply trying to survive in a postwar economy.

It was against this backdrop that Indians once again rose up to serve their country when the call came.

The Korean "Police Action"

The Korean War (1950–53) was the first undeclared war the United States ever fought. President Harry S. Truman called it a "police action" when he committed U.S. troops to operations on the Korean Peninsula in June of 1950. The Korean War is also sometimes called "The Forgotten War," but a total of 5,720,000 Americans saw military service during this period.

Unfortunately, no records were kept that made a distinction between Indian and white soldiers, and thus there is no official documentation of the contributions Indians made in this war. However, many Indian vets from the Korean conflict are alive and well and willing to share their war and postwar experiences.

For example, Alex Seowtewa, a Zuni Pueblo Indian artist, fought in Korea as a young man. He remembers the conflict this created within him because of the teachings of his traditional Zuni grandfather. "Never point a gun at a human being," his grandfather had taught, and so Alex had to go completely against his training and conscience to execute what he felt were his duties as an American citizen.

After he fought overseas, he returned to the Zuni reservation, near Gallup, New Mexico, to deal with the results of his *internal* war. His first attempt at coping with the problem was through alcohol. Weekend after weekend, Alex found himself sleeping off another binge in the Gallup drunk tank.

Finally, after an intense session of self-evaluation, following a particularly rough weekend, Alex came to grips with the turmoil in his gut and set himself on a new path. Integrating both the teachings of his grandfather and the experiences of his own life, he constructed a personal philosophy for life in two worlds that allowed him to balance the requirements of one with the demands of the other.

Increasingly, this became the way most Indian people had to learn to function in order to survive in modern America: a balancing act.

For other Native American men at the time, military service merely became a means of economic self-support. Take Ronald Stewart, a Crow Indian vet, for instance. "I joined the army in 1952 at the age of twenty," he said. "I needed a job and really didn't have any skills. After sixteen weeks of basic training, I was sent to the frontline in Korea. I served in the army until 1954 and was discharged. I wasn't treated any different than any of the other soldiers I served with. The only problem I got now is getting into a VA hospital. I go over there and try to get some services, they turn me down. It seems like others can get whatever they want. That kind of bothers me."

In the 1950s, the drive for tribal termination pressed on at the federal level, and several small tribes were officially taken off the federal books.

However, many people inside and out of government circles began viewing this policy as a sneaky way for the federal government to renege on its treaty obligations and responsibilities to Indians, and eventually this policy was abandoned.

Vietnam

As the United States began its involvement in Vietnam in the early 1960s, a new consciousness was developing among a generation of young Americans, including urban-based, politically savvy Indians who had mastered the art of living in two worlds. And as the Vietnam War escalated, the civil rights movement grew in strength, and various ethnic movements such as the Black Panthers became vocal and violent, so did the demands and actions of the newly formed American Indian Movement (AIM).

Indian rights and the recognition of tribal sovereignty were two of the main goals of the AIM organization, contrasting sharply with many federal policies and goals of the time, which continued to view Indians as wards of the government who were to be dictated to rather than listened to.

In spite of mounting conflicts and controversies between tribal peoples and the U.S. government, Indians enlisted in the military for service in Vietnam in record numbers, as in previous wars. Many say they did so because of family traditions going back many generations.

Andrew Lewis, an Indian painter from New Mexico, is one such Vietnam vet. "Everyone in my family has been through the military," he said. "My grandmother was a Red Cross nurse in World War I. My grandfather was a captain in World War I. My uncle was in World War II. My mother was a Red Cross nurse during the Korean War, and my father is a veteran of the Korean War, as well.

"Now, my older brother went into Vietnam in the early '60s. But myself, why I went—I just wanted to go. I had friends who went in. My family had been in, so I might as well go. I wanted to see how my attitude would change in the military life. I was born at home on the Pueblo and didn't have a birth certificate, so I could say I was old enough to enlist. I went in when I was only fourteen years old."

Creek Indian Vietnam veteran Willie Haney of Oklahoma had experiences in the war common to many other Indian vets. He shared these comments in a documentary film about Indian Vietnam vets called *A Time to Heal*, which was produced by the author.

"We have seen movies of the Vietnam War," he said. "Yet our Indian people are not portrayed there. You see the black people, the Hispanic people, the white people, but no Indians are there. Yet every time you'd be out in the field in 'Nam, the first thing an officer would do is say, 'Chief, you take point.' The man may have never lived in the country in his life, but if he was an Indian, it was always, 'Chief, take the point.'"

Haney's comments reflect the stereotypical views that many non-Indians have toward Indians, views often derived from Hollywood westerns. These films frequently depicted Indians with innate tracking and hunting skills that almost bordered on the supernatural, and Indian males are often referred to as "chief," a derogatory use of the word.

Haney continued. "One of the things we realize is that a lot of Indians during 'Nam, or anytime, are usually quiet, kind of set back, which may be one of the reasons that movies don't show too many Indians. But every time we are called upon, Indian people are always there. We want people to know that we, as an Indian people, are always ready to fight for our country. This is our homeland. We give it all we've got."[6]

It is interesting to note that one of the first casualties of Vietnam was a young Navajo volunteer, and one of the most highly decorated Indians of that war was Billy Walkabout, a Cherokee who was awarded the Distinguished Service Cross, five Silver Stars, and five Bronze Stars, and who was wounded six times. However, these are the kinds of facts that went unnoticed by the media and the general public during the Vietnam War years.

Crow vet Carson Walks-Over-Ice remembered one decorated native vet that he personally knew. "The Special Forces had an all-Indian team, an 'A-Team.' No one knew about them because they were strictly hush-hush. They were in Laos, China, Russia, Cambodia, Africa, and Thailand.

There was one guy I knew in that outfit, named Medicine Bull from Ft. Peck. He had six Silver Stars. Out of the twelve that were in that outfit, he was one of only two who made it back. He died several years ago—drank himself to death in Seattle."

Medicine Bull's wartime experience likely was shared by many other native vets, for it was in Vietnam that many Native American soldiers found themselves in a crisis of conscience. It was difficult for many Indian soldiers to deal with the images of villages filled with women and children being burned and routed, simply because they were fighting for their homeland. After all, their own tribal histories were filled with similar stories of native people being killed and forced from their lands.

Like many of their white brethren, they also put their lives on the line for love of homeland, but uniquely, many Indian soldiers began to find it hard to understand how that patriotism brought them to fight indigenous villagers in rice paddies in a tiny country thousands of miles from home who, from all appearances, were no real threat to the American homeland.

Later, after the Vietnam War ended, it also did not escape the notice of Native American veterans that they were not represented in the Vietnam Veterans memorial statue in Washington DC. Consequently over the last few decades, many tribes have erected their own memorials to tribal vets who served in Vietnam.

Coping During Peacetime

In 1981, several American Indian Vietnam vets came together and formed the Vietnam Era Veterans Intertribal Association to help bring recognition and healing to Indian vets from that war. They held the first annual powwow of the association that year in Anadarko, Oklahoma. Since then, tribal chapters of the organization have sprung up all across the country.

John T. McIntosh, a Cherokee Vietnam vet, helped form one of the chapters in Oklahoma, because the organization's goals were very near to his heart. He said, "I'd always wanted to do something like this because

I knew that the Vietnam Veteran had been really short-changed because of what he'd been through, and the way that some of the American people had felt. And I always thought that if there was something that could be done to heal those wounds between the American people and the Vietnam veteran, then I wanted to be a part of it because I was there, and I know there are wounds between myself and the way some of the people feel towards me."[7]

George Whitman, a Yuchi Indian vet, joined the Indian color guard established by the Oklahoma chapter to present the colors at parades, powwows, dedications, and funerals. He commented, "When I put that uniform on, it brings back memories of friends that were [in Vietnam], and some of them that didn't make it back. To me, I'm just carrying on maybe what they would have done if they had come back. It's kind of left up to the ones who did make it back to do these things for the Vietnam veterans.

"It's a good feeling," he went on, "because at most powwows, all the Indians respect veterans. No matter where you go, Indian veterans are always respected. That makes you feel good. It doesn't make you feel like you did something wrong. It makes you feel good out there, like you draw power from it. To me, when I'm out there dancing, it feels like all of nature is coming together and it's giving you power."[8]

George's brother, Richard Ray Whitman, took a stance on the other side of the fence, protesting against the Vietnam War. He joined AIM in the early 1970s and actively took part in the various protests sponsored by that organization against the war and against the American government's treatment of Indians in general. These two brothers' lives took different directions during those years, but each respected the other's right to follow his own conscience.

By war's end, over forty-one thousand American Indians had fought in Vietnam. Many had come face to face with an enemy that resembled themselves: indigenous peoples fighting for the right to determine their own futures. This discovery was added to the already harsh realities of this unpopular war.

Like warriors of old, many returning Indian Vietnam veterans were sincerely welcomed back into their home communities with honor pow-wows and cleansing ceremonies. This is one reason that many Indian vets have not suffered from the "postwar-stress syndrome" experienced by so many other Vietnam veterans. These traditional tribal ceremonies continue in contemporary times to purge the emotional and spiritual wounds of battle and restore the warrior to a harmonious place within the community.

The Gulf War/Operation Desert Storm

Unfortunately, stereotypes and ethnic ignorance about Indians didn't end with the Vietnam War. With over three thousand American Indian soldiers stationed in Kuwait during the Gulf War (1990–91), Marine Brigadier General Richard Neal referred to enemy territory as "Indian Country." This slang military term, obviously left over from the Indian Wars of the 1800s, apparently continued to be used during the Vietnam War and into the Gulf War and was applied to enemy territory in any nation.

Leaders of the National Congress of American Indians, which represents tribal governments all across the United States, immediately asked for an apology from the military for the "offensive, ignorant, and insensitive" comment. A spokesman for the military command in Saudi Arabia explained that "Indian Country" is a term that was used in Vietnam to mean hostile territory, but a Pentagon spokeswoman said that the term had no official definition in military manuals.

Military records, provided by the Pentagon public affairs office, show that approximately twelve thousand Native Americans served in the Middle East during the Gulf War, and possibly as many as twenty-four thousand were serving in all branches of the military just before Desert Storm began.

One thing that was obvious from television and print news coverage of the Gulf War was that an increasing number of women had stepped into combat and combat support roles, a trend reflected within Native American communities, as well.

A review of tribal newspapers of the time reveal that tribal communities all across the United States were intensely involved in ceremonial activities aimed at both honoring their young warriors involved in Operation Desert storm *and* bringing them safely home. It was apparent that patriotism among American Indians was as strong as ever.

Unfortunately, the last soldier killed in combat in that war was Manuel Michael Davila, aged twenty-two, Sioux.

Operation Enduring Freedom

The terrorist attack of 9/11 touched Native Americans, as it did all Americans, deeply and immediately. On that day, more than three hundred tribal leaders from Indian reservations all across the country were gathered for a meeting in Washington DC. Their responses to the fateful events of that day were, of course, a mixture of sorrow, disbelief, and anger.

A press release issued the same day by California's Morongo Band of Mission Indians summed up native reaction. "This is a terrible and sad day in American history," the statement said. "The entire community sends our deepest condolences to the families of the people who lost their lives this morning in the heinous, demented terrorist attacks on the World Trade Center in New York and the Pentagon in Washington, D.C. As in every major crisis that this country has faced, we stand with all of America in offering our resources and support in every way."[9]

Within days, outpourings of native generosity began finding their way to New York City. Four Mohawks drove a van full of urgently needed rescue supplies and cash donations to the City. The Mohegan tribe of Connecticut pledged $1 million to help the victims and families of the tragedy, and hundreds of thousands of dollars came from other gaming tribes around the country.

"Operation Enduring Freedom" was the name assigned to America's first military response to the 9/11 terrorist attacks. The name primarily referred to the war in Afghanistan and the initial search for Al-Qaeda leader Osama bin Laden. The number of Native Americans serving in the military at that time hovered around eighteen thousand, though records don't indicate how many were deployed in Afghanistan.

However, the loss of one of their own was never felt more deeply than during those years following 9/11, years of heightened American patriotism, years that Native Americans seemed to feel a part of the American fabric as never before. That was obvious on one cold December day in 2006 at Mandaree, North Dakota, when Army National Guard Corporal Nathan Goodiron was laid to rest. According to the *Indian Country Today* newspaper, the twenty five-year-old Hidatsu soldier died of wounds received in Afghanistan on Thanksgiving Day.

Approximately fifteen hundred people, including the state's governor, John Hoeven, attended the funeral. Governor Hoeven called Nathan "a true warrior and a true hero; he didn't set out to be a hero, but his principles and his character made him one."[10]

In 2003, Operation Enduring Freedom and the search for bin Laden was given a backseat when America launched its offensive against Sadam Hussein in Iraq.

Operation Iraqi Freedom

As with the war in Vietnam, the war in Iraq became quite controversial, both within and outside of native communities. While most contemporary Indian people support our troops wherever they may be fighting, some do not support the political decisions that bring America into a particular war.

However, no one disputes the fact that, once again, Native Americans responded to the call to duty when, in January 2003, America's invasion of Iraq began.

Private Lori Ann Piestewa, a Hopi from Tuba City, Arizona, came from a family that had a long military tradition, with both father and grandfather having served in the U.S. Army. She was already enlisted in the army and serving in the Quartermaster Corps with her friend Jessica Lynch when their unit was deployed in February of that year. Lori's 507th Army Maintenance Company was a support unit made up primarily of clerks, repairmen, and cooks.

Riding in a Humvee that was part of a caravan of support vehicles, Piestewa and her company became lost during the opening days of the war. They were ambushed in Nasiriyah, in southern Iraq, on March 23, 2003, and their vehicle was struck by a rocket-propelled grenade.

Piestewa and Lynch were severely wounded and taken prisoner. Piestewa died soon afterwards. The rescue mission that later saved Jessica Lynch from captivity became one of the early success stories of the war, but her friend, the Hopi soldier, was rarely mentioned.

Piestewa was awarded the Purple Heart and Prisoner of War Medal, and the army posthumously promoted her from private first class to specialist.

Lynch repeatedly said that Piestewa was the true hero of the ambush and named her daughter Dakota Ann Lynch in honor of her fallen friend, whose own middle name was Ann. Additionally, many agencies honored Piestewa's memory with memorials, including the renaming the offensively named Squaw Peak near Phoenix as Piestewa Peak.[6]

Piestewa was the first woman killed in the Iraq War and is the first Native American woman to die in overseas combat. And unfortunately, she won't be the last.

The Tradition Continues

Through the stories and events recorded in these pages, we've seen that Native Americans continue in the proud warrior traditions practiced by many of their ancestors, despite the ignorance and misunderstanding of their ways demonstrated by the federal government and the American people. Understanding the motives and actions of Indian people has always been hard for the general public, but this has never deterred Native Americans from acting with courage from the heart.

*   *   *

"Native Americans fly the American flag at our homes and display yellow ribbons to show our support for our troops. We will quietly go to our sweat lodges and pray. Our drums will beat to honor our warriors. We will join hands in our circle of prayer as the drumbeat courses through our veins and becomes our heartbeat.

"Tobacco offerings and burning sage will float heavenward to carry our prayers. The pipe will be smoked. Honor songs will be sung. Feathers will be earned. We will fight and we will die, beside non-Indians. As the sirens sound and the bombs fall, we honor our warriors. We will pray for their safety as we pray for peace. Tomorrow depends upon it."

—Native American veteran

PART FOUR

Enemies and Allies:
The Paradox of
Native American Service

Proud units of Native American vet color guards exist all over the United States and present the colors at a variety of Native American gatherings including conferences, powwows and public ceremonies. The color guard pictured here is a unit of Southern Cheyennes from Oklahoma. Photo by the author.

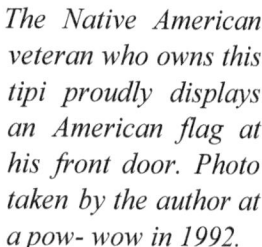

The Native American veteran who owns this tipi proudly displays an American flag at his front door. Photo taken by the author at a pow-wow in 1992.

This design, displayed on a t-shirt hanging in the Oneida Tribal Museum, dem- onstrates the pride Native American veterans feel regarding their military service. Photo taken by the author in Oneida, Wisconsin, c. 1992.

PART FOUR—ENEMIES AND ALLIES: THE PARADOX OF NATIVE AMERICAN SERVICE

As alluded to earlier in this book, the reasons Native Americans have volunteered for military service, at a rate that far exceeds other ethnic groups, are complex. Many speak of honor and duty, the same rea- sons other Americans give. Others talk about tribal traditions that span hundreds of years—the original "homeland security," you might say. Whatever the reasons Native Americans risk their lives to face an enemy, the feelings among Indians regarding service run deep. But who defines the enemy?

According to Sam Keen, author of *Faces of the Enemy*, we often create our enemy. Before the weapons come the images. This is a practice common to world civilizations, from ancient China to the Greeks and Romans. Generation after generation, we find excuses to dehumanize each other, particularly if we wish to justify genocide. We characterize the enemy in very specific ways—as an unjustified aggressor, a faceless, dehumanized stereotype deserving of our violence. This allows us to reserve our rational thought for the tactics we will use to destroy them.

In national propaganda, the enemy may be portrayed as an enemy of God, the agent of the devil. The enemy is portrayed as crude, rude, and uncivilized. The enemy is seen as a torturer, a systematic sadist who delights in inflicting pain. The enemy is rapist, destroyer of motherhood and female honor. And the enemy is cast as a barbarian, of another race and therefore less than human.[1]

Seventy years of Hollywood westerns capitalized on all of these "enemy" images, giving audiences such films as *The Searchers*, *Red River*, and *Arrowhead*, among many others, in which all Indian warriors are depicted as vicious sub-humans intent on torturing, maiming, and brutalizing innocent settlers. John Wayne, Charlton Heston, and other stars made fortunes by playing heroic "saviors" in these films, which validated Anglo-Americans as the rightful heirs to this great land.

However, Hollywood was not the first to dehumanize Native Americans in order to justify conquest and settlement. The process began five hundred years ago with the Spanish, as part of a premeditated campaign to dispossess the indigenous peoples of the Americas of their lands and resources.

R. Brian Ferguson of Rutgers University studied the stories and images generated by the explorers and conquerors who followed Columbus into the New World. He says they often dwelt on lurid stories of unbridled native violence.2 Because Spanish law made cannibals fair game for immediate enslavement, European explorers often created and disseminated false stories of indigenous cannibal buffets as a pretext and justification for their destruction.

The image of the Native American as brutal savage and the primary antagonist to white heroes became a seminal part of the myth of the Wild West. The vast majority of magazine articles and dime novels that perpetuated this image were written by people who either knew nothing of native peoples or who were serving an agenda to exterminate them.

As a matter of fact, the entire dime-novel publishing industry that flourished from 1860 to about 1915 began when the publishing firm of Beadle & Adams in New York City launched *Malaeska, the Indian Wife of the White Hunter*, by Mrs. Ann S. Stephens. It was the first entry in a series entitled *Beadle's Dime Novels*, and the author of this tale of the "wild frontier" was a stout, fifty-year-old woman who hailed from and had never left New England.

Unfortunately, many of the false images and lurid stories of "savage natives" were accepted as true and became part of our recorded his- tory. The Apache—who in actuality had a well-organized, chaste, deeply devout, and physically clean way of life—were a favorite subject of racist libel in fiction. The Apache were labeled as filthy, devil-worshipping, human-trophy-gathering beasts.

However, because of their constant cleansing in sweat lodges and washing with sand when water was scarce in the desert, it was not the Apache who could be smelled for miles off, but the white mountain men—and it was the mountain men who, in reality, boasted of raping

Indian women and using their severed breasts for purses. But the power of the media was potent even in the last century.

One example of the difference between prejudiced image and reality comes from the writings of military wife Ada Vogdes, who lived with her husband, a general, at an army fort on the plains for a while in the 1870s. Before coming to the fort, she, like so many other ladies living on the eastern seaboard, had heard many tales of the "fiercely savage heathens" of the plains and dreaded her move to the fort. The very thought of living so close to Indians caused her to fear for her life.

When the great Sioux war chiefs, Red Cloud, Red Leaf, and Big Bear came to the fort, her position as the general's wife forced her to interact with and help entertain these visitors. After spending only a brief time with these men, her attitude markedly changed. She wrote that these men were gentlemen filled with grace and dignity, and she spent many delightful hours in their company.[3]

But when a Native American went to war for the United States, whether as a scout for the cavalry or a marine in the Second World War, he found himself surrounded by the echoes of the myths of the savage, yet mystically attuned, warrior. Much of the perpetuated mythology, it turned out, was often used as politically expedient propaganda.

Crow Indian Vietnam vet Carson Walks-Over-Ice was one of many who experienced the stereotyped myth. "One thing that's funny is that Indians are never usually put together in a unit," he said. "I don't know why, but the army has a policy not to put Indians together. In 'Nam, they called me 'chief' and expected me to do the long-range reconnaissance patrol. They thought I could see in the dark and that kind of thing. I told them I was not a chief, but they persisted, because that's the stereotype of the Indian."

Northern Cheyenne vet Joe Walks-Along echoed this experience. He said, "There was a lot of unspoken assumption that an Indian was a natural-born warrior, and so I was selected to go out on patrol regularly. Nobody wanted to go on patrol, because that was so dangerous—you were so close to the enemy. They called me 'chief' a lot, but I'm not really a chief. I'm with the Kit Fox Society [a traditional Cheyenne warrior society], so I'm not a chief."

"When I first got to Nam, I was doing road checks on Highway 1," added Northern Cheyenne Vietnam vet Windfield Russell. "I met this other Indian guy from Anadarko [Oklahoma] and we went out on listening posts in the bush. The commander used to always call us for this kind of duty, because we were Indians, and he thought we were bet- ter than those other guys to go out into the jungle; we could detect the enemy better."

Vietnam Marine vet Apesanahkwat of the Menominee tribe recalled, "One time they transferred these guys over to our outfit, and there was an Indian guy in there, named Sherman Swift Eagle. We were out on company maneuvers, up in a mountain range, where we come across some tracks in a riverbed there. I was walking point, so I held up the column, and I was feeling them tracks, you know. The commander came up, and Swift Eagle was right behind me. I looked up at Swift Eagle and said, 'Looks like about forty-five minutes.' Swift Eagle felt in there and he said, 'More like a half-hour.' And that Captain said, 'Goddam, you Indians are good.'

"Me and Swift Eagle just busted out laughing," continued Apesanahkwat, known as A.P. to friends. "Those tracks must have been about three weeks old. That was pretty funny, but typical of the way it was over there. I'll tell you something about every Indian veteran that I know served in Vietnam. They always had us walking point.

"I used to ask my lieutenant, who was a black man: 'You know I'm getting ready to transfer back to the States, how come you're making me walk point? I can't see no better than you.' He says, 'I know that, but these guys feel better with you out there.' So they pretty much evenly divided the Indians among the platoons so each platoon had enough Indians to use as point men.

"They respected what they perceived—that stereotype of a skill we are born with to hear and see and smell and all of that. And sometimes you tried hard to live up to that."

Even as they fought, Indian soldiers were the subject of both ridicule and propaganda. World War II army publicity photos sent to the folks back home often posed Indian soldiers in ridiculous, caricature-like poses that reenacted the stereotypes of Indian warriors. Even today, as we try to bring Native American history closer to what really happened and what tribal American peoples were really like, there is resistance from the image-makers of the dominant culture, because those historical cultural icons are so powerful and so familiar.

As noted in Part One, when it comes time for an Indian warrior to return to his home community, his people have ways to welcome and honor him (or her). In these communities, warfare is acknowledged both as a natural part of life's struggles to protect tribal values and also as a disruption of family and community. While war is forced upon the community and upon an individual, veterans who return are to be honored whether they won or lost the conflict.

Not only should veteran warriors be honored, according to American Indian practice, but they should also be cleansed of the stains of battle and restored to a harmonious position within the community. And, consequently, many tribal cultures include both private and public ceremonies and social customs for doing so. For thousands of veterans and their families who attend powwows, the ceremonies, dances, and commemorations are times of genuine healing and community building.

For the families of Indian war veterans, sharing the stories of wartime struggles and sacrifice are an important part of their personal recovery and survival as a people. Such storytelling is another of the many Indian cultural practices that contribute to the health of both the individual and the community.

Charles Chibitty, a World War II Comanche codetalker and mem- ber of the Native American Church talked about the spiritual forces he believed protected him. "When they asked me to be a codetalker, I was proud," he said. "We saved a lot of lives when [the Germans] could not break the code. Before I went overseas, there was one man at home— ever since I was little he always called me son. We went back to his house where his old peyote ground is, and he put four peyote buttons on the ground and prayed—he said God gave us this medicine to use when we need it. 'It's going to take you over there and bring you back,' he said. 'When you get scared, you take one out, chew it little bit and pray.' I felt fear because there was a lot of artillery mortars coming in. I came back—I got wounded, but I came back—that old man's prayers went with me."

For all the hardships and prejudices that Indian soldiers found, they also had an immeasurable advantage. They had "good medicine" and powerful faith in that medicine. For many Indian people, the term "medicine" often refers to a combination of rituals, herbal substances, prayer, and faith that carries power to accomplish something that might include physical or emotional healing, protection, or simply effectiveness in one's endeavors.

Codetalker Harold Foster shared this about his preparation for war, his service and his return: "My Navajo religion is my religion that I'll never forget. They did a protection ceremony for me before I went overseas, and that's what brought me back. And when I got back, they did another one to purify my soul. This one medicine man did that for me. It takes four days. It's called the Enemy Way.

"I did pray many times when I was exposed to danger on the main battle line, as a codetalker and a signal man. I prayed as my mother and father taught me, to the Heavenly Being and to Mother Earth. When I came back, my mother told me, 'Son, since you left, almost every morning I have gone to my sacred hill and prayed, using my sacred corn pollen, that you would come back.' Maybe that is the reason I came back all in one piece."

What follows is the testimony of several Indian veterans who were positively affected by the native rituals and beliefs of their people.

Vietnam vet Harold Barse, one of the founders of the Native American Vietnam Veterans Association, commented, "Tribal societies have known all along that you have to do something in order to bring the warrior back into society, through cleansing ceremonies, sweats, to rid the per- son of the contamination of war. The Vietnam generation is probably the first generation of Indian vets to be born and raised in the city— not reservation Indians—and we have to make the effort to go back and learn our ways if we want to know anything about them and be able to use them to help us."

Oneida veteran Ted Christjohn said this about his postwar experiences: "After my service, I came back here to the Oneida reservation, but at first I had a very hard time. I went on a two-year binge of drinking. I couldn't handle it, and I ended up in jail. Now I'm going through sweat ceremonies and learning more about my tribe's beliefs, and that helps a lot. I just went through a ceremony up on the Menominee Reservation with those guys up there, what's called a White Feather Ceremony. And that was really something."

Crow Indian vet Eddie Little Light: "My uncles were in the Native American Church, and they held a peyote meeting for me before I went overseas and made me a medicine pouch to carry with me at all times. Carson Walks-Over-Ice and I came back together, and we were honored by the tribe. They held a victory dance during the annual Crow Fair. I had a hard time getting readjusted. I couldn't sleep at night. I almost had a nervous breakdown. I would wake up at night in a cold sweat and start to go outside to do things I had done in 'Nam. I started drinking to help me cope. But I had a Crow uncle who helped me get through it with informal counseling and in the sweats and taking me to powwows."

Fellow Crow veteran William Charles Stewart: "While in Korea, I was a squad leader. My clan uncles held a give-away for me before I left, and one of them sent a little bundle with me to take overseas for protection. They said to bring it back with me and give it back to them.

"After I came back and gave that bundle to him, he told me it was just dirt that he had picked up from the riverbank. But he had stood on the riverbank and prayed in the Indian way and said: 'My nephew is going across the water and will take this dirt and bring it back. When he gets back, I'll return this dirt to the same place I got it from. Thank you.'

"These clan uncles held another give-away for me for making it back. Then they took me into a sweat tipi and prayed for me to purify me. They said they were glad to see me make it back, and they prayed for a better future for me."

As the stories and comments of these veterans attest, the actions, attitudes, and experiences of Native American warriors stand in stark contrast to the stereotypes disseminated and perpetuated by the movies and the media. We all have much to learn from these indigenous men and women who heed the call to service and action.

*   *   *

Just as the Cherokee were removed, in the great Trail of Tears, from their North Carolina homes to the plains of Oklahoma, so has the major contribution of the American Indian veteran been removed from, or never fully included in, the national history of America.

To create the United States, the nation's white forefathers first destroyed the many Indian nations already thriving throughout this land. It is a shameful tale of broken treaties, murderous military campaigns, and near-genocide whose legacy remains visible today in a federal agency, the Department of the Interior's Bureau of Indian Affairs, that willfully mismanaged billions of dollars of funds belonging to the very Native American individuals the agency was created to protect (*Cobell v. U.S. Department of the Interior*).

For those Indian veterans who fought to protect the rights of all Americans, much of the past discrimination within the military finally seems to be coming to an end. Native American Heritage Month (November) is now one of several ethnically and culturally related events to be observed by the U.S. Department of Defense, and attempts to better understand Indian peoples and cultures are evident in all branches of the U.S. military.

Native American people, men and women, will continue to answer America's call to duty and will continue to sacrifice and serve, in hopes that one day all Americans—black, white, red, and yellow—will truly be treated as equals.

APPENDIX I
Profiles in Service

PROFILES IN SERVICE

Thousands of Native Americans have served in the armed forces with dis- tinction, and all their stories can't be told in these pages. However, the few men and women profiled here represent a small sampling of the bravery and valor exhibited by Native American soldiers throughout history. The source for the information printed below, except the final entry, is Native Americans and the Military: Today and Yesterday, *published by the U.S. Army Public Affairs Information Branch in March, 1984. This document is reprinted here in its entirety with permission.*

Sgt. I-See-O, Army Scout, 1889–1913

Known as a peacemaker in later life, the man called I-See-O was born near Larned, Kansas about 1851. He enlisted in the Army's unit of Indian Scouts in 1889 at Fort Sill, Oklahoma, and became a courier, messenger and eventually a counselor to Major General Nelson A. Miles.

In his early days at Fort Sill, the Scout met Lt. Hugh Scott, and the two became friends. Later they traveled together in that region wherever conflict developed between tribes or between Indians and whites. Indians came to trust I-See-O's advice and respected Lt. Scott's fairness. I-See-O is credited with preventing much bloodshed on both sides.

When I-See-O retired from military service in 1913, Scott, now Major General Scott and Chief of Staff of the Army, arranged for I-See-O to receive a pension for the rest of his life.

In a letter to I-See-O written in 1919, Scott said, "You and I worked well together at that time, and the Indian people of Oklahoma owe you a great deal of thanks … You and I together brought all those Oklahoma tribes through the same troubles which brought about the death of so many Sioux Indians without firing a single shot, so the white people owe much to you as do your own people."

I-See-O died on March 10, 1927, and was buried in his uniform as he had requested.

Sgt. William Major, Apache Scout
Recipient of the Expert Marksman Badge

Apache Indian William Major enlisted in the Army at Fort Apache in 1921. During his 27 years of service, he was a carpenter, truck driver, and military policeman. As was the practice for many Indian Scouts, Major also hunted deer to supplement the soldiers' diet.

Sgt. Major earned the Expert Marksman Badge by hitting a bulls-eye target with 10 rounds at 500 yards.

He loved the Army and in his later years, loved to tell visitors to the fort about the day he and four other Apache Scouts retired. "It was a fine thing," he is reported to have said. "We rode our horses in review, and they all saluted us. Now I am the only one living."

The Sergeant was indeed one of the last Apache Scouts to serve at Fort Huachuca, Arizona. He died in 1983.

Major General Clarence L. Tinker, Osage
Recipient of the Soldier's Medal

Clarence Tinker was born in 1887 near Pawhuska, Oklahoma, to an Osage father and German mother and grew up speaking both the Osage and English languages.

By 1922, he was a Commanding Officer in charge of the 16th Squadron stationed at Fort Riley, Kansas. He went on to eight other post commands during is military career. While serving in London in 1926, he earned the Soldier's Medal for rescuing a naval attaché from a burning plane, and in 1927, he assisted the Army in creating routes for airmail.

Major General Tinker was lost in action near Pearl Harbor, Hawaii, on June 7, 1942, while leading a squadron of bombers on a mission against the Japanese. At the time he was Commander of the Army Air Forces in Hawaii.

The Oklahoma City Air Depot was renamed "Tinker Field" in October of that year to honor "a gallant and courageous soldier and airman who brought credit to his forbears, his state and his nation." Five years later the air field's name was changed again to Tinker Air Force Base.

General Tinker was inducted into the National American Indian Hall of Fame located in Anadarko, Oklahoma, in 1966.

Jack C. Montgomery, Oklahoma Cherokee Congressional Medal of Honor Recipient

Born in Long, Oklahoma, Jack Montgomery entered the Army at Sallisaw, Oklahoma, and reached the rank of First Lieutenant in the 45th Infantry Division. The deeds for which he was awarded the Medal of Honor occurred during combat in Italy in 1945.

His Medal of Honor Citation reads: For conspicuous gallantry and intrepidity at risk of life above and beyond the call of duty on 22 Feb. 1944, near Padiglione, Italy. Two hours before daybreak a strong force of enemy infantry established themselves in three echelons at 50 yards, 100 yards, and 300 yards respectively in front of the rifle platoons commanded by Lt. Montgomery. The closest position, consisting of four machine guns and one mortar, threatened the immediate security of the platoon position.

Seizing an M1 rifle and several hand grenades, Lt. Montgomery crawled up a ditch to within grenade range of the enemy. Then, climbing boldly onto a little mound, he fired his rifle and threw his grenades so accurately that he killed eight of the enemy and captured four more.

Returning to his platoon, he called for artillery fire on a house, in and around which he suspected that the majority of the enemy had entrenched themselves. Arming himself with a carbine, he proceeded along the shallow ditch, as withering fire from the riflemen and machine gunners in the second position was concentrated on him. He attacked this position with such fury that seven of the enemy surrendered to him, and both machine guns were silenced. Three German dead were found in the vicinity later that morning.

Lt. Montgomery continued boldly toward the house, 300 yards from his platoon position. It was now daylight, and the enemy observation was excellent across the flat open terrain, which led to Lt. Montgomery's objective. When the artillery barrage had lifted, Lt. Montgomery ran fearlessly toward the strongly defended position.

As the enemy started streaming out of the house, Lt. Montgomery, unafraid of treacherous snipers, exposed himself daringly to assemble the surrendering enemy and send them to the rear.

His fearless, aggressive and intrepid actions that morning accounted for a total of 11 enemy dead, 32 prisoners and an unknown number of wounded. That night, while aiding an adjacent unit to repulse a counter-attack, he was struck by mortar fragments and seriously wounded.

The selflessness and courage exhibited by Lt. Montgomery in alone attacking three strong enemy positions inspired his men to a degree beyond estimation.

Ernest Childers, Oklahoma Creek Indian Congressional Medal of Honor Recipient

Oklahoma Creek Indian Ernest Childers was born in Broken Arrow and reached the rank of Second Lieutenant in the Army's 45th Infantry Division. His 1943 Medal of Honor Citation reads: For conspicuous gallantry and intrepidity above and beyond the call of duty in action on 22 Sept. 1943 at Oliveto, Italy.

Although Lt. Childers had previously just suffered a fractured instep he, with eight enlisted men, advanced up a hill toward enemy machine-gun nests. The group advanced to a rock wall overlooking a cornfield and Lt. Childers ordered a base of fire laid across the field so that he could advance. When he was fired upon by two enemy snipers from a nearby house, he killed both of them.

He moved behind the machine-gun nests and killed all occupants of the nearest one. He continued toward the second one and threw rocks into it. When the two occupants of the nest raised up, he shot one. The other was killed by one of the eight enlisted men.

Lt. Childers continued his advance toward a house farther up the hill and, single-handed, captured an enemy mortar observer. The exceptional leadership, initiative, calmness under fire, and conspicuous gallantry displayed by Lt. Childers were an inspiration to his men.

Admiral Joseph J. Clark, Oklahoma Cherokee
Navy Cross and Numerous Decorations

Admiral Joseph "Jocko" Clark, a veteran of three wars, was promoted to the rank of full admiral after receiving numerous battle decorations including the Navy Cross. He retired from the U.S. Navy after 40 years of service.

Clark was born near Pryor, Oklahoma, and graduated from the Naval Academy in 1917. He first served aboard the USS North Carolina during World War I escorting convoys across the Atlantic Ocean. He then qualified as a pilot in 1925, becoming one of the Navy's early aviators. During World War II he commanded two ships: the USS Suwannee and the USS Yorktown. He then commanded aircraft carrier divisions in Task Force 58 in the western Pacific Ocean. He earned 12 battle stars in the Pacific Theater and one in the Atlantic.

Finally, during the Korean War, Clark commanded Task Force 77 and later the Seventh Fleet.

Clarence "Tinq" Rogers, Prisoner of War

"Tinq" Rogers, a Cherokee, enlisted in the Army in May of 1941 at Fort Bragg, North Carolina. He was shipped to Manila, Philippine Islands, in October of that same year, as a member of the 803rd Engineers Company.

In the Philippines, Corporal Rogers was part of the team that was building roads near the Dell Carmen Airport. He was captured by the Japanese in April, 1942, after five days and nights of heavy fighting in the area.

He was one of the many American soldiers forced on the "Bataan Death March" for seven days and nights. Prisoners of war barely had anything to eat and were kept in crowded, unsanitary camps during this march.

Along with other Army engineers, Rogers was forced to work for the Japanese building roads and bridges, and then at the Caban Atican Prison Camp, was forced to perform manual labor on a farm.

In September, 1943, the Japanese moved him to the Japanese mainland where he worked in a foundry. There he was beaten and had to sleep on the floor of an unheated building. He was made to walk to work through five foot snow in straw boots and denim clothing.

In 1944, he contracted double pneumonia and was incapacitated for seven months. When he returned to the foundry, his weight dropped to 94 pounds due to a cut in the workers' rations.

When the war ended, Rogers recuperated in American Army hospitals for about seven months before he was discharged in May, 1946, at Fort Bragg.

PFC Charles George, Eastern Cherokee
Medal of Honor Recipient

Private First Class Charles George died in the Korean conflict on November 30, 1952, when he fell on a bursting grenade and smothered it to save his fellow soldiers. For this brave and selfless act, he was posthumously awarded the Congressional Medal of Honor.

He was further honored later in 1959 back in Cherokee, North Carolina, when the people of that community named their high school gymnasium after him. Private George had attended school there and had been a member of that tribe.

Sgt. John Burgess, Cherokee
Purple Heart and Numerous Decorations

Sergeant John Burgess was killed in action in Vietnam on April 19, 1969 and was posthumously awarded three medals for his valorous service. His Bronze Star citation states that Sgt. Burgess disregarded his own safety, took up an exposed position and then returned fire on enemy positions. He then moved among his unit giving instructions and encouragement to his men until he was mortally wounded by hostile fire.

He received an additional special Bronze Star with an Oak Leaf Cluster for valorous actions on April 18, 1969. That citation states: Sgt. Burgess' personal bravery and devotion to duty were in keeping with the highest traditions of the military service …"

Finally, Burgess received the Silver Star with First Oak Leaf Cluster for gallantry in action involving close combat with an armed hostile force in Vietnam. In part, the citations states: Sgt. Burgess distinguished himself by exceptionally valorous actions on February 28 and March 1, 1969, while serving as an Armored Vehicle Commander with Troop C, 3rd Squadron, 5th Cavalry, on a combat mission in Quang Tri Province … In an area where friendly forces were heavily engaged with a large enemy element, Sgt. Burgess directed his vehicle into the midst of the hostile emplacements and played a vital role in routing the enemy … When a vehicle in front of him was hit by a rocket propelled grenade, he moved his own vehicle into the line of fire to provide cover as the wounded men were evacuated.

"Sgt. Burgess' extraordinary heroism … was in keeping with the highest traditions of the military service and reflects great credit upon himself, the 9th infantry division and the U.S. Army."

Bernie Whitebear, Lakes Indian (Sin-Aikst)
Army Green Beret

Indian activist Bernie Whitebear, born Bernard Reyes on the Colville Reservation in 1937, enlisted in the army in 1957 at the age of 20. He was sent to Fort Ord, California, for basic training, and then went on to Fort Campbell, Kentucky, to become a paratrooper in the 101st Airborne division.

His sense of humor and easy-going style earned Bernie many friends during his term of service. He came to enjoy jumping out of airplanes, and he carried his camera with him on jumps so he could take pictures of his army buddies floating down in their parachutes.

He went on to become a Green Beret, which called for even more intensive training, and after the end of his tour of duty in 1959, he joined an Army Reserve Special Forces team of Green Berets in South Tacoma, Washington, to continue his service.

Bernie had faced prejudice against Indians much of his life and knew firsthand of the hardships born by low income urban Indians, so on his return to civilian life, he dedicated himself to the struggle for Indian rights. In 1970, he founded the *United Indians of All Tribes Foundation*, which continues to serve the needs of the Indians of Seattle to this day. Bernie passed away in July, 2000, after a lengthy battle with cancer.[*]

*source: Reyes, Lawney, *Bernie Whitebear: An Urban Indian's Quest for Justice.* Tucson, Arizona: University of Arizona Press, 2006.

NATIVE AMERICAN WOMEN IN SERVICE

(This section is quoted verbatim with permission from the Department of Defense. The source is a DOD Web site: www.defenselink.mil/specials/nativeamerican01/women.htm.)

Very little is recorded or known about the contributions of Native American women to the United States military. "The Women In Military Service For America" Memorial Foundation is attempting to fill this gap by encouraging Native American women veterans to register with the Memorial so that their stories may be recorded and preserved. They are also conducting research on the contributions of Native American women of earlier eras.

Historians have only recently rediscovered and verified the actions of an Oneida woman, Tyonajanegen, at the battle of Oriskany during the American Revolution (1775–1783). As mentioned in Part Two of this book, Tyonajanegen was the wife of the Oneida war chief Hanyery. She fought at her husband's side on horseback during the battle, loading her husband's gun for him after he was shot in the wrist.

The story of Sacajawea, the Shoshone woman who accompanied the Lewis and Clark expedition of the early 19th century, is somewhat better known. Since this expedition was carried out under U.S. Army supervision and coordination, it was considered a military operation. Much of what is common knowledge about the expedition's only Indian participant is myth, however. Sacajawea has been remembered as a guide. In reality, she served as an interpreter for members of the expedition, who were unfamiliar with the Indian language. "Bird Woman's" service is described in the journals kept by Army Captains Meriwether Lewis and William Clark during the expedition.

Four Native American Catholic Sisters from Fort Berthold, South Dakota worked as nurses for the War Department during the Spanish American War (1898). Originally assigned to the military hospital at Jacksonville, Florida, the nurses were soon transferred to Havana, Cuba. One of the nurses, Sister Anthony died of disease in Cuba and was buried with military honors.

Fourteen Native American women served as members of the Army Nurse Corps during World War I, two of them overseas. Mrs. Cora E. Sinnard, a member of the Oneida Tribe and a graduate of the Episcopalian School of Nursing in Philadelphia, served eighteen months in France with a hospital unit provided by the Episcopal Church. Charlotte Edith (Anderson) Monture of the Iroquois Nation also served as an Army nurse in France. Charlotte was born in 1890 in Ohsweken, Ontario, Canada. In 1917, she left her job as an elementary school nurse to join the Army Nurse Corps. She later referred to her service in France at a military hospital as "the adventure of a lifetime." Charlotte passed away in 1996, at the age of 106.

Nearly 800 Native American women served in the military during World War II. Elva (Tapedo) Wale, a Kiowa, left her Oklahoma reservation to join the Women's Army Corps. Private Tapedo became an "Air WAC," and worked on Army Air Bases across the United States. Corporal Bernice (Firstshoot) Bailey of Lodge Pole, Montana, joined the Women's Army Corps in 1945 and served until 1948. After the war, she was sent to Wiesbaden, Germany, as part of the Army of Occupation. Beatrice (Coffey) Thayer also served in the Army of Occupation in Germany. Beatrice remembers being assigned to KP with German POWs, who were accompanied by armed guards. Beatrice was in Germany when the Berlin Wall went up, and remained in the Army until the 1970s.

Alida (Whipple) Fletcher joined the Army during World War II and trained as a medical specialist. She was assigned to the hospital at Camp Stoneman, California, which was an Army port of embarkation for the Pacific. Alida was on duty the night two ships loaded with explosives collided at a nearby ammunition dump, killing approximately 400 sailors and wounding many more. The wounded were brought to the hospital where Alida worked. She remembers that night as the most tragic of her life.

First Lieutenant Julia (Nashanany) Reeves, a member of the Potawatomie Indian Tribe of Crandon, Wisconsin, joined the Army Nurse Corps in 1942, and was assigned to one of the first medical Units shipped to the Pacific. The 52nd Evacuation Hospital Unit was sent to

New Caledonia before its members had received their Army uniforms. When the hospital ship *Solace* arrived at New Caledonia, Julia was assigned temporary duty aboard the ship. The following year, Julia was transferred to the 23rd Station Hospital in Norwich, England, where she was stationed during the invasion of Normandy. She remained in Norwich through V-J Day, returning shortly afterward to the United States. During the Korean War, Julia mobilized with the 804th Station Hospital.

Private Minnie Spotted-Wolf of Heart Butte, Montana, enlisted in the Marine Corps Women's Reserve in July 1943. She was the first female American Indian to enroll in the Corps. Minnie had worked on her father's ranch doing such chores as cutting fence posts, driving a two-ton truck, and breaking horses. Her comment on Marine boot camp "Hard but not too hard."

Ola Mildred Rexroat, an Oglala Sioux from Pine Ridge Indian Reservation, South Dakota, joined the Women's Airforce Service Pilots (WASP) directly out of high school. Her job was to tow targets for aerial gunnery students at Eagle Pass Army Air Base in Texas. Towing targets for student gunners was a fairly dangerous assignment, but "Rexy" was happy to be able to contribute to the war effort in a meaningful way. After the war ended, Ola joined the Air Force and served for almost ten years.

During the 1950s and 1960s, fewer women felt the call to military service (*reason unknown*). The services, however, were in desperate need of womanpower during the Korean conflict and the Vietnam War, and conducted extensive recruitment campaigns aimed at young women. Many Native American women answered their country's call. Sarah Mae Peshlakai, a member of the Navajo Tribe from Crystal, New Mexico, enlisted in the Women's Army Corps in 1951 and served until 1957. Peshlakai trained as a medical specialist and was assigned to Yokohama Army Hospital in Japan, where she helped care for casualties from the Korean battlefields.

Verna Fender entered the Navy during the Korean Conflict and trained at Bainbridge, Maryland. She was severely injured during basic training and was sent to a Navy hospital for physical rehabilitation. Undeterred, Verna returned to Bainbridge and completed her training. The Navy assigned Verna to its base in San Diego, California, where she completed her 3-year term of enlistment, working in the departments of berthing and sectioning, supply, and ordnance. Shirley M. Arviso, a Navajo of the Bitter Water Clan, served in the Navy from 1953 through 1963. She was the Communications Officer in charge of a group of people who decrypted classified messages.

Pearl Ross, a member of the Arikara Tribe from the Fort Berthold Reservation, joined the Air Force in 1953, and trained as a medical specialist. Her first assignment was to the Air Force hospital in Cheyenne, Wyoming. Pearl was then assigned to Offutt Air Force Base in Nebraska, where she worked in the 865th Medical Group at SAC HQ. During the Vietnam era, she saw many men who had been wounded in the com- bat theater. Pearl volunteered for overseas duty, but was turned down because the Air Force was hesitant to send women to Vietnam.

Linda Woods enlisted in the Air Force in the late 1950s and was on duty when President Kennedy was assassinated. She remembers that the air base where she was stationed went on full alert. A later assignment took her to the southern United States during the Civil Rights movement. As a non-white, she found the environment somewhat difficult; however, she retained pride in her uniform as a woman of color.

Barbara Monteiro joined the WAC in 1963 and took her basic and secretarial training at Ft. McClellan, Alabama. Her first duty assignment was to Ft. Huachuca, Arizona, where she worked for three years in the travel office and motor pool in support of troop readiness during the Vietnam War. In 1966, Monteiro was assigned to Ft. Richardson, Alaska, where she served as an administration specialist at the Education Center for a year. Lance Corporal Valla Dee Jack Egge of Dougherty, Oklahoma, served in the U.S. Marine Corps in the early 1960s as the executive secretary to two commanding generals of the Parris Island Marine Corps Base, South Carolina.

Increasing numbers of women, including Native Americans, entered the military in the 1970s and 1980s. Patricia White Bear joined the Navy in 1981. She trained as an Instrumentman and served at sea repairing, adjusting and calibrating the wide variety of mechanical measuring instruments used aboard ships. Dolores Kathleen Smith, a Cherokee, graduated from the Air Force Academy in 1982. She completed navigator training and was assigned to a KC-135 unit. She served in the operational plans division of her unit and also as an instructor before retiring as a captain from the Air Force in 1990.

Darlene Yellowcloud of the Lakota Tribe was inspired to join the Army because so many of the men in her family had served. Her grandfather, Bear Saves Life, was killed in action in France during World War I. Her father, brothers, brothers-in-law, uncles and cousins were all veterans. Darlene was assigned to the U. S. Army in Korea as a Specialist 4th Class. Lawnikwa Spotted-Eaglefortune joined the Army in 1988, and attended Basic Training at Fort Dix, New Jersey. Acting as a guide-on carrier, she was injured when another carrier grounded a guide iron through her foot into the ground. She still has the scar, and now serves as a member of the Virginia Air National Guard.

As of 1980, at least sixty Native American women were serving in the Eskimo Scouts, a special unit of the Alaska National Guard. The Eskimo Scouts patrol the western coastline of Alaska and the islands separat- ing Alaska and Russia. The Scouts are the only members of the National Guard who have a continuous active duty mission. This unit was organized during World War II, and the wives of scout battalion members have always been involved in patrol missions. Women were admitted as official members in 1976, and only then began to receive pay, benefits and recognition for their work. Scouts currently patrol ice flows in the Bering Straits, monitor movements on the tundra, and perform Arctic search and rescue efforts as required.

Native American women lost their lives while in the service of their nation. Katherine Matthews of Cherokee, North Carolina, joined the Navy in the late 1970s and trained as an Aviation Machinist's Mate. She died while serving in California in 1985. Terri Ann Hagen, a former Army medic, was a member of the Army National Guard when she was killed fighting a fire on Storm King Mountain in Colorado in 1994.

APPENDIX II
The Record of Service

CHART OF NATIVE AMERICAN MILITARY SERVICE

World War I	8,000 served in the Army
	6,000 served in the Navy
World War II	25,000 served. Awards included:
	71 Air medals, 51 Silver Stars,
	47 Bronze Stars,
	34 Distinguished Flying Crosses, 2
	Congressional Medals of Honor
Korean Conflict	Unknown number served
	1 Congressional Medal of Honor
Vietnam era	41,500
Desert Storm era	24,000 (3,000 deployed in Kuwait)
Iraq War era	17,500

Source: U.S. Dept. of Interior, Bureau of Indian Affairs

Serving Today:

According to DOD records, approximately 18,000 Native Americans serve in all branches of the U.S. military today.*

Source: Office of Public Affairs, Department of Defense, the Pentagon, Washington DC

NATIVE AMERICAN RECIPIENTS OF THE CONGRESSIONAL MEDAL OF HONOR

Source: All information in this section is taken verbatim from www.army. mil/CHM-pg/topics/natam/natam-moh.html and is used with permission from the Pentagon Public Affairs Office. (Note: these records are part of the U.S. public domain.)

The Indian War Period

ALCHESAY—Rank and organization: Sergeant, Indian Scouts. Place and date: Winter of 1872–73. Entered service at: Camp Verde, Ariz. Born: 1853, Arizona Territory. Date of issue: 12 April 1875. Citation: Gallant conduct during campaigns and engagements with Apaches.

BLANQUET—Rank and organization: Indian Scouts. Place and date: Winter of 1872–73. Birth: Arizona. Date of issue: 12 April 1875. Citation: Gallant conduct during campaigns and engagements with Apaches.

CHIQUITO—Rank and organization: Indian Scouts. Place and date: Winter of 1871–73. Birth: Arizona. Date of issue: 12 April 1875. Citation: Gallant conduct during campaigns and engagements with Apaches.

CO-RUX-TE-CHOD-ISH (Mad Bear)—Rank and organization: Sergeant, Pawnee Scouts, U.S. Army. Place and date: At Republican River, Kans., 8 July 1869. Birth: Nebraska. Date of issue: 24 August 1869. Citation: Ran out from the command in pursuit of a dismounted Indian; was shot down and badly wounded by a bullet from his own command.

ELSATSOOSU—Rank and organization: Corporal, Indian Scouts. Place and date: Winter of 1872–73. Birth: Arizona. Date of issue: 12 April 1875. Citation: Gallant conduct during campaigns and engagements with Apaches.

FACTOR, POMPEY—Rank and organization: Private, Indian Scouts. Place and date: At Pecos River, Tex., 25 April 1875. Birth: Arkansas. Date of issue: 28 May 1875. Citation: With 3 other men, he participated in a charge against 25 hostiles while on a scouting patrol.

JIM—Rank and organization: Sergeant, Indian Scouts. Place and date: Winter of 1871–73. Birth: Arizona Territory. Date of issue: 12 April 1875. Citation: Gallant conduct during campaigns and engagements with Apaches.

KELSAY—Rank and organization: Indian Scouts. Place and date: Winter of 1872–73. Birth: Arizona. Date of issue: 12 April 1875. Citation: Gallant conduct during campaigns and engagements with Apaches.

KOSOHA—Rank and organization: Indian Scouts. Place and date: Winter of 1872–73. Birth: Arizona. Date of issue: 12 April 1875. Citation: Gallant conduct during campaigns and engagements with Apaches.

MACHOL—Rank and organization: Private, Indian Scouts. Place and date: Arizona, 1872–73. Birth: Arizona. Date of issue: 12 April 1875. Citation: Gallant conduct during campaign and engagements with Apaches.

NANNASADDIE—Rank and organization: Indian Scouts. Place and date: 1872–73. Birth: Arizona. Date of issue: 12 April 1875. Citation: Gallant conduct during campaigns and engagements with Apaches.

NANTAJE (NANTAHE)—Rank and organization: Indian Scouts. Place and date: 1872–73. Birth: Arizona. Date of issue: 12 April 1875. Citation: Gallant conduct during campaigns and engagements with Apaches.

PAINE, ADAM—Rank and organization: Private, Indian Scouts. Place and date: Canyon Blanco tributary of the Red River, Tex., 26–27 September 1874. Entered service at: Fort Duncan, Texas. Birth: Florida.

Date of issue: 13 October 1875. Citation: Rendered invaluable service to Col. R. S. Mackenzie, 4th U.S. Cavalry, during this engagement.

PAYNE, ISAAC—Rank and organization: Trumpeter, Indian Scouts. Place and date: At Pecos River, Tex., 25 April 1875. Birth: Mexico. Date of issue: 28 May 1875. Citation: With 3 other men, he participated in a charge against 25 hostiles while on a scouting patrol.

ROWDY—Rank and organization: Sergeant, Company A, Indian Scouts. Place and date: Arizona, 7 March 1890. Birth: Arizona. Date of issue: 15 May 1890. Citation: Bravery in action with Apache Indians.

WARD, JOHN—Rank and organization: Sergeant, 24th U.S. Infantry Indian Scouts Place and date: At Pecos River, Tex., 25 April 1875. Entered service at. Fort Duncan, Tex. Birth: Arkansas. Date of issue: 28 May 1875. Citation. With 3 other men, he participated in a charge against 25 hostiles while on a scouting patrol.

World War II

BARFOOT, VAN T.—Rank and organization: Second Lieutenant, U.S. Army, 157th Infantry, 45th Infantry Division. Place and date: Near Carano, Italy, 23 May 1944. Entered service at: Carthage, Miss. Birth: Edinburg, Miss. G.O. No.: 79, 4 October 1944. Citation: For conspicuous gallantry and intrepidity at the risk of life above and beyond the call of duty on 23 May 1944, near Carano, Italy. With his platoon heavily engaged during an assault against forces well entrenched on commanding ground, 2d Lt. Barfoot (then Tech. Sgt.) moved off alone upon the enemy left flank. He crawled to the proximity of 1 machinegun nest and made a direct hit on it with a hand grenade, killing 2 and wounding 3 Germans. He continued along the German defense line to another machinegun emplacement, and with his tommygun killed 2 and captured 3 soldiers. Members of another enemy machinegun crew then abandoned their position and gave themselves up to Sgt. Barfoot. Leaving the prisoners for his support squad to pick up, he proceeded to mop up positions in the immediate area, capturing more prisoners and bringing his total count to 17. Later that day, after he had reorganized his men and consolidated the newly captured ground, the enemy launched a fierce armored counterattack directly at his platoon positions. Securing a bazooka, Sgt. Barfoot took up an exposed position directly in front of 3 advancing Mark VI tanks. From a distance of 75 yards his first shot destroyed the track of the leading tank, effectively disabling it, while the other 2 changed direction toward the flank. As the crew of the disabled tank dismounted, Sgt. Barfoot killed 3 of them with his tommygun. He continued onward into enemy terrain and destroyed a recently abandoned German fieldpiece with a demolition charge placed in the breech. While returning to his platoon position, Sgt. Barfoot, though greatly fatigued by his Herculean efforts, assisted 2 of his seriously wounded men 1,700 yards to a position of safety. Sgt. Barfoot's extraordinary heroism, demonstration of magnificent valor, and aggressive determination in the face of pointblank fire are a perpetual inspiration to his fellow soldiers.

CHILDERS, ERNEST—Rank and organization: Second Lieutenant, U.S. Army, 45th Infantry Division. Place and date: At Oliveto, Italy, 22 September 1943. Entered service at: Tulsa, Okla. Birth: Broken Arrow, Okla. G.O. No.: 30, 8 April 1944. Citation: For conspicuous gallantry and intrepidity at risk of life above and beyond the call of duty in action on 22 September 1943, at Oliveto, Italy. Although 2d Lt. Childers previously had just suffered a fractured instep he, with 8 enlisted men, advanced up a hill toward enemy machinegun nests. The group advanced to a rock wall overlooking a cornfield and 2d Lt. Childers ordered a base of fire laid across the field so that he could advance. When he was fired upon by 2 enemy snipers from a nearby house he killed both of them. He moved behind the machinegun nests and killed all occupants of the nearer one. He continued toward the second one and threw rocks into it. When the 2 occupants of the nest raised up, he shot 1. The other was killed by 1 of the 8 enlisted men. 2d Lt. Childers continued his advance toward a house farther up the hill, and single-handed, captured an enemy mortar observer. The exceptional leadership, initiative, calmness under fire, and conspicuous gallantry displayed by 2d Lt. Childers were an inspiration to his men.

EVANS, ERNEST EDWIN—Rank and organization: Commander, U.S. Navy. Born: 13 August 1908, Pawnee, Okla. Accredited to: Oklahoma. Other Navy awards: Navy Cross, Bronze Star Medal. Citation: For conspicuous gallantry and intrepidity at the risk of his life above and beyond the call of duty as commanding officer of the U.S.S. Johnston in action against major units of the enemy Japanese fleet during the battle off Samar on 25 October 1944. The first to lay a smokescreen and to open fire as an enemy task force, vastly superior in number, firepower and armor, rapidly approached. Comdr. Evans gallantly diverted the powerful blasts of hostile guns from the lightly armed and armored carri- ers under his protection, launching the first torpedo attack when the Johnston came under straddling Japanese shellfire. Undaunted by damage sustained under the terrific volume of fire, he unhesitatingly joined others of his group to provide fire support during subsequent torpedo attacks against the Japanese and, outshooting and outmaneuvering the enemy as he consistently interposed his vessel between the hostile fleet units and our carriers despite the crippling loss of engine power and communications with steering aft, shifted command to the fantail, shouted steering orders through an open hatch to men turning the rudder by hand and battled furiously until the Johnston, burning and shuddering from a mortal blow, lay dead in the water after 3 hours of fierce combat. Seriously wounded early in the engagement, Comdr. Evans, by his indomitable courage and brilliant professional skill, aided materially in turning back the enemy during a critical phase of the action. His valiant fighting spirit throughout this historic battle will venture as an inspiration to all who served with him.

MONTGOMERY, JACK C.—Rank and organization: First Lieutenant, U.S. Army, 45th Infantry Division. Place and date: Near, Padiglione, Italy, 22 February 1944. Entered service at: Sallisaw, Okla. Birth: Long, Okla. G.O. No.: 5, 15 January 1945. Citation: For conspicuous gallantry and intrepidity at risk of life above and beyond the call of duty on 22 February 1944, near Padiglione, Italy. Two hours before daybreak a strong force of enemy infantry established themselves in 3 echelons at 50 yards, 100 yards, and 300 yards, respectively, in front of the rifle platoons commanded by 1st Lt. Montgomery. The closest position, consisting of 4 machineguns and 1 mortar, threatened the immediate security of the platoon position. Seizing an Ml rifle and several hand grenades, 1st Lt. Montgomery crawled up a ditch to within hand grenade range of the enemy. Then climbing boldly onto a little mound, he fired his rifle and threw his grenades so accurately that he killed 8 of the enemy and captured the remaining 4. Returning to his platoon, he called for artillery fire on a house, in and around which he suspected that the majority of the enemy had entrenched themselves. Arming himself with a carbine, he proceeded along the shallow ditch, as withering fire from the riflemen and machine gunners in the second position was concentrated on him. He attacked this position with such fury that 7 of the enemy surrendered to him, and both machineguns were silenced. Three German dead were found in the vicinity later that morning. 1st Lt. Montgomery continued boldly toward the house, 300 yards from his platoon position. It was now daylight, and the enemy observation was excellent across the flat open terrain which led to 1st Lt. Montgomery's objective. When the artillery barrage had lifted, 1st Lt. Montgomery ran fearlessly toward the strongly defended position. As the enemy started streaming out of the house, 1st Lt. Montgomery, unafraid of treacherous snipers, exposed himself daringly to assemble the surrendering enemy and send them to the rear. His fearless, aggressive, and intrepid actions that morning, accounted for a total of 11 enemy dead, 32 prisoners, and an unknown number of wounded. That night, while aiding an adjacent unit to repulse a counterattack, he was struck by mortar fragments and seriously wounded. The selflessness and courage exhibited by 1st Lt. Montgomery in alone attacking 3 strong enemy positions inspired his men to a degree beyond estimation.

REESE, JOHN N., JR.—Rank and organization: Private First Class, U.S. Army, Company B, 148th Infantry, 37th Infantry Division. Place and date: Paco Railroad Station, Manila, Philippine Islands. 9 February 1945. Entered service at: Pryor, Okla. Birth: Muskogee, Okla. G.O. No.: 89, 19 October 1945. Citation. He was engaged in the attack on the Paco Railroad Station, which was strongly defended by 300 determined enemy soldiers with machineguns and rifles, supported by several pillboxes, 3 20mm. guns, 1 37-mm. gun and heavy mortars. While making a frontal assault across an open field, his platoon was halted 100 yards from the station by intense enemy fire. On his own initiative he left the platoon accompanied by a comrade, and continued forward to a house 60 yards from the objective. Although under constant enemy observation, the 2 men remained in this position for an hour, firing at targets of opportunity, killing more than 35 Japanese and wounding many more. Moving closer to the station and discovering a group of Japanese replacements attempting to reach pillboxes, they opened heavy fire, killed more than 40 and stopped all subsequent attempts to man the emplacements. Enemy fire became more intense as they advanced to within 20 yards of the station. From that point Pfc. Reese provided effective covering fire and courageously drew enemy fire to himself while his companion killed 7 Japanese and destroyed a 20-mm. gun and heavy machinegun with hand grenades. With their ammunition running low, the 2 men started to return to the American lines, alternately providing covering fire for each other as they withdrew. During this movement, Pfc. Reese was killed by enemy fire as he reloaded his rifle. The intrepid team, in 21/2 hours of fierce fighting, killed more than 82 Japanese, completely disorganized their defense and paved the way for subsequent complete defeat of the enemy at this strong point. By his gallant determination in the face of tremendous odds, aggressive fighting spirit, and extreme heroism at the cost of his life, Pfc. Reese materially aided the advance of our troops in Manila and providing a lasting inspiration to all those with whom he served.

Korean War

GEORGE, CHARLES—Rank and organization: Private First Class, U.S. Army, Company C, 179th Infantry Regiment, 45th Infantry Division. Place and date: Near Songnae-dong, Korea, 30 November 1952. Entered service at: Whittier, N.C. Born: 23 August 1932, Cherokee, N.C. G.O. NO.: 19, 18 March 1954. Citation: Pfc. George, a member of Company C, distinguished himself by conspicuous gallantry and outstanding courage above and beyond the call of duty in action against the enemy on the night of 30 November 1952. He was a member of a raiding party committed to engage the enemy and capture a prisoner for interrogation. Forging up the rugged slope of the key terrain feature, the group was subjected to intense mortar and machine gun fire and suffered several casualties. Throughout the advance, he fought valiantly and, upon reaching the crest of the hill, leaped into the trenches and closed with the enemy in hand-to-hand combat. When friendly troops were ordered to move back upon completion of the assignment, he and 2 comrades remained to cover the withdrawal. While in the process of leaving the trenches, a hostile soldier hurled a grenade into their midst. Pfc. George shouted a warning to 1 comrade, pushed the other soldier out of danger, and, with full knowledge of the consequences, unhesitatingly threw himself upon the grenade, absorbing the full blast of the explosion. Although seriously wounded in this display of valor, he refrained from any outcry which would divulge the position of his companions. The 2 soldiers evacuated him to the forward aid station and shortly thereafter he succumbed to his wound. Pfc. George's indomitable courage, consummate devotion to duty, and willing self-sacrifice reflect the highest credit upon himself and uphold the finest traditions of the military service.

HARVEY, RAYMOND—Rank and organization: Captain, U.S. Army, Company C, 17th Infantry Regiment. Place and date: Vicinity of Taemi-Dong, Korea, 9 March 1951. Entered service at: Pasadena, Calif. Born: 1 March 1920 Ford City, Pa. G.O. No.: 67, 2 August 1951. Citation: Capt. Harvey Company C, distinguished himself by conspicuous gallantry and intrepidity above and beyond the call of duty in action. When his company was pinned down by a barrage of automatic weapons fire from numerous well-entrenched emplacements, imperiling accomplishment of its mission, Capt. Harvey braved a hail of fire and exploding grenades to advance to the first enemy machine gun nest, killing its crew with grenades. Rushing to the edge of the next emplacement, he killed its crew with carbine fire. He then moved the 1st Platoon forward until it was again halted by a curtain of automatic fire from well fortified hostile positions. Disregarding the hail of fire, he personally charged and neutralized a third emplacement. Miraculously escaping death from intense crossfire, Capt. Harvey continued to lead the assault. Spotting an enemy pillbox well camouflaged by logs, he moved close enough to sweep the emplacement with carbine fire and throw grenades through the openings, annihilating its 5 occupants. Though wounded he then turned to order the company forward, and, suffering agonizing pain, he continued to direct the reduction of the remaining hostile positions, refusing evacuation until assured that the mission would be accomplished. Capt. Harvey's valorous and intrepid actions served as an inspiration to his company, reflecting the utmost glory upon himself and upholding the heroic traditions of the military service.

RED CLOUD, MITCHELL, JR.—Rank and organization: Corporal, U S. Army, Company E, 19th Infantry Regiment, 24th Infantry Division. Place and date: Near Chonghyon, Korea, 5 November 1950. Entered service at: Merrilan Wis. Born: 2 July 1924, Hatfield, Wis. G.O. No.: 26, 25 April 1951. Citation: Cpl. Red Cloud, Company E, distinguished himself by conspicuous gallantry and intrepidity above and beyond the call of duty in action against the enemy. From his position on the point of a ridge immediately in front of the company command post he was the first to detect the approach of the Chinese Communist forces and give the alarm as the enemy charged from a brush-covered area less than 100 feet from him. Springing up he delivered devastating pointblank automatic rifle fire into the advancing enemy. His accurate and intense fire checked this assault and gained time for the company to consolidate its defense. With utter fearlessness he maintained his firing position until severely wounded by enemy fire. Refusing assistance he pulled himself to his feet and wrapping his arm around a tree continued his deadly fire again, until he was fatally wounded. This heroic act stopped the enemy from overrunning his company's position and gained time for reorganization and evacuation of the wounded. Cpl. Red Cloud's dauntless courage and gallant self-sacrifice reflects the highest credit upon himself and upholds the esteemed traditions of the U.S. Army.

SOURCES:
Citations, Interviewees, Bibliography, and Archives

Citations

Part One

1. Starkey, Armstrong. *European and Native American Warfare, 1675–1815.* Norman, OK: University of Oklahoma Press, 1998.

2. Weatherford, Jack. *Native Roots.* NY, NY: Crown Publishers, 1991.

3. Truman, Harry S. "America's Treatment of the Indians." Independence, MO: Presidential papers of the Harry S. Truman Library (public domain).

4. Brown, Dee. *Bury My Heart at Wounded Knee.* NY, NY: Holt, Rinehart and Winston, NY, 1971.

Part Two

1. Johansen, Bruce. *Forgotten Founders: The Iroquois and the Rationale for the American Revolution.* Ipswich, MA: Gambit, Inc. Publishers, 1982.

2. *Pennsylvania Journal & Weekly Advertiser.* Philadelphia, PA. Sept. 3, 1777.

3. Waldo, Albgence. *The Diary of Dr. Albigence Waldo.* Washington DC: National Archives, American Revolutionary War Papers, 1777.

4. Nabokov, Peter, ed. *Native American Testimony.* NY, NY: Viking Penguin, 1991.

5. "The Battle at Pea Ridge," *New York Illustrated News.* NY, NY: April 12, 1862.

6. Ambrose, Stephen E., ed. *A Wisconsin Boy in Dixie: Civil War Letters of James K. Newton.* Madison, WI: University of Wisconsin Press, 1961.

7. Union and Confederate War Department Papers, National Archives, Washington DC.

8. Armstrong, William H. *Warrior in Two Camps: Ely Parker*. Syracuse, NY: Syracuse University Press, 1978.

9. Ibid.

10. Act of Congress, July 28, 1866; National Archives, Washington DC.

11. National Archives, Washington DC.

12. Glass, Laurence C. "A Short History of the Indians in the U.S. Military" (unpublished manuscript), 1982.

13. Downey, Fairfax and Jacobsen, Jacques Noel, Jr. *The Red/Bluecoats: The Indian Scouts, U.S. Army*. Ft. Collins, CO: Old Army Press, 1973.

14. Dunlay, Thomas W. *Wolves for the Blue Soldiers: Indian Scouts and Auxiliaries with the US Army 1860–1890*. Lincoln, NE: Univ. of Nebraska Press, 1982.

15. Brown, Dee. *Bury My Heart at Wounded Knee*. NY, NY: Holt, Rinehart and Winston, 1971.

16. *New York Times*, December 27, 1893.

17. Roosevelt, Theodore. *The Rough Riders*. NY, NY: Charles Scribner and Sons, 1899.

Part Three

1. "Transmitting Messages in Choctaw," Report to Captain Spence, Commanding General, 36th Division, Washington DC, January 23, 1919. U.S. Military Archives.

2. "Germans Confused by Choctaw Code Talkers," *Bishinik* (Choctaw Tribal Newspaper). August, 1986.

3. "France to Honor Choctaw Code Talkers," *Bishinik*. October, 1989.

4. Bureau of Indian Affairs, Records Group 75, National Archives, Seattle Branch.

5. "Code Talkers Recognition Act"—proposed congressional legislation introduced several different times by different senators/representatives but never passed into law.

6. Robinson, Gary. *A Time to Heal.* Documentary short film, 1988.

7. Ibid.

8. Ibid.

9. *Indian Country Today* (newspaper) online archives.

10. Ibid.

11. Davidson, Osha Gray. "A Wrong Turn in the Desert," *Rolling Stone.* May 27, 2004.

Part Four

1. Keen, Sam. *Faces of the Enemy.* NY, NY: Harper Collins, reprint edition, 1991.

2. Ferguson, R. Brian. "Tribal Warfare," *Scientific American*, 1992: pp. 108–113.

3. Riley, Glenda. *Women and Indians on the Frontier, 1825–1915.* Albuquerque, NM: University of New Mexico Press, 1984.

4. National Archives, Washington DC.

Part Five

1. Primary Source: "Native Americans and the Military: Today and Yesterday," published by the U.S. Army Public Affairs Information Branch, March, 1984.

2. Department of Defense Web site: www.defenselink.mil/specials/nativeamerican01/women.htm.

Contemporary Witnesses/Interviewees*

(presented alphabetically)

George Amiotte (Lakota), Vietnam Veteran

Mary Anderson (Pima), Quoted from Lakota Times

Apesanahkwat (Menominee), Vietnam Veteran

Harold Barse, Vietnam Era Veterans Inter-Tribal Association Alison Bernstein, Author, *American Indians and World War II* Mike Berryhill (Creek), Vietnam Veteran

Schlict Billy (Choctaw), WWII Codetalker—European Theater

Dee Brown, Author, *Bury My Heart at Wounded Knee*

Charles Chibitty (Comanche), WWII Veteran

Amos Christjohn (Oneida), WWII Veteran

Erwin Christjohn (Oneida), Korean Veteran

Ted Christjohn (Oneida), Vietnam Veteran

R. Brian Ferguson, Author/Professor

Harold Foster (Navajo), WWII Codetalker

Carl Gorman (Navajo), WWII Codetalker

Paul Greenberg, Newspaper Columnist

Duane Hale, PhD (Creek), Historian/Professor

Nathan Hart (S. Cheyenne), Former Director, Oklahoma Indian Affairs Commission

Tom Holm, PhD (Cherokee), Vietnam Veteran/Professor

Sam Keen, Author, *Faces of the Enemy*

Laura Larkin (Oneida)

Eddie Little Light (Crow), Vietnam Veteran

Douglas Long (Wisconsin Winnebago), Korean Veteran

Jan Malcolm (Oneida), Vietnam Veteran, Oneida Museum Director

Joe Medicine Crow (Crow), WWII Veteran/Tribal Historian

Barney Old Coyote, PhD (Crow), WWII Veteran, Historian/Professor

Alfonso Ortiz (San Juan Pueblo), Anthropologist/Author (deceased)

Alice Petrivelli (Aleut)

Ministri Philemonof (Aleut)

Carol Red Cherries (N. Cheyenne), Army Veteran/Tribal Supreme Court Judge

Windy Shoulderblade (N. Cheyenne), Vietnam Veteran
Sherry L. Smith (N. Cheyenne), U.T.E.P.
John Stands-In-Timber (Cheyenne), Author/Historian
Ronald Stewart (Crow), Korean War Veteran
William Charles Stewart (Crow), Korean War Veteran
Joe Walks-Along (N. Cheyenne), WWII Veteran
Carson Walks-Over-The-Ice (Crow), Vietnam Veteran
    Jack Weatherford, Author/Anthropologist, *Indian Givers*
Ruth Williams (Navajo), Desert Storm Veteran
Russell Winfield (N. Cheyenne), Vietnam Veteran/Tribal Police Officer

All interviews were conducted in the early 1990s by the authors.

Bibliography and Suggested Reading:
Books and Articles

General Sources: Indians/Military History

1. Prucha, Paul. *A Bibliographical Guide to the History of Indian-White Relations in the United States.* Chicago, IL: Newberry Library, University of Chicago, 1977.

2. Hirschfelder, Arlene and Byler, Mary and Dorris, Michael. *Guide To Research On North American Indians.* Chicago, IL: American Library Association, Chicago, 1983.

3. Glass, Laurence C. "A Short History of The Indians in The U.S. Military" (unpublished article), 1982.

4. *Native Americans and the Military: Today and Yesterday*, U.S. Army Command Information Branch, Ft. McPherson, GA, March, 1984, SP 3–84.

5. Hill, Edward, ed. *Guide To The Records In The National Archives of The U.S. Relating To American Indians.* Washington DC: NARA, 1981.

6. Freeman, John F., ed. *A Guide To Manuscripts Relating To The American Indian In The Library of The American Philosophical Society.* Independence Square, Philadelphia: Amer. Philosophical Society, 1966.

7. *American Indians Today, Answers To Your Questions*, BIA: Washington, DC, 1991.

8. Lang, Walt. *United States Military Almanac.* NY, NY: Military Press/ Crown Publishers, 1989.

9. Heller, Jonathan, ed. *War and Conflict: Selected Images from the National Archives, 1765–1970.* Washington DC: NARA, 1990.

Warfare: Psychology/Nature of War, etc.

1. Holmes, Richard. *Acts of War—The Behavior of Men In Battle.* NY, NY: The Free Press/Simon & Schuster, 1989.

2. Dyer, Gwynne. *War: The Lethal Custom.* NY, NY: Carroll and Graf Publishers, 2005.

3. Keen, Sam. *Faces of the Enemy.* NY, NY: Harper Collins, 1991.

4. Hass, Jonathan, ed. *The Anthropology of War.* Cambridge, MA: Cambridge University Press, 1990.

Indian Warfare

1. Wellman, Paul. *Indian Wars and Warriors East.* Boston, MA: Houghton Mifflin Co., 1959.

2. Wood, Nancy C. *War Cry on a Prayer Feather.* NY, NY: Doubleday, 1979.

3. LaFlesche, Francis. *War Ceremony and Peace Ceremony of the Osage Indians.* Washington DC: U.S. Government Printing Office, 1939.

4. Hofsinde, Robert. *Indian Warriors and Their Weapons.* NY, NY: William Morrow and Company, 1965.

5. Mails, Thomas E. *Dog Soldiers, Bear Men and Buffalo Women, A Study of the Societies and Cults of the Plains Indians.* Rutledge, NJ: Prentice-Hall, 1973.

6. Taylor, Colin. *The Warriors of the Plains.* London, England: Hamlyn Publishing Group, 1975.

7. Worcester, D. E. "The Weapons of American Indians," *New Mexico Historical Review* 20, July, 1945: pp. 227–238.

8. Cooke, David C. *Fighting Indians of America.* NY, NY: Donald Mead, 1966.

9. Mishkin, Bernard. *Rank and Warfare Among Plains Indians.* Seattle, WA: University of Washington Press, 1966.

10. Forbes, Jack D. *Warriors of the Colorado.* Norman, OK: O.U. Press, 1965.

11. Johnson, Dorothy M. *Warrior for a Lost Nation: Biography of Sitting Bull.* Philadelphia, PA: Westminster Press, 1969.

12. Ferguson, R. Brian. "Tribal Warfare," *Scientific American.* January, 1992: pp. 108–113.

13. "Militarization and Indigenous Peoples, Parts I & II" *Cultural Survival Quarterly,* Vol. 11, Nos. 3 & 4, 1987.

14. Weatherford, Jack. *Native Roots.* NY, NY: Crown Publishers, 1991.

15. Blanchard, Kendall. *The Mississippi Choctaws at Play.* Urbana, IL: University of Illinois Press, 1981.

Colonial Era

1. Malone, Patrick M. "Changing Military Technology among the Indians of the Southern New England, 1600–1677," *American Quarterly* 25, March, 1973: pp. 48–63.

2. Mahone, John K. "Anglo-American Methods of Indian Warfare, 1676–1794," *Mississippi Valley Historical Review* 45, September, 1958: pp. 254–275.

3. Mahone, John K. *Indian and English Military Systems in New England in the 17th Century.* Providence, RI: Brown University, 1971.

4. Cwiklik, Robert. *King Philip and the War with the Colonists.* Englewood Cliffs, NJ: Silver Burdett Press, 1989.

5. Smoyer, Stanley C. "Indians as Allies in the Inter-colonial Wars," *New York History* 17, Oct. 1936: p.411–22.

6. Lincoln, Charles. *Narratives of the Indian Wars, 1675–1699.* New York: Charles Scribner's Sons, 1913.

7. Penhallow, Samuel. *The History of the Wars of New England with the Eastern Indians* (1700–1725) Philadelphia, PA: Oscar H. Harpel, 1859.

Revolutionary War

1. O'Donnel III, James H. *Southern Indians in the American Revolution.* Knoxville, TN: University of Tennessee Press, 1973.

2. Shaw, Helen L. *British Administration of the Southern Indians* (Unpublished manuscript). Library of Congress, 1931.

3. Mohr, Walter. *Federal Indian Relations 1774–1788* (Unpublished manuscript). Library of Congress, 1933.

4. Washington, George. "Washington's Valley Forge Papers" (Unpublished manuscript). U.S. Army Archives: Washington DC, 1778.

5. Sullivan, Thomas. *Journal of the Operations of the American War* (Unpublished manuscript). Library of the American Philosophical Society: Philadelphia, PA, 1778.

6. Abler, Thomas S., ed. *Chainbreaker: The Revolutionary War Memoirs of Governor Blacksnake.* Lincoln, NE: University of Nebraska Press, 1989.

7. Stone, William. *Life of Joseph Brant.* NY: George Dearborn and Co., 1838.

Civil War

1. Abel, Annie Heloise. *The American Indian as Participant in the Civil War.* Lincoln, NE: University of Nebraska Press, 1992.

2. Rampp, Larry C. and Donald L. *The Civil War in the Indian Territory.* Austin, TX: Presidial Press, 1975.

3. "Civil War Reports" (Unpublished manuscript). U.S. Army Archives: Washington DC, 1865.

4. Baird, David, ed. *A Creek Warrior for the Confederacy—The Autobiography of Chief G. W. Grayson.* Norman, OK: University of Oklahoma Press, 1988.

5. Franks, Kenneth A. *Stand Watie.* Memphis, TN: Memphis State University, 1979.

6. Brown, Dee A. *The Galvanized Yankees.* Urbana, IL: University of Illinois Press, 1963.

7. Armstrong, William H. *Warrior in Two Camps: Ely S. Parker, Union General and Seneca Chief.* Syracuse, NY: Syracuse University Press, 1978.

Indian Wars (1800s)

1. Downey, Fairfax. *Indian Wars of the U.S. Army, 1776–1865.* Garden City, NY: Doubleday and Co., 1963.

2. Dillon, Richard H. *North American Indian Wars.* London, England: Magna Books, 1994.

3. Marshall, S.L.A. *Crimsoned Prairie.* NY: Scribner, 1972.

4. Schmitt, Martin H. and Dee Brown. *Fighting Indians of the West.* NY: Bonanza Books, 1948.

5. Prucha, Francis P. *A Guide to Military Posts of the United States, 1789–1895.* Madison, WI: U.S. National Park Service, 1964.

6. Wheeler, Col. Homer W. *Buffalo Days (40 Years in the Old West).* Indianapolis, IN: Bobs-Merrill Co., 1925.

7. Rickey Don. *Forty Miles a Day on Beans and Hay.* Norman, OK: University of Oklahoma Press, 1963.

8. Utley, Robert M. *Frontier Regulars: The U.S. Army and the Indian* (1866–1891). NY: MacMillan Pub. Co., 1973.

9. Longstreet, Stephen. *War Cries on Horseback (1815–1875).* London, England: W.H. Allen, 1970.

10. *Wildlife on the Plains and the Horrors of Indian Warfare.* Facsimile edition of the original work published in 1891. Arno Press, 1969

11. Riley, Glenda. *Women and Indians on the Frontier, 1825–1915.* Albuquerque, NM: University of New Mexico Press, 1984.

12. Tillet, Leslie. *Wind on the Buffalo Grass: An Indian account of the Battle of the Little Big Horn.* NY: Thomas Y. Crowell, 1976.

13. Wiltsey, Norman B. *Brave Warriors.* Caldwell, Idaho: Caxton Printers, 1963.

14. Brandes, Raymond, ed. *Troopers West.* Frontier Heritage Press, 1970.

15. Pratt, Richard Henry and Utley, Robert, M, ed. *Battlefield and Classroom: Four Decades with American Indians (1867–1904).* Lincoln, NE: University of Nebraska Press, 1987.

16. Secoy, Frank. *Changing Military Patterns on the Great Plains.* Monograph of the American Ethnological Society, No. 21. J.J. Augustine, Locust Valley, NY, 1953.

17. Riddle, Jefferson C. *Indian History of the Modoc War* (reprint of a 1914 publication). Saratoga, CA: Urion Press, 1974.

18. Ferguson, R. Brian and Whitehead, Neil L., eds. *War in the Tribal Zone: Expanding States and Indigenous Warfare.* Santa Fe, NM: Santa Fe School of American Research Press, 1992.

Indian Scouts

1. Warfield, Colonel H.B. *With Scout and Cavalry at Fort Apache.* Tucson, AZ: Arizona Pioneers Historical Society, 1965.

2. Downey, Fairfax and Jacobsen, Jacque Noel, Jr. *The Red/Bluecoats: The Indian Scouts, U.S. Army.* Fort Collins, CO: Old Army Press, 1973.

3. Danker, Donald F. "The North Brothers and the Pawnee Scouts," *Nebraska History* 42, Sept. 1961: pp. 161–179.

4. Innis, Ben. *Bloody Knife: Custer's Favorite Scout.* Fort Collins, CO: Old Army Press, 1973.

5. Mason, Dr. Joyce Evelyn. *The Use of Indian Scouts in the Apache Wars, 1870–1886.* Dissertation. Bloomington, IN: Indiana University, 1970.

6. Smith, Sherry L. *The View from Officers' Row, Army Perceptions of Western Indians.* Tucson, AZ: Univ. of Arizona Press, 1990.

7. Swett, Morris. "Seargent I-See-O, Kiowa Indian Scout," Oklahoma City, OK: *Chronicles of Oklahoma* 13, Sept. 1935: pp. 341–354.

8. Hollis, Marjor General Robert P. "The Army's Legendary Sgt. I-See-O," *Army* 27(6). Washington DC: June, 1977: pp 41–45.,

9. Dunlay, Thomas W. *Wolves for the Blue Soldiers: Indian Scouts and Auxiliaries with the US Army 1860–1890.* Lincoln, NE: Univ. of Nebraska Press, 1982.

Spanish American War (1898)

1. Roosevelt, Theodore. *The Rough Riders.* NY: Charles Scribner and Sons, 1899.

Mexican Border War (1916)

1. U.S. Army Records at Ft. Huachuca, Arizona, 1867–1947 (Unpublished). Ft. Huachuca Museum.

World War I

1. Records of the American Expeditionary Forces (WWI), 1917–23, Record Group 120. National Archives, Washington DC, 1920.

2. "From Scout To Doughboy: The National Debate Over Integrating American Indians into the Military, 1891–1917," *Western Historical Quarterly* 17, No. 4. Logan, UT: Western History Assoc., October, 1986.

3. Wise, Jennings C. *The Red Man in the New World Drama.* Washington DC: W.F. Roberts Co., 1931.

4. Parker, Arthur C. "The American Indian in the World War," *Southern Workman,* February, 1918.

5. *New Mexico Historical Review* (Indians of New Mexico in WWI) A. I, page 426. B. II, pages 41–2. C. X, pages 79–83 and 313–5. D. XI, pages 18–25.

6. Hale, Dr. Duane. "Forgotten Heroes: American Indians in World War I," *Four Winds*. Austin, TX: Autumn, 1982.

7. Barsh, Russell. *American Indians in World War I*. Dissertation, Seattle, WA: University of Washington.

World War II

1. Bersnstein, Alison R. *American Indians and World War II*. Norman, OK: University of Oklahoma Press, 1991.

2. "Indians At Work"(1941–45), Published by The Civilian Conservation Corps, Indian Division, Dept. of Interior; Seven issues were devoted to Indians serving in WWII.

3. *Indians in the War*. Published by Dept. of the Interior, Office of Indian Affairs, Chicago, 1945.

4. Wolfert, Ira. *American Guerilla in the Philippines*. NY, NY: Simon and Schuster, 1945.

5. Medal of Honor Historical Society (list of Medal of Honor winners), 1012 S. Hammerschmidt, Lombard, Illinois.

6. Paul, Doris A. *Navajo Code Talkers.* Philadelphia, PA: Dorrance & Co., 1973.

7. Clark, Ida Clyde. *American Women and the World War*. NY, NY: D. Appleton and Co., 1918.

8. *New Mexico Magazine.* (Navajos and WWII):

    A. Kay, E. "Big Trouble Comes-We All Fight." Oct. '41: p.14

    B. Kirk, R. "Dedication For War." Mar. '42: p.7

    C. Higgins, H. "Navajo Warriors." Oct. '43: p.12

9. Neuberger, Richard L. "The American Indian Enlists," *Asia and the Americas* 42. Nov. 1942: pp. 628–31.

10. Sergeant, Elizabeth. "The Indian Goes to War," *New Republic* 107. Nov. 30, 1942: pp. 708–09.

11. Kawano, Kenji, photog. *Warriors: Navajo Code Talkers.* Flagstaff, AZ: Northland Publishing Co, 1990.

12. Holm, Tom. "Fighting A White Man's War: The Extent and Legacy of American Indian Participation in World War II," *Journal of Ethnic Studies*, 9:2. Tucson, AZ: University of Arizona.

Vietnam

1. Holm, Tom. "Indian Veterans of the Vietnam War: Restoring Harmony Through Tribal Ceremony," *Four Winds*. Austin, TX: Autumn, 1982.

Gulf War, Operation Iraqi Freedom and Modern Times

1. Various Tribal Newspapers.

2. *News From Indian Country*, various articles.

3. Combs, Beverly. "The American Indian Still Fights On For His Country," *The Times* (Magazine). Sept. 5, 1983.

4. *Stars And Stripes* (newspaper), various articles; P.O. Box 1803, Washington DC 20013. 202-829-3225. John Carroll, editor.

5. *Indian Country Today* newspaper, various articles.

Sources of Additional Information on American Indians in the Military Archives/Collections/Contacts

This list consists of the various agencies and individuals that were contacted in the course of doing research for this project and may be useful to others who are researching projects on this or related topics.

National Archives

1. General Research Reference Room, 203, (Books, guides, etc.)

2. Microfilm Reading Room, 400, (open until 9 p.m.). Almost everything in the archives has been published on microfilm, requires an "M" # and roll #; microfilm copy machines available.

3. Military Reference Branch

    A. Revolutionary War to 1917—Room 11w: Army enlistment records, muster rolls, Adjutant General's correspondence, etc.

    B. 20th Century: WWI, WWII, Korea—Room 11e

    C. Vietnam Records—National Records Center, Suitland, Maryland

4. Civilian Reference Branch—Room 13e: Records from: Dept. of Interior, BIA, CCC, Indian schools, Commissioner of Indian Affairs personal papers, etc.

5. Still Picture Branch, 18th floor, 202-501-5455

    A. Army Signal Corps Collection

    B. U.S. Marine Corps Collection

    C. Dept. of Navy Photo Collection

    D. Office of War Information

    E. BIA Collection

6. Motion Picture Branch, Room G-13, 202-501-5449

    Newsreel footage, U.S. Marine Corps, Dpt. of Navy, Army Signal Corps, Private Collections. Some available on videocassette for viewing, others on 16mm and 35mm film. Viewing equipment must be reserved in advance.

7. National Archives Publication Sales, Room G-9. Guides to the archives and collections.

Department of Defense

Dept. of Defense Still Media Records Center

Code SSRC, Washington DC 20374-1681

*Photos taken since 1973 are considered active.

Smithsonian, Various Buildings on the Mall

1. National Museum of Natural History, 10th @ Constitution

    A. American Indian Program, JoAllyn Archambault, Anthropologist

    B. Anthropological Archives: 250,000 records, manuscripts, and photos relating to American Indians. Includes the archives of NCAI and the National Tribal Chairman's Association.

    C. Human Studies Film Archives: International collection of films, including footage of American Indians. example: Dixon-Wanamaker Expedition to Crow Agency, 1908 and Sanderson's Northwest Indian Footage, c.1926–32.

2. National Museum of American History, 12th @ Constitution

    A. American Indian Program, Rayna Green, PhD

    B. Division of Armed Forces History, Don Kloster

3. National Air and Space Museum, 7th @ Independence

    Library; Air Force Photo Collection (1861–1954), includes: Army Air Service, Army Air Corps—150,000 negatives of aircraft, personnel, bases, etc.

4. National Museum of the American Indian, National Mall;

    A. Rick West's Office, Andrea Hanley

    B. Public Affairs Office

Library of Congress

1. North American Indian Reference Librarian: Patrick Frazier, Jefferson Bldg.

2. Prints and Photo Collection, Madison Bldg., 3rd floor

   718 entries for Indian graphic material: Indians in their natural habitat, Civil War, Dixon-Wanamaker Expeditions, Individual portraits of warriors in regalia, scouts, etc.

3. Computer Catalog Center, Jefferson Bldg. (ties in to major collections, including photos; printouts available.)

Other Sources for Military Photos & Info in Washington DC

1. Center for Military History, HQDA

   Historical Properties Branch

   Attn: DAMH-HSO

   Washington DC 20314

   *This center has the Army War Art collection and all U.S. Army Museum collections.

2. Center For Military History, HQDA

   Organizational History Branch (Army unit histories)

   Attn: DAMH-HSO

   Washington DC 20314

3. Marine Corps Historical Center

   Washington   Navy   Yard

   Washington DC 20374-0580

4. Office of Public Affairs (Media and Authors)

   Dept. of Defense

   Room 2E765, The Pentagon

   Washington DC 20001

5. U.S. Naval Historical Center 202-433-2765

   Curator's Branch

Bldg. 108, Washington Navy Yard

Washington DC 20374

<u>National Museum of the American Indian (New York City Location)</u>

1. Indian Film & Video Collection; Elizabeth Weatherford/Millie Seubert

2. Photo Collection; Karen Firth/Lee Calendar

3. Research Branch, Bronx; American Indian Warfare

<u>U.S. Army Military History Institute</u>

Carlisle Barracks, PA 17013

Dr. Richard Summers, Archivist

*Civil War collection and other historical eras

<u>U.S. Naval Institute Library</u>

Preble Hall; Annapolis, MD 21402

*Collection of paintings, prints and photographs

<u>Mathers Museum</u>

603 East 8th; Bloomington, Indiana 47405

*8,000 images, Joseph K. Dixon photographer. Early 1900s, WWI, Indians

<u>Bettman Archive, Inc.</u>

136 East 57th St.; NY, NY 10022

*4 million items: History of Civilization, WWI, WWII (source for a few photos in the book *American Indians in World War II*).

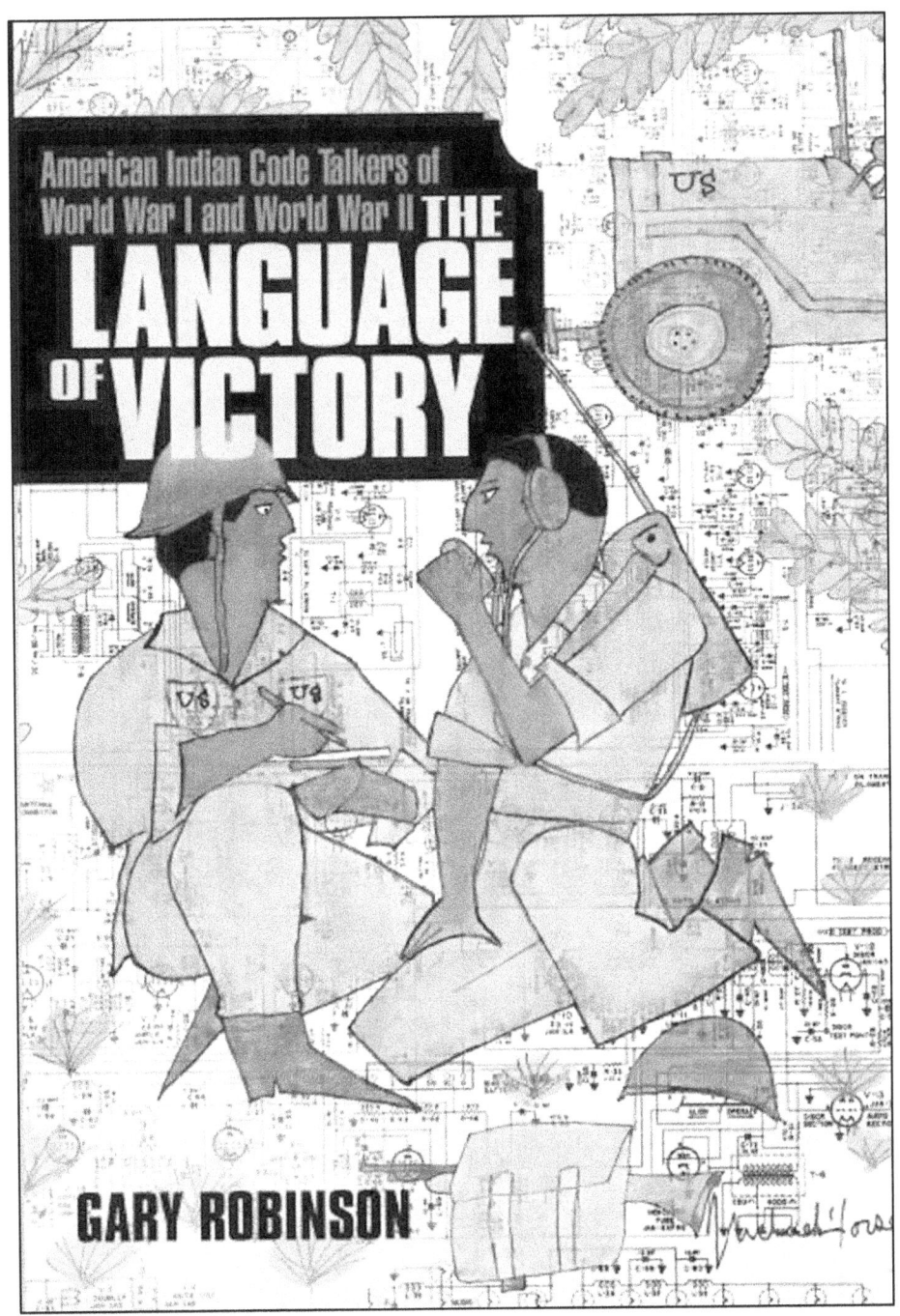

THE LANGUAGE OF VICTORY
American Indian Code Talkers of WWI and WWII

(Original copyrights 2010 & 2014)

Look for the companion *Language of Victory*
documentary, which features never-before-seen
footage and interviews with Choctaw, Comanche
and Navajo Code Talkers of World War II.
The link can be found on page 281
of this book.

INTRODUCTION

By now almost everyone in the United States has heard of the Navajo Code Talkers of World War II. Several books have been written on the subject, multiple documentary films have been produced, and Hollywood even made a movie about them (***Windtalkers***, 2002, starring Adam Beach). So much attention has been given to the Navajo code talkers that one might think they were the *only* code talkers.

But a growing number of Americans have begun to hear about the "other" code talkers, such as the <u>originals</u>, the Choctaw Code Talkers of World War I. Several magazine and newspaper articles, at least one book, and a PBS documentary have told their story.

But few people outside American Indian communities know that, according to various sources, at least <u>twenty</u> American Indian languages were used to send secret U.S. military messages during World War I and World War II, messages that were never decoded by the enemy.

Time after time, during both world wars, American military commanders credited our nation's military victories, in part, to the unerring delivery of undecipherable messages sent and received by American Indian soldiers fluent in their own tribal languages, languages thought to have been obsolete before that time, languages that many natives had been punished for speaking in government-run boarding schools.

In 2008, Congress passed the Code Talker Recognition Act designed to bring recognition and honor for, in the words of the Act, "the dedication and valor of Native American (*American Indian*) code talkers." Sioux Army veteran and Commander of National American Indian Veterans (NAIV) Don Loudner, was part of a group instrumental in getting that legislation passed, a group that included Chief Gregory Pyle of the Choctaw Nation of Oklahoma; Judy Allen, Public Relations Director for the Choctaw Nation;

Wallace Coffey, the former Chairman of the Comanche Nation; Lanny Aseperme, councilman and veteran from the Comanche Nation; and Andrea Page, a Sioux college instructor living in New York at the time.

This book explores the history of military communications and the unique place that American Indian code talkers, and their languages, have in that history and the history of America. The text includes never-before-published interviews with a few Comanche, Navajo, and Choctaw code talkers, most of whom are now, unfortunately deceased. This project also documents the long-overdue recognition and honor that finally came to be bestowed on the multi-tribal code talkers, including the creation of the Congressional medals awarded to the tribes and individuals whose languages were used as military codes.

Finally we'll reflect on what might have been lost if tribal languages had died, if tenacious native peoples hadn't struggled to preserve and pass on their spoken words, words that became the weapons of war spoken in the *language of victory*.

One final introductory note: NAIV has officially adopted the use of the term "American Indian" instead of "Native American" when speaking of America's indigenous people. They do so because technically any person born in the United States is a native American, just as any person born a Texan is called a native Texan. NAIV believes that the term American Indian more accurately reflects the historical term that a majority of indigenous peoples themselves prefer and accept. In deference to and respect for the National American Indian Veterans organization, this author uses American Indian in the pages of this book accept when quoting other speakers or federal legislation.

THE LANGUAGE OF VICTORY
TABLE OF CONTENTS

CHAPTER ONE

MILITARY COMMUNICATIONS:
AN OVERVIEW

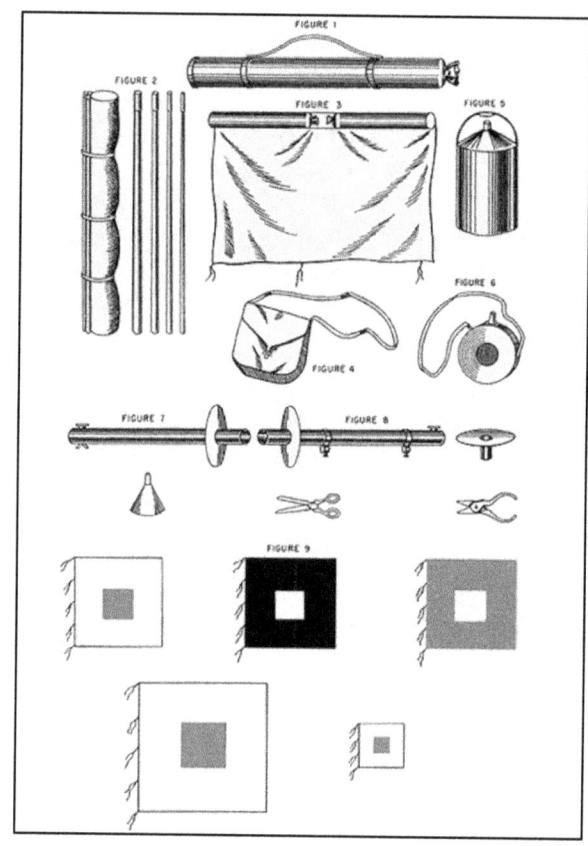

Early U.S. Army Signal Corps Field Kit with flags for signaling.

Army Signal Corps code class – WWII era

Communicating effectively has always been an important part of waging war and keeping the peace. Military commanders must be able to communicate orders to their units in the field to execute their strategies and win battles, and reports must be sent from the battlefront back to headquarters so that commanders know if their strategies are working.

Over the centuries, as armies grew larger and more complex, and as the distances between headquarters and the front lines increased, it became more and more difficult to orchestrate various military components into one successful operation. Thus separate communications units developed to handle the complexities of military communications. And, of course, an extremely necessary component of these communications is secrecy - the enemy must not be able to find out what your plans are - where and how and when you're going to strike. Secrecy and surprise are the key elements when it comes to winning victories.

As long as military units remained relatively small and engaged in close hand-to-hand combat, a commander's booming voice provided an effective means for transmitting orders on the battlefield. Armies also successfully used musical instruments, such as trumpets and bugles, as signaling devices. But for long-distance communications, ancient commanders often relied on runners or mounted messengers.

The use of messengers for delivering all kinds of messages developed in most societies in ancient times, and, in some cases, this method still constitutes a valuable means of direct communication to an intended receiver over long distances.

Legend has it that in 490 B.C., a Greek runner delivered to Athens the news of Greece's victory over the Persians at a place called Marathon, and then the runner died from the exertion. This heroic feat is said to have given rise to the athletic event known as the marathon.

Later, military leaders such as Alexander the Great, Hannibal, and Caesar developed elaborate systems of relays by which messages were carried from one messenger post to another by messengers mounted on horseback, traveling at top speed. In that way, they were able to maintain contact with their homelands during far-off military campaigns and to transmit messages with adequate speed.

At the close of the 12th century, the Mongolian warlord Genghis Khan not only established an extensive system of messenger posts from Europe to his Mongol capital, but he also made use of homing pigeons as messengers, as well. As his military victories grew and the lands falling under his command stretched, he established pigeon relay posts across Asia and much of Eastern Europe. Because he was both political and military ruler of his domains, it was necessary for him to send kingly orders to all sectors of his kingdom, and he effectively used both human and fowl messengers to transmit instructions to his subordinates.

Many American Indian societies used foot messengers to communicate not only military messages, but other types of important social messages as well. A prime example of the effective use of the "Indian runner" was during the Pueblo Revolt of 1680, in which the American Indians of New Mexico threw off the oppressive yoke of Spanish rule. Popé, the spiritual and military mastermind of the revolt, prepared a set of knotted ropes for each of his runners to carry to the far-flung pueblo villages strewn up and down the Rio Grande River. Each knot on the cord represented a day's count until the fateful day of revolution, when all of the Pueblos would rise up against the hated outsiders. And rise up they did, expelling the Spaniards from their midst, but unfortunately for the pueblos, not for good.

Of course, the process of delivering messages on foot is comparatively slow and is really only effective when the distances are not too far.

American Indians used several other means of communications for warfare and hunting that proved both appropriate and successful within their natural lifestyles. Certain animal calls signaled that warriors were in place and ready for attack. Smoke signals might represent the call of danger or the return to safety and peace. Drums were sometimes used to summon warriors or neighboring camps. Charcoal and ochre markings placed in pre-arranged locations could indicate the location of game or an enemy. Trail signs made of stacked stones or tree cuts could indicate the direction for hunters or warriors to follow or the direction to avoid. Tribes of the Plains, who spoke different languages, developed a system of inter-tribal sign language made up of arm and hand gestures that allowed for the effective exchange of information.

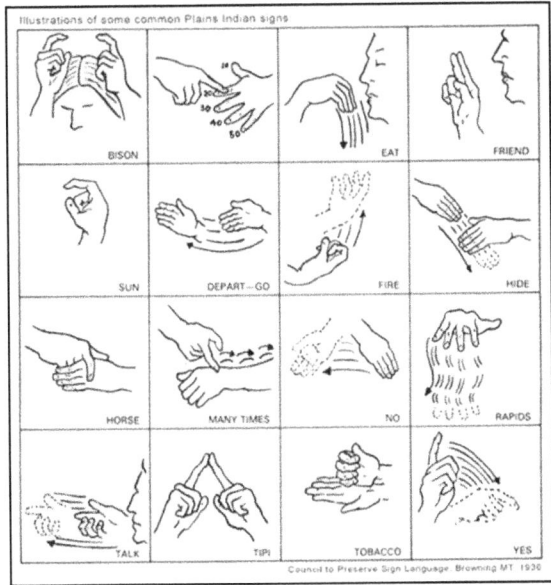

Plains Indian Sign Language

Back in Europe near the end of the 18th century, the French engineer Claude Chappe developed a sort of visual telegraph system of communication that employed towers or poles with movable arms near the top. The raising or lowering of the arms in the proper combinations indicated specific letters, words, or phrases. Using this system, messages could be sent over long distances in hours rather than days. In the early 1800s visual telegraph duties, known as semaphores, were assigned to units of engineer troops. Various forms of these "optical telegraphs" were developed and used by different European nations.

At the same time that these elementary methods of signal communication were being evolved on land, a comparable development was going on at sea. Early signaling between naval vessels was by prearranged messages transmitted by flags, lights, or the movement of a sail.

The idea of using coded messages came into use in Europe in the 16th century. Many codes were based simply on the number and position of signal flags or lights or on a number of cannon shots. In the 17th century the British admirals and ship commanders developed regular codes for naval communication, and near the end of the 18th century, British Admiral Richard Kempenfelt devised a plan of flag signaling similar to the one still in use today. Of course, these methods have been refined and improved through the decades.

In the United States, various branches of our fledgling country's military came into being through acts of Congress in the 1780s. And each branch of service put to use the best in existing means of military communications.

However the most significant development of signal communication for wartime use came after the invention of the electric telegraph by Samuel F.B. Morse. He successfully demonstrated electric communication between Washington, D.C., and Baltimore in 1844, and immediately provided a completely new means of rapid signal communication. His Morse Code, in which letters of the alphabet are communicated through a series of dots and dashes, used an electric key and sounder. This new technology was soon put to military use to supplement the various means of visual signaling.

In the U.S., the new device saw limited service during the Mexican War (1846-1848), because it still had a few bugs and was disastrously unreliable. So the Army only used the telegraph to communicate from their Washington office to offices in Baltimore, Philadelphia, and New York. As a precautionary measure, however, each telegraphed message was followed up with a letter.

In 1867, the British Navy adopted a system of "flash signaling," which was developed by a member of their high command. This was essentially an adaptation of the Morse code to lights. But the first actual application of the telegraph in time of war was made by the British in 1854 during the Crimean War. However its capabilities were not well understood, and therefore it was not widely used. Three years later, the Brits made full use of the telegraph in the East Indian Mutiny of 1857 and its use was a deciding factor in victory.

The United States Army became the first army in the world to create a separate communications unit, beginning with the appointment in 1860 of a signal officer to the War Department's Army staff. This event marked the official beginning of the U.S. Army Signal Corps. The flag-signaling system then put to use had been developed by an assistant Army surgeon, Albert J. Meyers, who had previously worked both as a civilian telegraph operator and an aid to the deaf. Combining these two experiences, he came up with the signaling system that became the Army Signal Corps' first wartime signaling system. Meyers was named the first Signal Officer and given the rank of Major.

Ironically, the first use of Myer's signaling system in the field was against the Navajos in October of 1860. Myer and his men accompanied troops on the campaign, maintaining communication between the columns, performing reconnaissance, and reporting by signals. The simplicity of the system, with its lightweight, portable equipment, made it well suited to use in the rugged terrain of the Southwest.

When the opening shots of the Civil War were fired the following spring at Ft. Sumter, South Carolina, the newly formed Army Signal Corps was called into action. Myer became its first instructor and operations supervisor.

As military signaling became more routine and systematic within the armed forces, signal security started to become a serious problem.

Enemy forces could learn the meanings of the messages that were being sent, and therefore anticipate the coming action. During the Civil War, the chief of staff of the Army of the Potomac expressed this very concern during an important battle when he ordered that signals not be used because the enemy could read them. The Chief Signal Officer at the time complained in his report of the battle that "the corps is distrusted and considered unsafe as a means of transmitting important messages. It is well known that the enemy can read our signals when the regular code is used."

To prevent Confederate forces from reading Union messages, the Signal Corps developed mechanized means of creating codes that could be changed on a regular basis, therefore making it next to impossible for an enemy to break the code. This became a regularly used technique that extended well into WWII. Both senders and receivers would be given a new code clue that would allow them to adjust their "cipher wheels" to find the matching code. As long as both ends of the transmission were on the same place on the wheel, coded messages could be sent without enemy translation.

Near the close of the 19th century, the wireless telegraph, or radio, made its appearance, and military leaders the world over quickly saw its potential for military and naval signaling. Development was rapid, and, by 1914, the new technology had been adopted and put to extensive use by the armies and navies of the world. With such widespread application, it soon became obvious that wireless telegraphy had its flaws when it came to military messaging: it lacked secrecy because messages could be easily heard by ally and enemy alike.

This led to the further development of extensive and complicated codes and ciphers as a necessary part of military signaling. And a new battlefield of the airwaves arose, pitting the cryptographer against the cryptanalyst on either side of any international conflict. A nation's ability to create an unbreakable communication code for wartime use became <u>the</u> ultimate challenge.

With the need for rapidly developed technical improvements to radio communications for wartime applications, American resources in the military, scientific and industrial fields joined forces to create better and more reliable means of transmitting messages during battle. Dramatic technical develops during and after WWI made it possible for Signal Corps personnel to consistently communicate vital messages that saved lives and won wars. But throughout all the technical advances in communications, it has always been the American soldier that has brought the courage, determination, and ingenuity necessary to make the equipment work under fire.

CHAPTER TWO

TRIBES AND TRIBAL LANGUAGES
BEFORE WORLD WAR I

A written Cherokee alphabet, using unique characters, was created by a Cherokee man named Sequoyah in the 1820s and was one of the very few early attempts to create a written version of an American Indian language.

D	a	S	ga		ka		ha
W	la		ma	Ɵ	na		hna
G	nah		qua	U	sa		s
	da	W	ta		dla		tla
G	tsa	G	wa		ya	R	e
	ge		he		le		me
Λ	ne		que		se		de
	te	L	tle	V	tse		we
	ye	T	i	Y	gi		hi
	li	H	mi		ni		qui
	si		di		ti	C	tli
	tsi		wi		yi		o
A	go		ho	G	lo		mo
Z	no	V	quo		so	V	do
	tlo	K	tso		wo		yo
	u	J	gu		hu	M	lu
	mu		nu		quu		su
S	du		tlu	J	tsu		wu
G	yu	i	v	E	gv		hv
	lv		nv	ε	quv		
R	sv		dv	P	tlv		
C	tsv	G	wv	B	yv		

Feb, 1919 Description of ʃimila ɀʃa ①

moɾʃaɀʃan aku ʼiti,
ʃaɾʃutʃ awilp asxoxoʼm,
 za.
kʼutaʼka mɔɾ. sam suki tuonus aʃtɔq,
kunaɀʃanin aʼinisuti kusmu aʃnikʼoʃi,
manoɢonoʃ ʼiʃkoʼm aɾaɀʼ,
ʼe lemes asɔlsk ɯn apakaʼs

This is a portion of one of the hundreds of thousands of pages of notes left by the anthropologist and linguist John P. Harrington who meticulously recorded many disappearing American Indian languages in the early 1900s.

As any fourth grade student knows, American Indian tribes have lived on the North American continent for thousands of years and have fought to defend their homelands, families, resources and ways of life from all outside threats, including European immigrants, American pioneers and the United States military.

Many tribes had well-developed warrior traditions that were more complex and contained more mental and spiritual depth than anything depicted in Hollywood westerns, and American history books are filled with the names of native warriors who put their lives on the line in defense of their people.

U.S. military leaders from George Washington to Andrew Jackson and Teddy Roosevelt recognized the unique abilities of American Indian warriors to win battles using unconventional means with almost supernatural force, and they put those skills to successful use time and time again. *(See the author's non-fiction book From Warriors to Soldiers to explore tribal warrior traditions and the history of American Indians in the military in more detail.)*

One of the things native people fought for, and continue to fight for, is their identity and the right to maintain that identity. Language is a central and defining element of anyone's culture and personal identity. Contained within a language are a people's view of the world, their sense of place within it, and their relationship to it. Destroy a nation's language and you also destroy its connection to it's own past and future.

People's ways of living, their histories, and their philosophies are all understood and communicated through language. Although most American Indians now speak English to some degree, many still consider their traditional languages to be very important. During the past 100 years, many tribal languages have been lost, or are now in danger of being lost. When the last speaker of a language passes away, that language becomes extinct, and therefore American Indian communities are working hard to keep their native languages alive.

As the United States strengthened its independence from European nations and grasped for larger pieces of the American continent, the nation's treatment of indigenous peoples fluctuated between the policies of annihilation, relocation and assimilation. In the 1700s and 1800s, many tribes were forced off their lands and confined to reservations where they endured hardships that included racism, poverty and efforts to eradicate their traditional cultures. Some of these efforts were part of a movement to "Americanize" the Indian .

The <u>Indian Removal Act</u> of 1830, which called for the relocation of tribes living east of the Mississippi River to lands west of the river, reflected the government's goal of removing Indians who were seen as impeding American expansion. While the law did not authorize the forced removal of tribal peoples, it authorized the President to negotiate land exchange treaties with tribes located in the eastern regions. A follow-up law, the Intercourse Law of 1834, prohibited U.S. citizens from entering tribal lands granted by any such treaties without permission, though it was often ignored.

Though the Indian Removal Act made the relocation of the tribes voluntary, it was often abused by government officials, including President Andrew Jackson. One infamous example of this abuse is the Treaty of New Echota of 1835, negotiated and signed by a small faction of Cherokee tribal members, not the tribal leadership. It resulted in the forced relocation of the tribe in 1838, during Andrew Jackson's administration, where an estimated 4,000 Cherokees died in the march from their traditional homelands in the Carolinas to the recently created Indian Territory, a march known as the *Trail of Tears.*

But in the decades that followed, white settlers encroached heavily into these western lands that had been set aside for tribes. American settlers eventually made homesteads from coast to coast, leaving no tribe untouched by the Americanizing influence of white traders, farmers, and soldiers.

In his State of the Union Address in December of 1871, Ulysses Grant stated that "many tribes of Indians have been induced to settle upon reservations, to cultivate the soil, to perform productive labor of various kinds, and to partially accept civilization. They are being cared for in such a way, it is hoped, as to induce those still pursuing their old habits of life to embrace the only opportunity which is left them to avoid extermination." The prevailing view towards the American Indian at the time is evident in Grant's statement: change or die.

In the 1890s, as the United States continued to expand, tribal lands were once again confiscated and reduced further in size to make way for more white settlers. In 1889, Congress authorized the opening for homestead settlement of tribal lands seized from the Indian Territory.

Languages were particularly targeted in the U.S. government's efforts to assimilate American Indians into the mainstream. The centerpiece of these efforts was the network of Indian Boarding Schools established in the late 1800s by the U. S.

government and various churches in different regions of the county. American Indian children were forcibly removed from their home communities and sent to these schools where they were forbidden to speak their own languages and punished if they did. The stated objective of these schools was to "kill the Indian but save the man." Unfortunately, nearly half of those subjected to the boarding school experience did not survive that experience.

In the boarding school strategy, the assault on a native child's tribal culture was complete. These children were forced to cut their hair and replace their traditional clothing with uniforms. They also had to replace their indigenous names, steeped in rich cultural traditions, with meaningless English ones.

They were taught that their cultures were inferior, and their own ancient religious practices were replaced with a rigid form of Christianity. Teachers were encouraged to use ridicule and humiliation to teach native youth to be ashamed of their "Indian-ness."

Boarding schools had a long-term negative effect on the self-esteem of Indian students and on possible continuation of native languages and cultures.

In spite of these culturally destructive, learned behaviors and beliefs, American Indian students did also manage to acquire knowledge of the workings of the white man's world and to learn skills that in some cases proved to be helpful later in life. One area that proved useful was, for those who joined the military, a regimented lifestyle, because the boarding school curriculum usually included some of the skills necessary for life in the military.

During the opening years of the 20th century, mainstream white America continued its national debate concerning the fate of American Indians. The "assimilationists," as they were known then, believed that Indians should continue to be mainstreamed in all aspects of life including clothing, customs, hair styles, housing, employment, religion, and education.

Separatists tended to believe that Indians were incapable of full integration into American society due to their inferior nature, a belief that continued to be applied to African Americans, as well.

American Indians, it seems, were seldom consulted regarding these issues. Many were eager to prove themselves within the national arena in all walks of life, while firmly maintaining their preference for practicing traditional native ways. To indigenous people, the two are not mutually exclusive.

With America's entry into World War I in 1917, several Indian tribes declared war on Germany independently of the United States, and thousands of American Indian men and women volunteered for military service, but were rejected because they did not speak or read English.

Simultaneously, many U.S. military leaders were still opposed to using Indians in regular service and needed convincing otherwise. Several prominent citizens with close ties to Congressional leaders finally paved the way for Indian participation in military service.

At the time, the Department of the Interior still operated about twenty five boarding schools, and those automatically became recruiting stations. At Virginia's Hampton Institute, one Lakota student, Charles Roy Morsea, gave a patriotic speech to his fellow students encouraging their enlistment. He explained that his father had served earlier in the Spanish-American War and was already fighting in France with General Pershing.

Despite a variety of barriers, more than 17,000 Indians saw active service in the army and navy during the First World War. Some two-thirds were volunteers, even though Indians weren't allowed to be citizens on a national scale until 1924 with passage of the Indian Citizenship Act.

Why did so many American Indian men enlist? Partly because tribal societies still regarded their warriors with the utmost respect. Native men had trained at a young age to develop the spiritual, mental, emotional, and physical strength needed to become warriors. Many tribes continued their warrior societies with their own ceremonies, songs, dances, and regalia. But they no longer had any means of achieving warrior status. So, many turned to military service as a way of achieving that honored status.

CHAPTER THREE

WWI AND THE BIRTH OF THE
AMERICAN INDIAN CODE TALKERS

World War I Field Telephone

The first: Choctaw Code Talkers of World War I

As mentioned in the previous chapter, at the outbreak of World War I in 1917, American Indians were not citizens of the United States, and to most Americans, the languages they spoke were considered obsolete. Little did anyone know that a few of these so-called obsolete languages, spoken by soldiers that weren't American citizens, would help turn the tide and win what became known as the Great War.

To the surprise of many of U.S. commanding officers, American Indian soldiers proved to be adept at learning to use complex equipment and speak other languages. However, their methods, as noted before, were not always orthodox.

For example, two Comanche soldiers from a unit endangered by not knowing the German strategy, waited 'til nightfall, stripped down and covered their bodies completely in whitewash. They crept out into No Man's Land (the zone between opposing enemy trenches) and waited by the enemy lines until daylight. There, they stood absolutely still, blending in with a collection of wooden posts, overhearing the enemy communications.

Personal accounts of American Indian heroism were numerous, and the contributions made by American Indian soldiers were noticed by British and French commanders. Ferdinand Foch, Marshall of France, wrote, "I cannot forget the brilliant service which the valorous Indian soldiers of the American army have rendered to the common cause, and the energy, as well as the courage, which they have shown to bring about victory…"

According to native soldiers, the use of tribal languages as codes did not arise from a brilliant strategic military plan devised by Army headquarters, but rather from desperate need on the field of combat. The Germans had become masters at listening in and decoding all U.S. Army field communications in Europe. Every planned battle or maneuver was effectively thwarted by German artillery, air and ground troops. They obviously knew what was coming, and America was losing the war.

Though reports from Army personnel give non-Indian military leaders the credit for the idea, it was Indian soldiers themselves who presented the idea of using one of their languages as a code. Having exhausted every other means of transmitting coded information, U.S. commanders believed it was worth a try.

Initially a group of eight Choctaws were trained in the use of field telephone set-up and use. Since there were no specific Choctaw words for many of the military terms they needed to communicate, many existing Choctaw words were substituted. For example, the First, Second and Third Battalions were called One Grain of Corn, Two Grains of Corn, and Three Grains of Corn respectively. The term adopted for machine gun was "little gun shoot fast." Thus an entire coded military vocabulary was developed.

Then, when it came time to test the system, one Choctaw was placed at each of the allied field camps to send and receive messages in the tribal language. The messages were then translated into English.

The remarkable results of this experiment were reported by Colonel A. W. Bloor, commander of the 142nd Infantry Division operating in France, in his memo to the headquarters of the American Expeditionary Forces.

Date: January 23, 1919, A.P.O. No. 796
From: C.O. 142nd Infantry
To: The Commanding General 36th Division (Attention Capt. Spence)
Headquarters - 142nd Infantry, A.E.F.
Subject: Transmitting messages in Choctaw

In compliance with memorandum, Headquarters 36th Division, January 21, 1919, to C.O. 142nd Infantry, the following account is submitted.

In the first action of the 142nd Infantry at St. Etienne, it was recognized that of all the various methods of liaison the telephone presented the greatest possibilities. The field of rocket signals is restricted to a small number of agreed signals. The runner system is slow and hazardous. T.P.S. is always an uncertain quantity. It may work beautifully and again, it may be entirely worthless. The available means, therefore, for the rapid and full transmission of information are the radio, buzzer and telephone, and of these the telephone was by far the superior, provided it could be used without hindrance, provided straight to the point information could be given.

It was well understood however, that the German was a past master of "listening in." Moreover, from St. Etienne to the Aisne we had traveled through a county netted with German wire and cables. We established P.C.'s in dugouts and houses, but recently occupied by him. There was every reason to believe every decipherable message or word going over our wires also went to the enemy. A rumor was out that our Division had given false coordinates of our supply dump, and that in thirty minutes the enemy shells were falling on the point. We felt sure the enemy knew too much. It was therefore necessary to code every message of importance and coding and decoding took valuable time.

While comparatively inactive at Vaux-champagne, it was remembered that the regiment possessed a company of Indians. They spoke twenty-six different language or dialects, only four or five of which were ever written. There was hardly one chance in a *million that Fritz would be able to translate these dialects and the plan to have these Indians transmit telephone messages was adopted. The regiment was fortunate in having two Indian officers who spoke several of the dialects. Indians from the Choctaw tribe were chosen and one placed in each P.C. (*Note: while this commander claims the idea came from within the Army's intelligence unit, several of the Choctaw soldiers claimed the idea was there's.)*

The first use of the Indians was made in ordering a delicate withdrawal of two companies of the 2nd En. from Chufilly to Chardoney on the night of October 26th. This movement was completed without mishap... The Indians were used repeatedly on the 27th in preparation for the assault on Forest Farm. The enemy's complete surprise is evidence that he could not decipher the messages.

After the withdrawal of the regiment to Louppy-le-Petit, a number of Indians were detailed for training in transmitting messages over the telephone. The instruction was carried on by the Liaison Officer Lieutenant Black. It had been found that the Indian's vocabulary of military terms was insufficient. The Indian (word) for "Big Gun" was used to indicate artillery. "Little gun shoot fast" was substituted for machine gun and the battalions were indicated by one, two and three grains of corn. It was found that the Indian tongues do not permit verbatim translation, but at the end of the short training period at Louppy-le-Petit, the results were very gratifying, and it is believed, had the regiment gone back into the line, fine results would have been obtained. We were confident the possibilities of the telephone had been obtained without its hazards.

A.W. Bloor, Colonel
142nd Infantry
Commanding.

According to research done by the Department of Defense, there were possibly 23 American Indian soldiers from different tribes who used their tribal languages to send and receive coded messages during World War I. Most of them were Choctaws, as the Choctaw language was most extensively used. However, the Comanche and Cherokee languages are also reported to have been used.

It's unfortunate that a respected history of the Army's Signal Corps, published by the U.S. Army Center of Military History, makes no mention of the American Indian code talker contribution during World War I.

As they proved successful in using their native language as a code, more Choctaws were quickly pressed into service, expanding the original eight to at least nineteen. Choctaw tribal documents list these names on their WWI Choctaw Code Talkers list: Tobias Frazier, Victor Brown, Joseph Oklahombi, Otis Leader, Ben Hampton, Albert Billy, Walter Veach, Ben Carterby, James Edwards, Solomon Louis,

Peter Maytubby, Mitchell Bobb, Calvin Wilson, Jeff Nelson, Joseph Davenport, George Davenport, Noel Johnson, Schlicht Billy and Robert Taylor. These men were members of the Army's 36th Division.

Later, a captured German officer confessed that his intelligence personnel "were completely confused by the Indian language and gained no benefit whatsoever from their wiretaps." Up until the time American Indian languages were spoken over military telephone lines, the Germans had successfully deciphered all coded messages because most Americans were of European origin and their sense of language, coded or otherwise, came from the languages of that continent. Consequently, Germans had a good idea of the different ways Americans might try to render English into codes. American Indian languages are not based on European tongues, so Germans had no reference when attempting to translate and decode native code.

"Within 24 hours after the Choctaw language was pressed into service, the tide of the battle had turned and in less than 72 hours the Allies were on full attack," Commander Bloor reported.

Of course, the tribes are very proud of the story of the original Code Talkers of WWI. The Choctaws of Oklahoma have erected a granite monument at the entrance to their capitol grounds that bears the engraved names of the men who used the language to help win World War I. Toward the end of the war, Cherokee, Comanche, Cheyenne, and Osage tribal members from Oklahoma also served as code talkers, according to Department of Defense documents.

It should be noted that the term "code talker" was not coined until WWII or shortly after. The WWI code talkers never referred to themselves this way nor did anyone else. It seems that these soldiers usually referred to their activity as merely "talking on the radio," by which they meant the field telephone.

CHAPTER FOUR

WWII: CODE TALKING PERFECTED

Comanche Code Talker Trainees of World War II

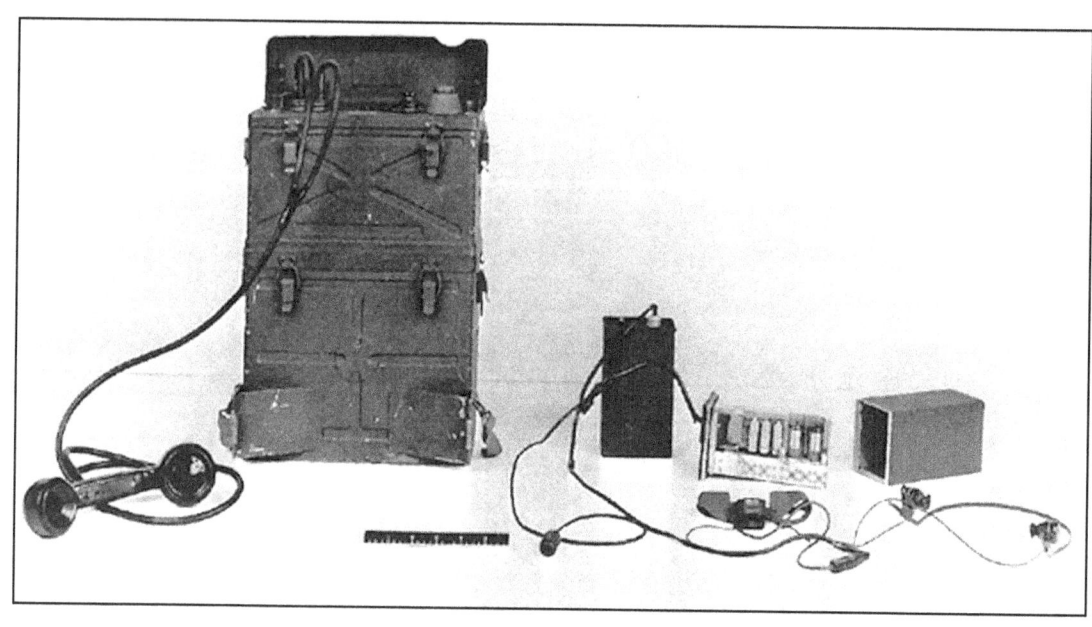

World War II U.S. Army Back-Pack Radio Telephone Gear

Before the outbreak of World War II, Adolf Hitler secretly sent an undercover team of German anthropologists to the United States in an attempt to learn American Indian languages, because he'd learned of the successful use of American Indian code talkers during World War I. However, it proved an overwhelming task for the Germans to learn the many tribal languages and dialects that existed.

Because of these Nazi anthropologists' attempts to learn tribal languages, the U.S. Army did not implement a large-scale code talker program for the European Theater of the Second World War. However, anticipating that the U.S. might be drawn into WWII, the director of the Fort Cobb Indian Conservation Corps camp of Oklahoma, a Comanche named William Karty, proposed that the Army begin using the Comanche language for coded communications. Karty's suggestion fell on receptive ears, and he was authorized to recruit volunteers for this special mission. The primary requirement was the ability to speak and understand English and Comanche fluently.

Comanche code talker Roderick Red Elk explains what happened. "There was a man that came down and talked to several of us for the purpose of joining the Army to become code talkers. This was December, 1940. I got sworn in January 1, 1941."

So, in December 1940, the army did recruit seventeen Comanches to become code talkers. These were Charles Chibitty, Haddon Codynah, Robert Holder, Forrest Kassanavoid, Wellington Mihecoby, Perry Noyabad, Clifford Otitivo, Simmons Parker, Melvin Permansu, Elgin Red Elk, Roderick Red Elk, Albert Nahquaddy Jr., Larry Saupitty, Morris Tabbyetchy (Sunrise), Anthony Tabbytite, Ralph Wahnee, and Willie Yacheschi.

After graduating from West Point in 1941, Lt. Hugh F. Foster joined the Army Signal Corps and was sent to Fort Benning, Georgia, where he was put in charge of training the Comanches who'd been recruited for code talking.

Assigned to the Fourth Infantry Division's Fourth Signal Company at Fort Benning, they received basic training, followed by phone, radio, Morse code, and semaphore training. These were the only American Indian soldiers that were officially trained to become code talkers for deployment in Europe.

Red Elk continues describing their experience: "...after basic training, they started us on the different types of communications, how to operate, tear down and repair the telephone, the radio..."

Most of these recruits had attended Indian boarding schools where they had become accustomed to military-style discipline and been punished for speaking their native tongue. Their mastery of military skills amazed the Army drill sergeant assigned to train them.

By October 30, 1941, the Comanches had completed their training and were conducting field exercises soon thereafter.

Comanches of the 4th Signal Company compiled a vocabulary of over 100 code terms using words or phrases in their own language.

Red Elk said that in the Army there are "a lot of military terms with no Comanche word for them, so we had to sit down and figure out a name for each, for instance, like "gun."

"We had just one name for gun (he says the Comanche word) which means "gun." In the military you have all types of guns. You got your artillery, you got your small arms, you got your machine guns, the different caliber machine guns. And we had to work out a word for each of those." *(Roderick Red Elk's complete interview appears in Chapter 6 of this book.)*

Using a substitution method similar to what the Navajo code talkers later developed, the Comanche code word for tank was "turtle", bomber was "pregnant airplane", machine gun was "sewing machine" and Adolf Hitler became "crazy white man."

Fourteen Comanche code talkers took part in the Invasion of Normandy. Two code-talkers were assigned to each regiment, the rest to 4th Infantry Division headquarters. Shortly after landing on Utah Beach on June 6, 1944, the Comanches began transmitting messages. Some were wounded but none killed, and they continued to serve in the 4th Infantry Division during further European operations.

The most well-known and most written about group of code talkers is, of course, the Navajo, for several reasons. First, they were the largest group. Four hundred twenty Navajos were recruited and trained as code talkers, though not all of them saw active combat duty. Second, their code was kept secret for the longest time, becoming de-classified in 1968, so the news made more of a public splash when it was finally revealed. And lastly, and most unfortunately, many of the Navajo code talkers claimed to be the only "true" code talkers, entirely dismissing other natives who'd used their tribal languages to send secret wartime messages. *(See this book's bibliography for multiple sources on the Navajo code talkers.)*

It has always been the position of National American Indian Veterans that any American Indian soldier who used a tribal language to communicate secret messages to one of his fellow tribesmen during combat should be considered a code talker. Congress validated this view when it issued the Code Talker Recognition Act in 2008, recognizing that some twenty American Indian languages had been used in this manner.

Even though the Comanches and the Navajos were the only <u>officially</u> trained code talkers who devised codes within their languages for use in WWII, as many as 100 other American Indian soldiers from as many as nineteen other tribes used their native languages to send coded communications. Many of these uses were not well documented because they spontaneously appeared on the battlefield in a time of great need where two or more Indians spoke the same language.

Among the Choctaws who brought their native tongues to war was Second Lt. Schlicht (pronounced "Slish") Billy of Pittsburgh County, Oklahoma. Because of high scores on intelligence tests he took after entering the Army, Billy was sent to several special schools to receive training that prepared him for a battlefield leadership position. When explaining how he came to use his language with other Choctaws during battle, Billy said, "we were more of an experiment, because we had it (the language) at hand right there."

Because enemy shelling often destroyed land lines, they had to use other means of communications. "When a shell hits," Billy remarked, "it tears up your communication lines - so we had these little "536 Radios." I went to school for that, so I had knowledge on how to use that. And we knew that the Germans were good at breaking codes and tying into our lines, things like that. So that was the fastest and easiest, and we had the language."

Billy said he regularly conversed in Choctaw when using field radios to coordinate military maneuvers. Quite often, Billy's Choctaw friend and machine gunner Davis Pickens was on the other radio. Pickens was usually positioned where he could do the most damage to the enemy. Speaking the Choctaw language, the men were able to communicate exact details and locations of targets without fear of the Germans intercepting the conversations.

Billy, who was also a trained platoon leader, commanded the first Platoon in Company F, known as Fox Company, 180th Infantry Division. Billy's regiment experienced more than 500 days of actual combat in Italy and France, and several wartime articles reported on the achievements of this brave platoon. *(His complete interview appears in Chapter 6.)*

Documentation is still being researched to determine the names of other WWII code talkers from other tribes. Native soldiers from more than nineteen tribes (not including Navajos, because they were previously honored by Congress.) had been identified to receive the Congressional medal.

CHAPTER FIVE

FINALLY COMES THE RECOGNITION

The Choctaw Nation's War Memorial dedicated to the
Choctaw Code Talkers of World War I

"Spirit of the Code Talker," created by artist Dan Pogue,
was unveiled in 2003 and stands in front of the Comanche tribal headquarters.

What the code talkers did during World War I, and how they did it, was not reported to the public for many years, and there seems to have been no real public recognition for their efforts in the years following the Great War. Boasting or even talking about wartime deeds was not in the nature of most of the returning native soldiers.

The Comanche code talkers of WWII, who served as part of the U.S. Army Signal Corps, and other tribal code talkers were given individual permission to speak of their wartime activities, though most did not talk about it outside their own tribal community, and again their accomplishments were not reported to the public.

However, the Navajos, who were part of the Marine Corps during WWII, were first recognized for their contributions to the war effort in an article published in the Marine Corps Gazette at the war's end. This article was reprinted in a publication issued by the Office of Indian Affairs (an office within the Department of the Interior) titled Indians in the War. The Office of Indian Affairs had been regularly printing and distributing a publication called Indians at Work that was created to publicize American Indian accomplishments and contributions to American society. During the war, several issues of this publication included native wartime facts. Fifteen thousand copies of Indians in the War were printed in 1946 in order to emphasize the "Indian contribution to the victory" in the second world war.

While Navajos were allowed to divulge information about their activities, it wasn't until 1968 that the Navajo code itself was declassified by the Marines. It was then that their fame really began to spread, and they were honored several times over the years.

Gradually, as word spread more widely about all of the tribal language codes and code talkers, the recognition came to the others. The Choctaw Nation of Oklahoma first honored the Choctaw Code Talkers of WWI in a special ceremony held at tribal headquarters in 1986. The French were next. In 1989, the French government gave the Comanche Code Talkers of WWII an honor called the "Chevalier of the National Order of Merit" in a special ceremony held in Oklahoma City.

In 1992, the governor of the state of Oklahoma issued a proclamation naming September 26 of that year as "American Indian Code Talker Day" in the state. This proclamation was shared with the public at an event held near Norman, Oklahoma, that day to honor the code talkers. (*This is covered in more detail in Chapter six.*)

In 1999, Charles Chibitty, then the last surviving Comanche Code Talker, was given the Knowlton Award by the Pentagon, a special honor from the Military Intelligence Association. He also received other honors from state and national organizations.

It wasn't until the year 2000 that the United States Congress passed legislation to honor any of the code talkers, and the Navajos were nationally recognized at that time. That law provided for the creation of special gold and silver Congressional Medals. The gold medals were issued to the original 29 Navajos who developed the code, and the silver medals were issued to those who served later in the program. On the back of the medal is printed a statement in the Navajo language that means "With the Navajo language they defeated the enemy."

The awards were given to the Navajo code talkers by President George Bush at a special ceremony held at the White House in 2001. At that time, the president said, "Gentlemen, your service inspires the respect and admiration of all Americans, and our gratitude is expressed for all time, in the medals it is now my honor to present."

The Comanche Nation commissioned sculptor Dan Pogue to create a statue to commemorate the Comanche code talkers, and his sculpture, called "Spirit of the Code Talker," was unveiled at the Comanche Nation headquarters during the tribal fair in 2003.

Even with this acknowledgement of a few of the WWII code talkers, other code talkers from the other tribes, and those from WWI, were still unknown and unheard of outside their own tribes.

The Code Talker Recognition Act of 2008

The comprehensive Code Talker Recognition Act of 2008 finally addressed the issue of the "unknown" code talkers and specifically expressed the nation's gratitude for "the dedication and valor of Native American (*American Indian*) code talkers." The movement to nationally acknowledge the contributions of the code talkers may have begun as early as 1998 when a petition on the issue began to be circulated.

The code talker bill, H.R. 4544, was passed by the House of Representatives on Sept. 25, 2008, and then passed by the Senate five days later. It was signed into law by President Bush on October 15, 2008, and became Public Law 110-420. The bill, as it was first introduced earlier that year, is reprinted below. (*Author's note: the legislation reprinted below uses the term Native American instead of American Indian throughout. I am merely reporting the bill verbatim and so have left that terminology intact.*)

One Hundred Tenth Congress
of the
United States of America
AT THE SECOND SESSION

Begun and held at the City of Washington on Thursday,
the third day of January, two thousand and eight.

An Act
To require the issuance of medals to recognize the dedication and valor of Native American code talkers.
Be it enacted by the Senate and House of Representatives of the United States of America in Congress assembled,

SECTION 1. SHORT TITLE.

This Act may be cited as the 'Code Talkers Recognition Act of 2008'.

SEC. 2. PURPOSE.

The purpose of this Act is to require the issuance of medals to express the sense of the Congress that--

(1) the service of Native American code talkers to the United States deserves immediate recognition for dedication and valor; and

(2) honoring Native American code talkers is long overdue.

SEC. 3. FINDINGS.

The Congress finds the following:

(1) When the United States entered World War I, Native Americans were not accorded the status of citizens of the United States.

(2) Without regard to that lack of citizenship, members of Indian tribes and nations enlisted in the Armed Forces to fight on behalf of the United States.

(3) The first reported use of Native American code talkers was on October 17, 1918.

(4) Because the language used by the Choctaw code talkers in the transmission of information was not based on a European language or on a mathematical progression, the Germans were unable to understand any of the transmissions.

(5) This use of Native American code talkers was the first time in modern warfare that such a transmission of messages in a native language was used for the purpose of confusing an enemy.

(6) On December 7, 1941, Japan attacked Pearl Harbor, Hawaii, and the Congress declared war the following day.

(7) The Federal Government called on the Comanche Nation to support the military effort during World War II by recruiting and enlisting Comanche men to serve in the Army to develop a secret code based on the Comanche language.

(8) The United States Army recruited approximately 50 Native Americans for special native language communication assignments.

(9) The United States Marine Corps recruited several hundred Navajos for duty in the Pacific region.

(10) During World War II, the United States employed Native American code talkers who developed secret means of communication based on native languages and were critical to winning the war.

(11) To the frustration of the enemies of the United States, the code developed by the Native American code talkers proved to be unbreakable and was used extensively throughout the European theater.

(12) In 2001, the Congress and President Bush honored Navajo code talkers with congressional gold medals for the contributions of the code talkers to the United States Armed Forces as radio operators during World War II.

(13) The heroic and dramatic contributions of Native American code talkers were instrumental in driving back Axis forces across the Pacific during World War II.

(14) The Congress should provide to all Native American code talkers the recognition the code talkers deserve for the contributions of the code talkers to United States victories in World War I and World War II.

SEC. 4. DEFINITIONS.

In this Act, the following definitions shall apply:

(1) CODE TALKER- The term 'code talker' means a Native American who--

(A) served in the Armed Forces during a foreign conflict in which the United States was involved; and

(B) transmitted (encoded and translated) secret coded messages for tactical military operations during World War I and World War II using their native tribal language (non-spontaneous communications)

(2) SECRETARY- The term 'Secretary' means the Secretary of the Treasury.

SEC. 5. CONGRESSIONAL GOLD MEDALS.

(a) Award Authorization- The Speaker of the House of Representatives and the President pro tempore of the Senate shall make appropriate arrangements for the award, on behalf of the Congress, of gold medals of appropriate design in recognition of the service of Native American code talkers during World War I and World War II.

(b) Identification of Recipients- The Secretary, in consultation with the Secretary of Defense and the tribes, shall--

(1) determine the identity, to the maximum extent practicable, of each Native American tribe that had a member of that tribe serve as a Native American code talker, with the exception of the Navajo Nation;

(2) include the name of each Native American tribe identified under subparagraph (A) on a list; and

(3) provide the list, and any updates to the list, to the Smithsonian Institution for maintenance under section 5(c)(2).

(c) Design and Striking of Medals-

(1) IN GENERAL- The Secretary shall strike the gold medals awarded under subsection (a) with appropriate emblems, devices, and inscriptions, as determined by the Secretary.

(2) DESIGNS OF MEDALS EMBLEMATIC OF TRIBAL AFFILIATION AND PARTICIPATION- The design of a gold medal under paragraph (1) shall be emblematic of the participation of the code talkers of each recognized tribe.

(3) TREATMENT- Each medal struck pursuant to this subsection shall be considered to be a national medal for purposes of chapter 51 of title 31, United States Code.

(d) Action by Smithsonian Institution- The Smithsonian Institution--

(1) shall accept and maintain such gold medals, and such silver duplicates of those medals, as recognized tribes elect to send to the Smithsonian Institution;

(2) shall maintain the list developed under section 6(1) of the names of Native American code talkers of each recognized tribe; and

(3) is encouraged to create a standing exhibit for Native American code talkers or Native American veterans.

SEC. 6. NATIVE AMERICAN CODE TALKERS.

The Secretary, in consultation with the Secretary of Defense and the tribes, shall--

(1) with respect to tribes recognized as of the date of the enactment of this Act -

(A) determine the identity, to the maximum extent practicable, of each Native American code talker of each recognized tribe with the exception of the Navajo Nation;

(B) include the name of each Native American code talker identified under subparagraph (A) on a list, to be organized by recognized tribe; and

(C) provide the list, and any updates to the list, to the Smithsonian Institution for maintenance under section 5(d)(2);

(2) in the future, determine whether any Indian tribe that is not a recognized as of the date of the enactment of this Act, should be eligible to receive a gold medal under this Act; and

(3) with consultation from the tribes listed in following subsection, examine the following specific tribes to determine the existence of Code Talkers:

(A) Assiniboine.
(B) Chippewa and Oneida.
(C) Choctaw.
(D) Comanche.
(E) Cree.
(F) Crow.
(G) Hopi.
(H) Kiowa.
(I) Menominee.
(J) Mississauga.
(K) Muscogee.
(L) Sac and Fox.
(M) Sioux.

SEC. 7. DUPLICATE MEDALS.

(a) Silver Duplicate Medals-

(1) IN GENERAL- The Secretary shall strike duplicates in silver of the gold medals struck under section 5(b), to be awarded in accordance with paragraph (2).

(2) ELIGIBILITY FOR AWARD-

(A) IN GENERAL- A Native American shall be eligible to be awarded a silver duplicate medal struck under paragraph (1) in recognition of the service of Native American code talkers of the recognized tribe of the Native American, if the Native American served in the Armed Forces as a code talker in any foreign conflict in which the United States was involved during the 20th century.

(B) DEATH OF CODE TALKER- In the event of the death of a Native American code talker who had not been awarded a silver duplicate medal under this subsection, the Secretary may award a silver duplicate medal to the next of kin or other personal representative of the Native American code talker.

(C) DETERMINATION- Eligibility for an award under this subsection shall be determined by the Secretary in accordance with section 6.

(b) Bronze Duplicate Medals- The Secretary may strike and sell duplicates in bronze of the gold medal struck pursuant to section 4 under such regulations as the Secretary may prescribe, at a price sufficient to cover the cost thereof, including labor, materials, dies, use of machinery, and overhead expenses, and the cost of the gold and silver medals.

SEC. 8. AUTHORITY TO USE FUND AMOUNTS; PROCEEDS OF SALE.

(a) Authority to Use Fund Amounts- There are authorized to be charged against the United States Mint Public Enterprise Fund such amounts as may be necessary to pay for the cost of the medals struck pursuant to this Act.

(b) Proceeds of Sale- Amounts received from the sale of duplicate bronze medals authorized under section 7(b) shall be deposited into the United States Mint Public Enterprise Fund.

Speaker of the House of Representatives.

Vice President of the United States and

President of the Senate.

(END OF LEGISLATION)

Code Talker Tribes

Soldiers in World War I and World War II from the following tribes are known to have used their languages as codes and are being included in the Congressional Medals bestowed as part of the Code Talker Recognition Act. This information, provided by the Department of Defense, indicates the number of individuals who were known to be code talkers from each tribe.

1. Assiniboine – WWII: 3*
2. Cherokee – WWI: 1; WWII: unknown number
3. Choctaw – WWI: 19: WWII: 4
4. Comanche – WWI: 1; WWII: 17
5. Creek – WWII: 2

6. Crow – WWII: 2

7. Hopi – WWII: 11

8. Kiowa – WWII: 3

9. Oneida – WWII: 2

10. Pawnee – WWII: 9

11. Ponca – WWII: 1

12. Seminole – WWII: 1

13. Sioux – WWI: 3; WWII: 16

14. Tlingit – WWII: 3

15. Cheyenne – WWII: unknown number

16. Menominee – WWII: unknown number

17. Meskwaki – WWII: unknown number

18. Chippewa – WWII: unknown number

19. Osage – WWII: unknown number

To successfully be able to send and receive coded messages, there has to be an even number of people who know that code: one to code the message and speak it into the radio or telephone, and a second one to hear the message, decode it and then pass it along to the intended recipient. This author can't explain how the Department of Defense determined the number of code talkers for each language or how there could be an uneven number of code talkers for some of these languages, but these are the numbers indicated by the DOD at the time of publication.

The Congressional Medals

Whenever Congress commissions the minting of medals, that process is executed by the United States Mint. The Mint has a well-established process for designing these medals, which was adapted for the design of the code talker medals. The process is as follows:

<u>Stage 1</u>   The U.S. Mint will initiate the formal design process by contacting appropriate officials of each tribe and requesting the appointment of an individual to serve as the official liaison to the U.S. Mint for the Code Talkers Recognition program.

Stage 2   The U.S. Mint, in consultation with the liaisons for the tribes, will develop unique themes for the obverse (heads side) designs for each eligible tribe. With respect to the reverse (tails side) designs, the U.S. Mint will develop a common design theme that will be adopted for the reverse of all medals produced under this program.

Stage 3   Based on the themes, the U.S. Mint artists will produce unique candidate obverse designs and a common reverse design, focusing on the aesthetic beauty, historic accuracy, appropriateness and coinability.

Stage 4   The U.S. Mint and the liaisons for each tribe will collaborate on the candidate obverse designs. Each liaison will appoint an historian, other responsible officials or experts, to participate in this collaboration to ensure historic accuracy and proper presentation of the candidate designs. The U.S. Mint will refine the candidate designs, as necessary, before presenting them to the Citizens Coinage Advisory Committee (CCAC) and the U.S. Commission of Fine Arts (CFA).

Stage 5   The CCAC and the CFA will review the candidate designs as required by law and make recommendations, and the U.S. Mint, in consultation with the tribal liaisons, may make changes to address such recommendations.

Stage 6   From among the final candidate obverse designs, the liaisons for the tribes will recommend their preferred obverse candidate designs. The U.S. Mint will request documentation from each tribe supporting the recommendations.

Stage 7   The U.S. Mint will present the recommended designs to the Secretary of the Treasury for approval.

From 2008 to 2013, the Department of Defense conducted a thorough search of its records to uncover as many American Indian code talkers as possible. During this same period of time, designers at the U.S. Mint worked with tribes to design the metals mandated by the Code Talker Recognition Act of 2008.

Finally, in November of 2013, Congressional medals were presented to thirty-three tribes, recognizing code talkers from both World War I and World War II. Unfortunately, most of the individual code talkers had already passed away by then. So, in many cases, the medals were presented to tribal representatives.

A proud nation finally said a long-overdue "Thank You" to these deserving men.

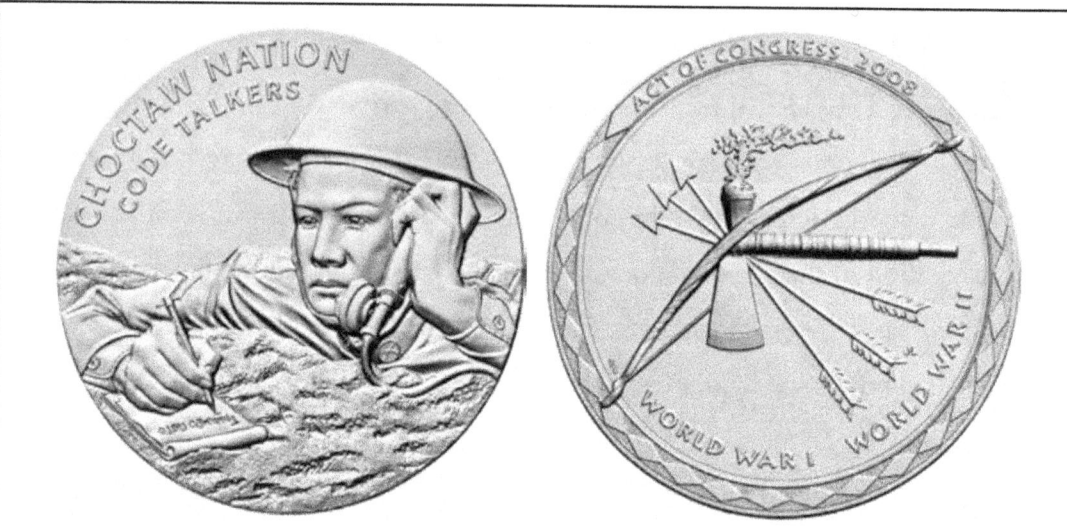

Pictured are the front and back sides of the Congressional gold medal presented to the Choctaw Nation in honor of their code talkers from WWI and WWII. All of the code talker medals can be viewed and replicas purchased from the U.S. Mint's catalog on the Internet at: www.usmint.gov. (Image courtesy of U.S. Mint.)

CHAPTER SIX

THE WWII CODE TALKER INTERVIEWS
RECORDED IN 1992

Powwow Grand Entry in Norman Oklahoma, September 1992,
where Choctaw, Comanche and Navajo code talkers were honored.

Proclamation issued by the Governor of Oklahoma naming
September 26, 1992, as American Indian Code Talker Day in the state.

In the early 1990s, the author was engaged in doing research that was meant to lead to a documentary television series about the history of American Indians in the U.S. military. As part of that research, he traveled to six states to visit a dozen reservations and a few urban communities to interview American Indian veterans.

As a part of that project, the author sent a film crew to capture footage of a unique event. In October of 1992, six code talkers from three tribes (Comanche, Choctaw and Navajo) gathered outside Oklahoma City to be honored by fellow American Indians at the first Powwow and Arts Festival hosted by the American Indian Cultural Society of Oklahoma. Dancers, singers, drummers and artists from many tribal communities in the state attended the three-day event held at the Cleveland County Fairgrounds in Norman, Oklahoma.

A young Cheyenne veteran named Nathan Hart was the chairman of the hosting organization, and he also served as the Executive Director of the Oklahoma Indian Affairs Commission at the time. Hart explained the goals of the organization and what the weekend event was all about:

"The American Indian Cultural Society was formed to provide educational and culturally-related events for the general public. One of our goals is to pay tribute to Indian people who've made great contributions to our people during their lives. We wanted to honor Navajo, Comanche, and Choctaw code talkers at our first annual pow-wow because of the significant roles they played during World War I and World War II.

"This is one of the few times that code talkers from these three tribes have ever been able to be together. We have heard very positive comments from each of the three groups simply because each has been able to meet for the first-time other code talkers they've heard so much about.

"I think paying tribute to these people is long overdue. They played a significant role in shaping American history, and the United States government has been slow in recognizing their contributions. But Indian people were quick to recognize their contributions.

"Finally I'd like to say that establishing a national monument to pay tribute to American Indian veterans is very appropriate. There are so many Indians who've served in the World Wars, Vietnam, and recently in Desert Storm, and I personally feel this would be a tremendous way to acknowledge the accomplishments of these people. "

Another significant participant in the activities was Comanche artist and flute player Doc Tate Nevaquaya, a personal friend of the Comanche code talkers and Cultural Director of the host organization who lived in Apache, OK. Mr. Nevaquaya composed a flute song in honor of the Comanche code talkers, which he performed during the event.

"That song is based on a Comanche riding song that I adapted to our modern melodies. The original song came from the 1800s and was sung by many of our warriors when they were returning from a hunt or war journey. They were more or less describing the success of the journey, and this particular song belonged to Chief Wild Horse of the Comanche. The old songs came from the heart and spoke to the spirit.

"I played this particular song for the code talkers because it was sung by our warriors in the 1800s who had to ride long distances and faced overwhelming odds against the white man's weapons in those days, so they expressed their gallantry as warriors when singing that song, and I wanted this song to express the warrior-ship of the code talkers. When they were in battle, they had a lot of endurance, and they could go for days if they had to, so that is why this flute song is for them."

Doc Tate Nevaquaya passed away in 1996 at the age of sixty-four.

As mentioned earlier, research for the television documentary took the author to several reservations to conduct interviews. This research included one additional code talker interview that took place at the Navajo Nation Inn in Window Rock, Arizona, the same year. He is the last code talker in the list. The seven code talker interviewees of 1992 were:

1. Schlicht Billy (Choctaw) 1921-1994
2. Charles Chibitty (Comanche) 1921-2005
3. Forrest Kassanavoid (Comanche) 1921- 1996
4. Roderick Red Elk (Comanche) 1922 – 1997
5. Albert Smith (Navajo) born 1925
6. William Dean Wilson (Navajo)
7. Harold Foster (Navajo)

Interview with Schlicht Billy (Choctaw)

Mr. Schlicht Billy (Choctaw) - U.S. Army code talker

SB: My name is Schlicht Billy. I live south of McAllister, Blanco, Oklahoma, and I am a full-blood Choctaw. I am 71 years old, and I was born in Pittsburgh County. And I lived all my life in that area even at the present time.

Q: Can you give me a few details about the events that led up to you joining the military?

SB: I knew as I read current events and newspaper accounts that we were preparing for a conflict but didn't know where, and I was at the right age. And more or less, curiosity led me to go in the service, because I knew it would be time very shortly that I would enter the service.

Q: Before you shipped out, did your tribe or your family hold any kind of a celebration for you?

SB: You know, we were many miles away from my people because we s hipped out from Hampton Roads, port of embarkation, that none of my families were there when we shipped out. Went to Africa back in 1943, June 22nd, when we sailed out to go to Africa.

Q: So there really wasn't an opportunity for your family to honor you in any way or to, you know, have a ceremony for you before you left?

SB: No, they didn't. The fact of the distance away from where they were living.

Q: So whenever you enlisted, what branch of the service did you enter?

SB: When I enlisted, I enlisted in the (U.S. Army) infantry unit, 180th infantry of the 45th division. That was in 1940, September 16th of 1940. And I was shipped to Fort Sill for basic training.

Q: And in speaking earlier with you, you talked about how you became a squadron leader, so you were not only just in the infantry, but you managed to work your way up and you said that you always had a job to do. Can you explain just a little bit about that, how you became a squadron leader?

SB: At the time when we were in the service, we took a test as to everything, just in general, the knowledge that you had - I.Q. tests. And that's one of the reasons that I guess they sent me to school a whole lot because my I.Q. was high enough, although from what I see now, I guessed at a lot of the things was on the test but, you know, I made a high score on that. From there on they always sent me to school on different phases of combat infantryman; on basic training of all the weapons in the infantry unit, and more specialized things like gas schools and how to direct artillery fire on the enemy, and a lot of map-reading classes, aero photos. And I had amphibious training, ship-to-shore landings, along with a unit called Frogman's school over at Massachusetts where the Kennedy's live, those people that were in high government positions in that area were trained at. And every day that we were in the service stateside, we always had some kind of school that we attended. So I had a well-rounded education in many things that some of the men didn't receive, like mountain training, that took place over in Virginia. And there was a winter training in Pine Camp, NY. That's cold country. And swamp training around Manny, Louisiana - how to survive. We worked in that area too. And as I see it, a lot of it we didn't get to use - but as it was what we did have knowledge of came in handy when the time was ripe for that type of use. And we were able to survive because I think we made an effort to really absorb what was taught to us, and we accomplished nearly all the missions that was given to us. I'll say that. As Indians I know we had many different tribes that were represented in my division, the 45th division, and the units that did take part in all those phases of combat, we always accomplished our missions. And I don't see where we were running or retreating or, you know, everything we done in order. We knew where we was going – the fundamentals that we learned, the basic fundamentals came into play where we went ahead and utilized what we had to fight with, whether it be tank support or aerial bombardments or many of the other things that we learned, like scouting and patrolling, how to go about in appreciation of the territory that you were fighting on. We even had schooling on topography of the countryside. We learned many military terms on those mountain ranges like Hogs-back or escarpments or base Camels-back, hogs-back, all types of names that they had. We knew what they were talking about when the time came to use those terms. And just like in our daily lives when you know what is expected of you and you had that training, you do a better job. I believe that's one reason why we weren't afraid as a combat unit. We have 511 days of actual combat time in that book that I have of the unit that I fought with. 511. So with a good leadership, determination, and that discipline – even today without discipline, we're just a mob. But in that day and time, they drilled into us the things that were essential, things that we could use. And like I mentioned earlier, that it is not so much as being afraid. We all have some kind of fears, but you know, if in leadership you want to know many men you are going to come back out with in a skirmish or going on a mission. To me that was better than anything that I could think of – is that it is somebody's son that I am leading.

Q: We had talked about that earlier about the sense of responsibility that you felt to bring back every one of those men. And also we talked about the natural born traits of an Indian that may have been traits that were more predominant in Indians that were the qualities that you are talking about that helped, helped the soldiers, the Indians, the discipline. And, also, I would like for you – if this is true – you came from a boarding school background. How did that experience of a regimented lifestyle at boarding school, how did that assist you or enhance your abilities as a soldier? Could you talk about that for a moment?

SB: Most of us came from a rural area that one time or another, as Indians, we like to hunt, and we could track things. Even a man, if the soil is wet, we could tell or have an idea how big of a man was going through that area, which way he was going. And you know how to hunt squirrels. If you are by yourself, you can do a whole lot of things. If the squirrel gets behind a tree and you're going to it, take a piece of stick and throw it on the back side of it and he will always turn toward you - basic things like that. And if we're going through an area where water is polluted and you and you know you're going to be thirsty, when your canteen runs dry. All right, we take a pebble, a smooth pebble, and put it in your mouth and you can go hours and hours and hours without drinking any water. Just small things like that help a combat man.

Q: I think you call those things common sense.

SB: Yes.

Q: Can you share some of your wartime experiences, maybe something that you remember vividly.

SB: Many of the experiences that I have - is like it happened yesterday, many of them. For instance, on invasions when you are going into a hostile shore, they had drilled us so that we knew exactly what area of the ship we was going to use to get off into the assault boats to go to the shore where people were shooting at you. Also I remember the preparation that they made, some of the seas were real rough at times, other times smooth, but of all invasions I had taken part in was an invasion of southern France. That was the easiest. Africa wasn't so bad going in there. But the war had just about ceased in that area where we was at. And the Island of Sicily – that's an island between Africa and the boot of Italy – they call it Sicily. There was 38 days to accomplish a mission there. We took care of those people there. British 8th Army went up the boot going towards Naples, Italy. We made, what they call an end-run, like a football player making an end-run. We landed at Salerno, another invasion where people are shooting at you. That's below Naples, Italy. After fighting there around almost a year in the mountains of Italy. You take one mountain, there's one a little higher. They're looking down at you. A general that was in command of that fortification for the German forces – his name was General Kiserling - he was a man that we had to deal with. And they had bunkers, fortifications, emplacements, everything well prepared years and years ahead and they were there to stay. We had to dig them out of there, maybe a platoon, maybe a squadron, maybe a company, bombed and shelled. I guess that is one area where we had more units fighting as allies that I ever took part in. I had these Moroccans out of Africa. I had these "Nisei" from the west coast of here in America. *(Author's note: Nisei was a Japanese term that meant a Japanese person born in the United States and holding U.S. citizenship.)* I remember when Pearl Harbor days when they put their parents in stockades or detention camps and those youngsters or young men that were old enough to be in the service, why they drafted them and made a unit – they called them "Niseis," little bitty fellows, Japs.

But, you know, they made good soldiers. We had Polish soldiers. We had the British soldiers, Canadian soldiers and some of the Italians fought with us to, but not many. But as a unit, that's what we had to fight the Germans. Remember Mussolini, he was a leader over there - they hung him. His own people did. And the Germans took over. That's where the big trouble was below Naples there. We fought them people from in that area all the way into, past Rome, Rome, Italy. I know I had to go across that Tiber River. It's on the outskirts of Rome. I saw that Vatican City. I saw that Coliseum, but you know they respected the wishes of that Italian government, the Pope, rather. Also the Americans, they respected the Holy place. So they didn't bomb and shell that out. Leading to the city they did - bridges and roads - and after we helped take Rome and went on past Rome, they pulled my unit out and they sent me back to Anzio (Italy). We got replenished with supplies, ammunition, guns, and clothing - everything that we needed, replacements, men that we lost along the way. And from there we went on to Southern France. We went to Naples, Italy, got on board. We sailed between two islands, Sardinia and Corsica. Went on between the two islands, went on to southern France where all the rich and famous goes I guess now. It was in that area – Leone and Monte Carlo. But you know, that was the easiest. Nobody gave us any bad time at all. We walked in there and it was like we was the kings in there. We went right on into France. We went up the Rhone Valley towards Nancy, France. And from there everything got harder. The Germans really put up resistance all the way into their homeland. We were getting closer and closer. Allied forces were coming in from around Normandy at that time. So we had many, many good men that fought that war, especially against the Germans, and boy they were well disciplined. But they were just like anybody else, they couldn't stop a bullet. And they would go down, too. There were paratroopers. There were mountain troopers. There were SS men. To me they were just humans…

Q:		And how many years were you in the service?

SB:		Six. You see I volunteered for three. And when my time was up I was in Africa. And they told me, they just laughed you know. As a matter of fact, I never was drafted see. I volunteered. The draft papers - my mother sent me my draft papers in Africa. And I told my commanding officer, I said, "Hey, I have to do to the draft board." And he laughed and he says, "Six months plus - the duration plus six" So that was my status of being in the service there.

Q:		How you were selected to be a code talker?

SB: Well, the language that I have--I already knew that, the language. We were more of an experiment with it because we had it at hand right there. There was something that needed to be told to our units - either we had these powered telephone lines on the ground, but we couldn't depend on that because there was shelling all the time. When a shell hits why it tears up your communication lines. So we had this little 536 radios. I want to school for that too. So I had knowledge on how to use that. And on flat country you could go maybe a mile or two with it. But in mountainous country, why, you couldn't get too much good communication out of it. But it served the purpose. And we knew that the Germans were good at breaking codes and tying into your lines and things like that. So that was the fastest and easiest, and we had the language. And it just so happened I could speak both languages, you know. And we had our own figures too, you know. On your grid coordinates, on your maps, battle condition maps, why we could use our own figures and relay the messages - like you want to send artillery shells to an objective, it could be a mortar pool or whatever it was. You didn't even have to say the guns. Just say "Fire control center" and them boys would be ready to go – these combat units, that are manning those guns back there. We had weapons that shoot up to 21 miles, those big 155 Howitzers. That's what we had. That's about the longest distance. And we had mortars that were 60- millimeter mortars, and we had 81millimeter mortars. 1,760 yard was the maximum on the little 60 mortars and we just utilized what was at hand because we had it. And one of the boys, he is deceased now, but he was a machine gunner. He had a chart of a section. That's they boy that I used to speak (Choctaw) with most of the time, when we wanted communications to the next unit. He'd relay it for me. I would tell him what I wanted. Since I was a platoon leader most of the time. I had 47 men under me that I was responsible for. And when I would call in to him the location where I was at and where he was at and I would have him get the best fields of fire because he can do the most damage to the enemy. And he had full authority to take that position wherever it was at. And one thing I had, too, in my favor, as a unit leader, they usually let me have anything I wanted - tank fire, or close support, airplane bombing or even ships at sea - they even sent me to school to learn how to control that fire from the ships, those 16-inch battle wagons. They called it "Jan Grid System"- J.A.N., Joint Army-Navy. That's what I trained for that, too. So I had a pretty good knowledge of the things I had to do.

Q: Tell us a little about how you used the Choctaw language to explain or to use the code for military terms whenever there wasn't a word in Choctaw that described the

214

military term, how would you improvise? Be sure and when you are telling me this, say as a code talker I used the Choctaw.

SB: I would say artillery; you're talking about large caliber weapons. When speaking about artillery you want a certain amount of concentration. It is said: (in Choctaw) "Tenapo Hochito" - that would be the large whatever you have at your batteries. It might be 105 millimeters. It might be 90's. It could be 155, or it could be chemical, chemical mortars was 4.2 millimeters. We could call in our own figures, what we wanted, what would be best. If it's a wooded area, maybe wanted a tree burst - we let them have a tree burst. And boy they sure do a lot of damage, with tree bursts. Because not much you can do when they burst in the air and scatter.

Q: Can you in your Choctaw language give just an example. Again, I know you just did but another example of maybe an order or something that you would use in code and then translate it into English.

SB: Okay. For instance, you were sent on a combat mission. In other words, you want to bring in a prisoner, and about the only way you know how is to cripple him and carry him in, or else you want to try to kill him and try to get the information from this enemy. And you can relay it this way: (in Choctaw) "Hatak ish benah. Stish na tagee Oh chayahou - Bring him back alive. Don't kill him." And that's what we would relay to the other men, whoever was with us, you know. You might have three people with you or maybe a dozen people. But they want to know. You have a set pattern where all needs to know that's going on. That is where we would try to do in all of our attacks. You know where the line of communications is. Where your water supply would be, where your ammunition dump is, and where your food supply, K rations or C rations or whatever it is, first aid stations. We knew that. So, it took all hands....

Q: As a code talker was there any, is there anything that stands out in your memory as being frightening or funny or a memorable experience that you had as a code talker?

SB: Yes, I know on one occasion, as a code talker, we were up in the mountains of Italy, around Venafro (Italy). This particular person that I was talking to, we were in what we called "pup tents." You have one half of the tent and that is a shelter half and you have the other half. You put them together and hopefully keep you dry. But it rained so hard and the tent was so soaked that he was sitting up, and he says, "You know why they call this a pup tent?" And I said, "No why?" He looked at me and he said, "Dogs have more sense than to sleep in one of these." (He chuckles.) Just, things like that. And on another occasion where we were fighting these other Germans way up on top of a mountain. We got halfway up the mountain and this young Indian, he says, "I'm going up and loosen them up." I said, "What do you mean, loosen them up?" He said, "I am going to get the cobwebs out of his head," he said. He was standing, looking up there, not concerned, and I said, "Hey, get down, boy. They're going to kill you." He said, "Well, we own half of it, don't we? I am going to go over to get the other half of that mountain." Things like that, to me now, when I think back, he had some kind of humor about him that he survived, in that particular battle anyway.

Q:		What honors or awards or medals have you received and what did you do to get those awards?

SB:		The awards that I received mostly everybody that has been in combat and has injuries caused by the enemy that sheds blood. Why, you start out with the Purple Heart. I am sure that everybody has seen a purple heart. Then you add the bronze star. The bronze star is… Many of the assignments that you receive towards advancing your unit or accomplishing the mission, if you do it satisfactorily, in a way that you been taught to do, and it is something out of the ordinary that you did, maybe using the knowledge of the area that you are fighting on or maybe outwit the enemy, you receive a bronze star for that. It is a medal similar to the Silver Star.

Q:		You said you had your own coordinates. You are talking about… You had a Choctaw relationship or a Choctaw word for those coordinates. Is that what you meant?

SB		The figures.

Q: In other words, you related those figures in Choctaw.

SB:		Yeah,

Q:		Okay, good.

SB:		I didn't bring all of my awards, like victory medal. Everybody that's been in that war brought the victory medal and stuff, but these are the ones. (He holds up his Purple Heart.)

Q:		Okay, look at the monitor. Are we ready?

SB:		This is the first medal that I received for being shot through the foot. We were advancing on the retreating enemy, and I was shot through the foot, and we had this sulfa medicine. All we do is kind of clean it up a little bit and put that sulfa and tape it up and go. I mean it throbbed a little bit, but we kept a-going. And that's your Purple Heart.

Along with this you get a bar that goes with it. Here's a bar that goes with it. (He holds that up.) That's the purple one here. I've got three oak leaf clusters in lieu of four of these (Purple Hearts). See I have been injured… First time they give a medal. The next, don't care how serious it is, all you get is this little oak leaf cluster to go with it on the bar, so there it is right there. (He holds up the medal and the bar so the cameraman can take close-up shots of them. Then he holds up another medal.)

Q: Okay, tell me about this.

SB: This is a Silver Star medal and this is a third highest that the American government gives to the soldiers that fought against the enemy, and it is known as, on the back side here is an inscription. It says: "For gallantry in action." And this was given for the leadership, and this is the first one that I received. All the days that I had command of the different units, different groups of people that come and go. Many times that they sent me a leader, he didn't last too long. He would either get killed or else he was wounded or they would replace him. I was usually the one that had to do the replacing. And that was the first. And it has a bar also that goes with it. (He holds up the bar.) There it is, this bar here goes with it, and they have got a lapel, a small replica that goes on your lapel of your uniform. And this oak leaf cluster in lieu of another silver star like this, they give me one of these that go with this bar. That was when I happened to be fortunate enough to take the German fortification away from that… And this is what that is for, that little bitty black looking oak leaf cluster. Instead of giving me another medal, they give me this one. (He holds up these medals so the cameraman can get close-ups.)

Q: When you were wounded?

SB: How many times I've been wounded?

Q: What were you wounded in that one?

SB: Yes.

Q: Can you relate that story? Was that the pillbox…. The German pillbox?

SB: In action against the Germans, on their own homeland, that was March 17, 1945 and it was in the Siegfried lines. There was a main fortification, and that was their homeland. They were defending their homeland, from those bunkers. Some of the doors as we captured this particular one that they, the doors, were six feet thick, steel reinforced concrete. And firing machine guns and different infantry weapons at it, just knocked the paint off. That's about all it done. That's how thick it was. And I had the mission with the unit that I commanded to take that German pillbox. And it was interlaced with 26 other pillboxes. I have a book here that it shows the overlay of the map where these fortifications were placed. They were placed in such a manner that it took care of each other. One of them shooting straight ahead, flanking fire and it looked impossible to go through any part of that - machine guns. You see, they had a cyclic way to fire the 1200 rounds a minute, their machine guns. We used them slow firing - 500 rounds a minute - what we were firing at them. They had 1200 rounds in those German schmeissers *(a type of submachine gun)*. And we were fortunate enough to go in and accomplish a mission that we were assigned to get, and there is an open country, something similar to that, ever where I go, even today, I was looking around about this countryside, I can see how in the world would I attacked this position? Hill side or smooth grounds or whatever. And it just is something that I learned that I always refer to it, some of the things that I have seen: how to attack it if I had to, you know. And that's one of the things we learned in a line of appreciation, and there is a little draw, just kind of a fold in the ground, that I saw down in what we call in Indian style. We didn't go all in big bunches spread out there in the open. We would go one at a time in there like a snake going through. That's after I got my men organized. After we started all right, and then we were pinned down. They really raked us good with artillery, mortars, and machine guns. Of course every one of them was helping one another. Just like a sewing machine or something – those burp guns. Anyway, when we got to this position where we were pinned down, that's when we took to the little old fold in the ground, crawling on our bellies, to get to this first fortification. I went to that door, and they had a big old lock on the door. I dropped to the ground and I said, "I'm not going to do any good here." So I thought and looked, and it had a little old ventilation system, something similar to that on top of this bunker. It was just like a cellar, where great big, bigger than this room here, where they had 26 bunks, and then they had generators and dynamos, food, and all kind of supplies in there, running water, and they were there to stay. And when I saw what was happening there, I went around the back door, thinking it might be open. Still - locked tight. So I looked around and I saw that ventilation. And I come back down, and I saw this little opening where this machine gun barrel was sticking out. They had a periscope sight in there, like a submarine, you know. The periscope sight would be sticking up, and they could look into the scope. They didn't have to expose themselves and I knew I was in trouble if I didn't do something with it. So I went on around and I threw a smoke grenade or a fragmentation grenade in there first. Nothing happened, nobody came out or nothing. So I had a smoke grenade that I tied on my belt and I pulled it out and I threw it in there. That's when I heard them about get choked down in there. That's when they began to come out of there. They was hollering, 'Comrade." And I had that 536 radio on and I radioed back to my company. I said "I've got a tiger by the tail here and I can't turn him loose." He said, "Don't turn him loose." When we got squared away and reorganized more and some of my men came right on where I was at. We occupied the outside positions but I secured it the best we knew how, right around that area. We had good cover. And when the smoke cleared, I sent those German prisoners back. I said, "You guys get on out of here. Get on back where I come from." (He points behind himself.) I figured some of the men would shoot them down, but they didn't. So I radioed back to the company commander and I said, "I have prisoners going you way. I have sent them back there." He said, "All right. We'll take care of them." So, we were busy, 26 of them ahead of us, all around about us that needed to be taken care of, cleared out. So we went ahead and accomplished our mission and about that time, the German force had begun to pull out of their positions and went out in the open, and they re-shelled the position they just lost. That's how they do counterattack. They catch you in the wide-open space. Boy, they let you have it with artillery. And that's what happened. That's the last round up for me that day. That's why I was wounded. What I was doing, the German emplacements, some of it was about 8 or 10 feet deep that the German engineers had dug for them for the route of escape. And they had some ladders sticking up from the hole to the top and I was checking one of them out and boy, I heard that big 170-millimeter mortar coming in, and boy it hit. And I hit blood shot all over me. I looked like I had measles. Next round came on in and hit the top of that, that's when they took me out of there. That's when my war days were over then. So I received two medals that day, the silver star of oak leaf clusters, plus another oak leaf cluster for the Purple Heart. On the invasions where you are invading enemy territory, they give you a little bitty arrowhead. When you make an invasion, see that little bitty black arrowhead. (He holds up another medal.) That's what you receive if you're surviving. But anyhow I got the invasion of Sicily, Salerno, Anzio, and Southern France where the people are shooting at you when you're going in there to them. That's what that's for. (He holds up the medal and turns it so the cameraman can get a close shot.)

Q: After you were wounded, how long did it take you to recover?

SB: Two years on the last wound. Partially paralyzed the left side of my body.

Q: And back to that battle, how many Germans were lost that day. Did you have a count or anything?

SB: That's one thing that is hard to determine after a battle, there's so many people involved in destroying the enemy that those that are in direct contact to that area where they have been shelled or when you are attacking, that would be the easiest way of accounting the casualties of the enemy, would be counting after a battle. That's the best way, but so many things involved in there. If there's a concentration of artillery on a given target, it is going to involve civilians and everybody else that is in the way there. But the Allied Forces always did warn these large cities to move out of there. And they gave them warning to move out of there. They are going to bomb it.

Q: Mr. Billy, when you were involved in that battle, were you afraid or were you just cool under fire? What was going through your mind?

SB: I was concerned about the mission, the route of our approaches and my line of communications that we had it pretty well intact because of that 536 radio we had. But the concern, as many battles as I had been in is bringing and leading the units out without too much casualties. I believe that is the best answer I can give you, is bringing all you can out from that particular battle, because if you don't find an enemy, you are going to go find him. It's like a bully in town, if you go looking for it, you're going to find it.

Q: Did you experience any prejudice in the military?

SB: None whatsoever. I didn't experience prejudice toward my leadership. We worked in harmony. Everything I asked of those young men they just automatic went right ahead and did the best they could. That's all you can ask of any combat man. I had a good team.

Q: You said that you had 3 or 4 members of your family in the military.

SB: I had three brothers that served in the service, but one of them served in the 90th division that came in on Normandy invasion, and the one that was with me, he got killed in 1943, July 18th when he died. He lasted 8 days in combat. But then, I had a younger brother, he came back. He was an 82nd airborne paratrooper. Other than that, why, I didn't have any immediate family other than cousins, but they were different branches of service, like the marines, and we weren't together in combat. They were scattered all over the country, all over the world.

Q: When you returned, were you given any type of ceremony?

SB: After I returned back to the United States, I couldn't ask for no better treatment. Everybody just couldn't do enough for us. Those that I came in contact with, like most of the folk, paralyzed or we were battered. If we want letters written, or somebody was there to help us, or read to us, you know. Anything that they could do for you to make you comfortable. And they had a lot of help too at that time, they had the Waves. They had the WACs. They had volunteers. They had their regular nurses. They had the doctors. They had the War Boards. I mean I couldn't ask for more. They even shined my toenails even. I mean that's the kind of treatment we had.

Q: You might explain… hospitalized for the 2 years….

SB: Yes. When I came back to the United States, the first place they sent me to was Fort Devins, MA, the hospital there in Boston. I trained there, too, about a year before going overseas. And I knew the country pretty well, and they were nice to me there at Ft. Devins. Then, to Walter Reed, that is in Washington, for further treatment of all paralyzed veterans. And after we got better, they sent us to Camp Edwards for a short stay there, and on to O'Reilly General Hospital, Springfield, Missouri. And they had all types of entertainment there for us too when we got there. They had these big-name bands back in the 40s. Les Brown and Cab Calloway and different people like that, entertainers. And they just more or less let us take it easy and we would take treatments and those of us who could walk a little bit, somebody would be helping us to gain our strength back. Everywhere we went people would try to feed us something: train stations, bus stations. They had facilities all ready. I don't know who sponsored all that. I can't remember that far, but they really took care of us.

Q: Can you tell me the extent of your injuries, maybe show where you still have shrapnel?

SB: Yes. To start out with, on my left arm here I have a piece of steel there that has been there since 1945, and they told me it would never hurt me, but it does hurt me. It stings and when wintertime comes, it aches. But I can live with that. It's in there. And I have got one in my shoulder, way down deep. And some seemed that I had cancer at one time. Told my wife about it. I knew better than that. There's a piece f steel in there, and it's got a growth around it, and the doctors told me that it would be all right. It wasn't necessary that they take it out. They could go in there deep and get it. And I had shrapnel in my head right there (points), but there they took skin grafts off of my leg and fill this up and I had an X there where another piece of steel. I'll tell you a story about the hospitalization over in Italy. They had a hospital, 36th General Hospital they called it, was a King Umberto's Palace, and they converted it into a hospital. And that's where they sent me. They had gold fixtures in their bathrooms and things like that at the time I was there. And when they stay there long, when they took the shrapnel out, and when they gave me a skin graft, kind of fill those up and, put skin grafts on my arm too, see. *(He points to his arm.)* Where the steel went in and I took the graft out of my stomach right there and ….

Q: Was it mostly for shrapnel wounds they gave you treatments?

SB: Yes, yes. Bullet wounds. I heal pretty fast. Got shot through the foot there one time too, right there. But it healed up. I used to heal rapidly.

Q: When you came back stateside, did you have any problems readjusting to civilian life? Was alcohol ever a part of that?

SB: No, I am fortunate. I didn't have any problems, even when I entered the hospitals, different hospitals. That's one of the questions that usually ask me. Do you sleep well? Do you have nightmares? Different things that bother you in combat days. I told 'em "No." That's one thing that I haven't experienced is having a hard time adjusting to civilian life. I have always been busy anyway. I believe that's one of the keys to life is staying busy. You can always find something. Helping others, somebody else, you know. Read a whole lot.

Q: So you think you had a good readjustment because you kept yourself mentally and physically active?

SB: Yes, that's right.

Q: And the last question. Do you see an interest or a need for a National Indian Veterans Memorial?

SB: I've always thought about that some years ago for I believe we ought to have a community where… maybe centrally located or where the need is. We know the need is everywhere. In my particular tribe we don't have as many Choctaws in there compared to the western tribes, you know. But you know it would be well if we had good counselors stressing education because without education we're going to have a hard road to travel. Our youngsters, I'm talking about. Old timers like me, why, it's not so bad. We adjusted years ago, how to take care of our own selves. But these young ones, drug abusers, alcohol, lack of education, that's one thing I would like to see our leaders in high government positions to…   In the leadership from a local level to help all young people because we aren't' going to be here but a very short time ourselves. Somebody is going to have to do something, and that something is education.

Q: Going back, can you restate for me in your own words?

SB: I do believe that we need a Veterans Memorial for the future cause of our young people in education and everything related to it.

Q: I am going to ask you one last question – How many other Choctaw code talkers did you serve with?

SB: In the beginning, scattered throughout the regiment, a regiment of men is composed of around 6,000 men - in that we were sparsely scattered according to your ability to take care of the job that you were assigned, maybe communications, and we weren't all in a group, but those that were able to converse with one another (in Choctaw), well that's what we did, because we knew the language and there was no problem there. Like we knew our figures. We could read and we could write it. And relate what was in store for us.

Q: But you don't know the exact number that served with you, Choctaw code talkers from OK?

SB: Well, to start out with we had around 17 Choctaws but like I say some of them were transferred to headquarters, some of them were sent off to school, like radio school, liaison people, and some of them were sent to… as runners between companies sending messages, you know. This individual would send message to the next unit or something, and that's how we survive, is just using our language because we had it at hand. We didn't need to go to no classrooms and study. We just talked to one another just like we did back home.

Q: That you were the ones defined as Choctaw code talker.

SB: Yes, as far as we know, I haven't heard of anyone else that was in the area where I was at that carried on a conversation. Like artillery training there was a Captain Crane that taught me to be a forward observer and to have communication with the fire control center in directing artillery fire on enemy targets. But the man died up in the mountains of Italy. He got hit with shrapnel, but we may start something in Pittsburgh, a little community down there that have asked me to help the children in a spelling bee, about two more months away, I suppose. I had some of them enrolled in my class and we took first prize among all the Choctaw communities round there, like Antlers, Clayton, even the city of McAllister. They have got Choctaws in there at a little school that I taught over there to read the Choctaw language and how to use it. Well, we came out 1st place and we had 54 sessions of spelling bee contests. And we came out first place. We work harder we may take it all again this year.

Q: So you carried on your tradition of using the language as a teaching tool. Thank you for sharing with us.

SB: Well, it has been my pleasure. I enjoyed it. I have enjoyed everything I have seen today here.

Q: That's good.

SB: The hospitality is great around here.

Q: Can you tell us about this photo?

Choctaw Platoon - 180th Infantry

SB: That picture of the platoon that I was in was taken at Fort Sill and it was Sept 16, 1940, when that was taken. I was a squad leader. Starting out I had 12 men in the unit that I had. That's the first assignment I had as a squad leader. I was in basic training at Fort Sill, just a beginner at that time. And from there we advanced to Camp Barkley, TX. That's in Abilene, TX. From there we went to Louisiana. From there to Ft. Devins, Massachusetts, Camp Edwards, MA. Then to Pine Camp, NY. Then back to Ft Devins. Then back to Camp Edwards. Then the port of embarkation. That was in Hampton Roads, VA. I remember the ship that we sailed on had 10,000 troops on one ship. And the name of the ship was Freddie Funston. It took us 22 days to go to Africa. We landed at Oran, Casa Blanca. Then we were in training in Africa, the northern port of Africa. They had the French units there that we trained with, getting ready for the invasion of the Island of Sicily. In the meantime nearly all of those men right there were transferred out to other places where they were needed for further training.

Interview with Roderick Red Elk (Comanche)

Mr. Roderick Red Elk (Comanche) - U.S. Army code talker

Q: Please tell me your name, your tribe and where you live.

RRE: My name is Roderick Red Elk. I live in Lawton, Oklahoma. My tribe is Comanche.

Q: How old are you and when and where were you born?

RRE: I am 70 years old. I was born out in the country in Cotton County. That is south of Walters, OK. Born in 1922, January.

Q: How did you become a code talker?

RRE: There was a man that came down and talked to several of us for the purpose of joining the Army to be code talkers. And we all went in around – this was December, '40, when he was recruiting us and we got sworn in. I got sworn in January 1, 1941. And we went from there to Fort Benning, GA, and took our training - just regular basic training with the Army. And after basic training, then they started us on the different types of communications: how to operate, tear down and repair, the telephone, radio. And then we had to – a lot of military terms there is not Comanche word for them. So we had to sit down and figure to a name for each, for instance, like gun. We just have one name for gun and that is "stawoy" (approximate spelling). It just means a gun. When you get in the military, you have all types of guns - you got your artillery, you got your small arms, you got your machine guns, the different caliber machine guns - and we had to work out a word for each one of those different types of weapons. The same way with airplanes. We had to identify airplanes. We had a word for airplanes. But we didn't have no word for bomber or fighter or a transport and we had to get together and come up with a name that everybody could understand and would relate to what we were talking about. Just for instance, like a bomber. We have words for airplane but a bomber, there's no such word for a bomber. So we got together and kicked it around. And we come up with the word in Comanche, "Esnoab," which means pregnant. You know, those bombers carried those big bombs under them like they had big bellies like a pregnant woman. And that's what we called a bomber.

Q: Can you give me another example? Say a sentence in Comanche and give me interpretation in English.

RRE: I have got one better than that I believe. Let me see. Let me straighten it out. Machine gun would be a better one. Okay. Just for instance, I'm with a regiment and we are getting a lot of machine gun fire, so I have to call back and relate the message to the artillery and point it, pin point it on the map for them. I tell them – I'd be speaking Comanche. I say: (Comanche words). I am saying this machine gun is really giving us heck, really shooting us. So then I tell them, the artillery will have a man over there that speaks the same (Comanche) language. I tell him. Then he relates it to the guns and say, about 5 or 10 minutes, and then all the machine guns are silent - the machine guns that's firing on us.

Q: What is the Comanche word for machine gun?

RRE: (He speaks in Comanche) In Comanche, that is a sewing machine, the only way we could associate that with a machine was a-rat-a-tat-tat, and you know, how you're sewing how that sounds. That sound is what we associate the machine gun with.

Q: What honors or medals have you won?

RRE: Well, I just received one yesterday at the Comanche Nation. They gave us an honor, a little plaque. And I received one from the French government. I think that was in '89. And before that I received another plaque from Comanche Homecoming. That's a group around Walters –at the annual powwow, and they give us a plaque. That's the only awards, just recently. Are you speaking of awards while we was in the Army?

Q: Yeah, your service medals.

RRE: Oh gosh. I can't remember them all. We were in five major campaigns so that would be five stars. Each campaign is a star, and I had a good conduct medal. You know you have to be a soldier and your conduct has to be good so long before you receive one of those. And every campaign that you are in you receive a medal and a ribbon for that. The bronze star is another one, and every time you get a bronze star, then they put you a cluster on it the next time. And if you get over five, that's about all they can get on there, they have to give you another award. And naturally, the Purple Heart, and that's when you are wounded. That's about all I can think of right now.

Q: Do you see that there is a need or an interest in a National Indian Veterans Monument or Memorial to be erected in honor of Indians who've served in the military, and if so, where do you think it should be located?

RRE: Yeah, I believe we should have a monument erected, but as far as the location goes, we would have some controversy there, because, you see, you got all different tribes in different states. I think each one should – each state should erect one in their state where they're – it's like the Navajo code talkers, now they are all a big bunch. I think they should have one there. And all the code talkers in Oklahoma should have one in Oklahoma, in a centrally located place.

Q: How many Comanche code talkers did you start out with in your group and how many are remaining today? That's the last question.

RRE: We started out with seventeen, and in the time we entered the war, there was only thirteen of us left. And up to date there was only three that actually went to war, and there is one, another one, there's four that's left, that's still surviving that was in the code talkers.

Q: That's what we needed.

Cam: Can we get from him one memorable story?

Q: Okay. Is there a memorable story as a code talker, either frightening or funny? A lot of them shared funny little anecdotes about the code talker's experience.

RRE: Yeah, I got one good one. As you know after we hit the beach we just - wherever the infantry hit resistance we would stop and we would clear the resistance, and then we would go. And we did that the first day from six o'clock in the morning until dark. So we pulled into this little—there in France they got what they call hedgerows. They use that for fence to keep your cattle and stock in. So we pulled into this place, and just as we pulled in, I said, "We are going to spend the night. You all settle down for the night." And about that time we hear an artillery go off and you know, after you been there awhile you can tell whether they are close or far, and this one was getting closer. And man, I scrambled for the nearest hedgerow and luckily there was already a foxhole dug there. So I just dive in this foxhole. I say, "This would be a good place to spend the night." So I just take my helmet off, and I laid my gun across my belly and laid flat on my back and went to sleep. I wake up the next morning in good daylight, I look on the other side on the foxhole, and there sits a German soldier with his rifle lying across his lap - his eyes wide open. And I just froze. I didn't know what to do. I thought well, one of us has got to make a move. So, I grabbed my gun and swung it over to him and he never moved. So I go over there and check him and sure enough – I slept with a dead enemy all night long and didn't know it.

Q: How did that make you feel?

RRE: I just showed the dead German how fast I could get out of the hole. (He chuckles).

Interview with Forrest Kassanavoid (Comanche)

Mr. Forrest Kassanavoid (Comanche), U.S. Army code talker

Q: Let's start with your name and your tribe.

FK: My name is Forrest Kassanavoid. In Comanche, that is pronounced "Kassanavoda" (approximate spelling). Kasa means "feather" and navoda means "to mark" so my grandfather's name was Kassanavoda which meant "marked feather." And I am a Comanche Indian of the Q'ata band and my sub clan is "Tipicui." Tipicui is Comanche that means mountain of rocks.

Q: And where do you live?

FK: I live at Indiahoma, Oklahoma. That is in western Comanche County, 20 miles west of Lawton.

Q: ow old are you and where were you born.

FK: I am 71 years old. I was born at Indiahoma. I was born in a tent. My grandmother was the one that brought me into the world.

Q: What are some of the most memorable experiences you had as a code talker? Is there one or two that stand out?

FK: I think the one that stands out the most with me was a message that was sent by one of the code talkers. It was not me but one of the other fellows. It was a message that was sent by Brigadier General Theodore Roosevelt, Jr., who was the Assistant Division Commander of the 4th Infantry Division, and he sent a message back to the command ship when they made their landing at Utah Beach in Normandy, when he realized that they had landed in the wrong spot. The 8th infantry, which was the first wave, made a landing and through some error from one other service, either the Coast Guard or the Navy who was bringing the troops in, they made an error, so they landed at the wrong spot and the reason they sent the message is that they didn't want the Germans or the enemy to know that they had made a wrong landing.

Q: What about an experience where you were involved?

FK: Where I was involved? Well, this is kind of a humorous - but I think one of the experiences that I remember that sticks in my mind the most is a friend of mine who was a code talker. One night we had moved up from our command post and we dug in along a hedgerow. Well, this one fellow—his name was Perry Knowubad from Cyril – he was one of the code talkers. He says, "Oh, I'm getting too sleepy. I am not going to dig a fox hole tonight." So he didn't dig one. So that night we got a raid by the Luftwaffe, and they were dropping butterfly bombs on us, so everybody was jumping in their foxhole, except him. He didn't have one to jump in. So he jumped into the garbage pit that the unit before us had dug, and they didn't cover it up. And boy, there was all these tin cans in there. And when he jumped in there he cut his body up, cut his feet and everything. And after he came out of there, they saw he was bleeding, so they sent him to the Aid Station, and he went there. And after they treated him, they tried to pin a purple heart on him. Of course, he had had several before, but he says, "I don't need that. I didn't get wounded. I got cut up by jumping in that garbage pit where all those tin cans were." (He laughs.) And I think that sticks with me more than anything. He was my buddy, and a close friend of mine but it was just the humor of the thing that stuck with me so long.

Q: That's good. And then one last question.

FK: Sure.

Q: What medals or honors awards have you won for your service?

FK: Well, I thin the one that – there's two of them that I think the most of and one is the European – the African-European-Middle East campaign ribbon with five campaign stars on it for the campaigns that we served in Europe. Now I think that is the greatest. That means more to me. And I think the second most important one that I cherish is the Order of Military Merit, which was awarded to us by the French government in 1980, I think it was 1989, here at the state capitol in Oklahoma city.

Q: One last question. Tell me your feelings as you come here for these two days to be honored with the other code talkers.

FK: Well, the thing that I was – I think it is great that they are doing this today in this time, but until just recently they began to recognize the accomplishments of these code talkers. And I felt that this should have been done some years ago for the simple reason that many of our Comanche code talkers have already passed on. There was seventeen of us, and there is only five of us living today who actually, you know, were code talkers. Now, there's two that didn't go overseas with us. One fellow lives in California. The other one lives in Oklahoma City. But no fault of their own, they were discharged, you know, for medical reasons. Us three that went over – there's only three of us left, and I felt that there's already been twelve that has passed on, and I felt that some recognition should have been given while those men were still living.

Q: Okay. That's what we needed. We really appreciate it.

Interview with Charles Chibitty (Comanche)

Mr. Charles Chibitty (Comanche) – U.S. Army code talker

(Mr. Chibitty holds a framed certificate he had recently received.)

Q: Mr. Chibitty, can you tell us about that award, what it means and when did you receive it?

CC: We got this Saturday evening, around about 4:30 at the Old Comanche Grounds where when I was a little kid about, I remember, about 5 years old. Its west of Lawton, a little town named Cash, and its two miles north. They call it the Old Craterville Park. I danced there in the late 20s when I was small, and Major General Hugh Forrester from Philadelphia brought it down and honored us with these certificates from the government, and give it to Forrest Kasanavoid, Roderick Red Elk and Albert Nahquaddy and myself.

Q: Okay, we'll begin the regular interview. I am going to ask you to tell us your name and your tribe and where you're from.

CC: My name is Charles Chibitty. I am a full-blood Comanche Indian, and I was raised near the Wichita Mountains near Lawton, Oklahoma in Comanche County. But now, after the WWII, my girlfriend came down to see me and I went to Tulsa for just a week, and I am still there after 47 years. I live in Tulsa, made my home there and probably be there the rest of my life.

Q: Can you tell me, as a codetalker, what are some experiences or an experience that stands out in your memory?

CC: Well, there's a lot of things that I could talk about. But the most thing that I never did forget, that we had a boy from New Jersey, and his name was Mullins. I never did know his first name. He was one of the replacements that came to us. But the boys nicknamed him "Moo," because he liked to read a funny book, and he had a funny book that had a Moo Mullins in it. And that night, he was sitting just arms reach from me, and there was a lot of mortar fire coming. And we dug down in a hole, and when it quieted down, we got back, and another one hit, and I ran to the nearest house, because they had a basement. And I looked back, and he was slumped over, and I ran back and picked him up, put him on my shoulder and carried him to safety. But I didn't know it, but the medics said he had a direct hit in his heart with the shrapnel. That I never did forget. He was a good friend of mine from New Jersey, and he also showed me a picture of a little girl that he was his daughter, and he never did see her. She was born after he was sent overseas. And I never forgot that one man.

Q: As you have been here these several days visiting with the code talkers, sharing stories – can you share with us some of what you shared with them?

CC: After 50 years - way back in 1941 when it started with the Comanches – you see the Navajos in the Pacific had a big territory to cover and there was over two hundred - about two hundred of them. The Comanches - you take France and Germany, you could put them in Texas and Oklahoma. That's the difference. There was 20 of us, and 15 of us went overseas. And I never did forget the words that we used. They have a – as I understand it they could write theirs, you know. We can't. You have to talk Comanche fluently, and then the other one would listen to it, and he could write it down in English and that way the Germans could listen all day, and it has never been written. I think here the University is trying to put it down in a book, but I don't think they have ever really been successful with it. If we have to do it again, we probably would. Let me give you and example. It's kind of funny in a way. We got a bit laugh of it. My older brother, he was a civilian - after we got on Utah Beach on D-Day in Normandy in France. And I told him he was a good mechanic, and he is a good auto mechanic - anyway to get a quartermaster ordinance, because he was married and had two kids. The next time I met him he came in from southern Germany, and his division moved next to mine. And me and him got together, and we were sitting there and he says, "Where can I get hold of one of you?" Because I was with the 22nd Infantry Regiment with the 4th Infantry Division. Let me have that telephone. So, I got a hold of one boy named Yekashak - he was with the 8th Infantry Regiment. And he, my brother, told him. He said, "I am your enemy." (He says a Comanche word) And he said, "I understand your Comanche language." He said, (He says a sentence in Comanche.) He said, "Go ahead and talk, I'll write it down." (More Comanche words.) And, Yekashak was one of us. He said, "Who are you?" And then my brother said again, (Comanche words). "I am your enemy." And Bobby, he said, "I am Charles' brother. My division moved close to yours and I am just talking to you." He got a big kick out of it. (He laughs.)

Q: So there were other members of your family that served in the military?

CC: I had a first cousin there, Larry Sawpitty. He was just raised up across the road from me up there, north of Lawton. And I was surprised to see him leave because he was always a homeboy, but he talked Comanche fluently, so he went with us. And it wasn't just before the Sentinel break through if you are familiar with it, and after we took the Cherbourg Peninsula - then there was a line there and we moved up and we laid telephone lines o the tanks. They had markers on there. And that night before the break through came on, we got a lot of shelling from the Germans with 88s. That was a deadly weapon – artillery. And my little cousin, he dug a hole, and he dug it next to a tree and that 88 hit the top of that with an air burst, and it really shot him up pretty bad - one through his head and one through his leg - and he laid there, he said, for about two hours before they found him. The next morning, I got a word from my sergeant from Coleman, Texas. He said, "Your little brother got hit. If you want to go see him, go ahead, take the jeep and go on back." And it wasn't over 5 miles, maybe a little over that, where the hospital was. And when I got there, they had already flew him to England. And then a few of the other boys, one in particular, Yakisha, Paul Yakisha, he would always say, "They ain't' built a bullet that can shoot me" And then when we was at Old Germany, he got hit in the back, just grazed him like somebody got a knife and cut it. He jumped up and run and when they had him on a stretcher, behind a jeep, him and another white boy that was wounded, and while it was snowing and sleeting and it was bad and it slowed down, and the two medics in front was looking forward, he jumped off and came back to where we was. So they clamped his wounds up with them clamps and he just stayed around headquarters then. Boy, we got after him. You ought to have went on back where you could have a hot meal and a good bed.

Q: Do you think that the Comanche's being such fierce warriors – you come from a long line of warriors – do you think that had anything to do with you being good soldiers, well disciplined?

CC: That's one thing that our commanding officer and this major general I was talking about – he was a Second Lieutenant fresh from West Point that came to work with us at Fort Benning, GA. Now he was a Two Star General. He was with us last Saturday at Lawton. And he was with us working on how to set things that we couldn't say. And as far as warriors, they always tell me the Comanche's were Lord of the Plains from Mexico, Oklahoma and Kansas, you know, and a little bit up to Colorado. And I've heard a lot of good things, a lot like the Battle of Adobe Walls. They knowed they was going to get killed and they said that little Gatlin gun came out. So they sang the song and went in, and all of them got killed. We carry that song high. We don't sing it just anywhere, unless it's for warriors. And as far as it has being - I don't know, when they asked us to do what we did, we gladly did and we probably would do it again if they asked us.

Q: Do you think - just kind of building on that one statement you made – you know American Indians have always either been stereotyped or there has been a lot of prejudice in this country against them, so why do you think American Indians are always first to serve the country.

CC: That's something that I always wondered, because in my younger days I went to the Fort Sill Indian School out of Lawton. And they had – if we talk Indian they would punish us. But we would get around and talk to each other in Indian, and when we seen them coming we'd hush up. But not only at Fort Sill. There was other schools. But later on in years now, they try to make us – I was caught in between the old traditional way and where modern kind of come up, and I am going to be 72 years old pretty soon, and way back in 1921, but I don't know I still feel it every once in a while. Give you and example that happened to me at - I was the only registered voter in a group of glass workers. They called us glazers. There was five of us sitting there. And this man up in

Tulsa - he was running the office - he went ahead and shook hands with those white boys, but he didn't shake hands with me. But he didn't know but I was the only registered voter sitting there. And somebody said "You going to vote for him?" I said "So and so, I wouldn't vote for him if he was running for a dog catcher." Those things shows up. But now I think everything is going to settle down, and everybody is going to try to love each other.

Q: So, even in light of that prejudice, as far as you're concerned, would you still serve your country, you would still go?

CC: I would, yes.

Q: What makes the difference - I mean why would you feel that way?

CC: This is our place. I made a speech for thirty students from Sicily, and I sang them a song, a Native American song. I still attend those religious – that was here before white man ever come here. We talk to that man (pointing up). We call him (Comanche word) "our Father." We didn't know - and then when they heard the word - I used the word "Jesus" in that song. And one of the students questioned – he said, "Where did you learn that word, Jesus, at?" And naturally, it kind of hit me a little funny. I said, "Well, a long time ago." I said, "That was an Italian man. He got in boats and he was coming this way. I think he was lost because he hit over here somewhere. They call him Columbus. And he had a book. They called it a Bible. And different churches went different ways and different Indians joined different churches - Catholic, Protestants and others - and we learned it from that book. Now, we use what we learned of what happened years ago, and we use that word, Jesus, because he was kind to everybody. He listened when you asked something from his God. And we use it in our native church. We've always used it." They bend in prayer somewhere. In this we'll never bend his prayers. He would always talk to God Almighty.

Q: That's good. Now will share with us your feelings about what is happening here at this honor of all you code talkers.

CC: It was a wonderful feeling to know that the Navajos and the few of us left here, the Comanches, that we did something for our country. Like it said in some of these deals we get, maybe we saved a lot of lives when they couldn't break the Indian language, the Navajo codetalkers or the Comanches. If we made that big contribution, I am glad I was part of it.

Q: OK that's good. Can you share with us some of the things you learned as a young boy – your traditional teachings?

CC: I was taught when I was a young man - always hold your head up and most of all, always respect the Elders. Always – not only your mother or uncles or aunts – but all Elders. If you see an old man, go over there and say a good word to him. Then you get that feeling that one of these days when somebody be good to me, I am going to be a man. I wanted to go where I could go and do things and be proud of what I am going to do. Just like when they asked us to be this Comanche codetalker. It made me proud that I would go, and I learned from them to always hold your head up and do what you think is best. And they said in that Native American Church, they got a line: It's a road of life. When you stay on that road and hold yourself up, and if you kind of fall off that road a little bit, people are going to bite at you a little bit. But if you can stay on that road of life, straight life, you're going to be a man and you're going do what you want to and be good at what you do. That way, that's what I got encouragement from folks that I would go and do what I was asked to do and do it with all the best of my ability.

Q: Before you went away, did your tribe or family hold any kind of traditional ceremonies for you?

CC: Before I went overseas, they was coming close. We knew that. And mama and them has always been a religious group of people, the Methodists. And they had a big church service for me. And also one man that lived a mile east and back north of Lawton and ever since I was little, he always called me son, Old Man Abe Manachacha. He said. "Before you go, son, I want you to come up to my house to see me." I had my uniform on. I went over there. We went back of his house. We sat down where his old peyote ground is. He put four peyotes on the ground and he prayed. He said, "God give us this medicine to use when we need it. I am going to put it in this little pouch." He says, "I want you to tie it around your neck. It is going to take you over there, and it is going to bring you back. When you get scared, you get fear, you take one out. Chew it a little bit. Put it in your hand and pray God Almighty. He is going to take care of you. With this medicine for Indians to use when they are in need or fear - when you fear, use it." And when my little cousin got hurt - I just got through talking about him not long ago. I felt fear because a lot of artillery and mortars were coming in. And I sat down and I talked, prayed and my little white friend that sat by me. He sat down with me. He listened. And I told him what I was doing. So I used one of those medicines. And when we got into

Old Germany and stuff didn't do right, I did the same thing. And I came back. That close. Several of my brothers got wounded. But I was close; That old man's prayers went with me. When I got home, I heard he had passed away. I will never forget him.

Q: Ok. That's good.

CC: Yesterday over there, they gave us these (points to a ribbon), and then all the veterans danced with us. There was one Comanche - a young man, tall. He said he served in Viet Nam." He said, "I heard about you all my life, Charles Chibitty. That name, I heard it. I got to meet you now. I am going to give this to you. Wear it for me. I earned it. My grandfather is George Espany." I used to play ball with his grandfather. He was older than I was. I was young. He said, "I am his grandson, and I am going to give this to you. Put it on when you put on your uniform, put everything, your other ribbons you got, your four battle starts and everything. Wear that. I earned it. I am going to give it to you." That's where I got it. You see we didn't have that extra infantry badge, but we were with the infantry all the time. And he knew that. He said, "I am going to give it to you. I am a veteran from Viet Nam." So I thanked him and I said I would wear it with pride.

Q: That's beautiful. We really appreciate it.

Interview with Albert Smith (Navajo)

Mr. Albert Smith (Navajo) – U.S. Marine Corps code talker

Q: Tell us your name and your tribe and where you live.

AS: My name is Albert Smith. My tribe is Navajo. I am from New Mexico. I am living in Gallup. My home is in Red Springs.

Q: Please tell us about your being president of the Navajo Code Talker Association. Tell us a little bit about the Association and when you took over the presidency.

AS: The Association, the Navajo Code talker Association, was formed in 1971. At the present time we have thirty-five active members, twenty-two non-active members. Those are the ones that come to see us maybe once or twice a year, and then out of the four hundred code talkers, we just have about a hundred that we come in contact with. The others, we're not sure. And out of that, eleven have been killed in action and a little over a hundred have passed away since then, since the end of the war.

Q: And when were you elected president?

AS: I have been president for nine years, off and on, but steadily for the past nine years.

Q: How old are you, and when and where were you born?

AS: I am 67 years old. I was born on the reservation before there was any hospital in the Hosta Butte area, and later on I lived in Red Springs. That's where I'll be moving to when I retire from the public life.

Q: What do you do? What has been your vocation?

AS: I was a schoolteacher for forty years. I retired in 1989. I have gone from Zuni Reservation, taught there 3 years. I was in Chimawa, Oregon for fifteen years. I spent one summer in Alaska when they were forming the Head Start. I was helping them out. And since that time I moved back to the Navajo Reservation to head one of the adult education, at one of the agencies. And then I retired. Now I am doing mainly the code talker work.

Q: What are some of the details of the events that led up to you joining the military? Did you enlist or were you drafted?

AS: I enlisted. The thing that came about was, they were having military induction at the school where I was. I was just fifteen, but one of my uncles was in the Philippines at the time and another uncle was on the east coast waiting to go to Europe, and we were debating whether we would be next, and we wanted to stay together, so I moved my age two years up, and the same way with my other brother. That's how we got in, but it didn't last very long because of the five Sullivan's that were killed in a battleship. They were all lost in one heavy bombing. And so that is what split us up. We didn't serve together.

Q: Before you went away to the service, did your family or tribe hold a ceremony or event for you?

AS: I went from school. I had a deferred, deferred over a month before school was out before I went in, but in the meantime my dad had some other things done for us.

Q: What branch of service did you go in to?

AS: I was in the Marines. This is where the Navajo code talkers were in. They were all in the Marines.

Q: Can you share some of the most notable experiences that you had over there that stand out in your memory?

AS: Why, it was just a special duty that we had to do. We were regular Marines, and then this was a special assignment that we did. We weren't always code talking. We did the regular duties as regular infantry Marines, like I started off as a radio infantryman with for company. After three battles, I moved up to the regiment, and then just before Iwo (Jima), I was assigned to the 7th Fleet, Admiral Nimitz's command, to do my work. But I did everything from communications center, a runner, a message center and guard duties and what not, besides my radio work.

Q: And how were you selected to be a code talker?

AS: All of us, those of us that were Navajos, we were assigned - after following our basic training, we were assigned to advanced training. That's when we were assigned to this special Navajo communication group, and that's where we memorized - you had to know enough English and also enough Navajo so that you wouldn't spend so much time learning the language at the same time that you were learning the new code. See, it was a code, but it was the language and then a code. So that even is you spoke Navajo, you couldn't decipher the language, the coded language.

Q: Was there any particular instance, as a code talker, that was frightening or funny or that stands out in your mind?

AS: Well, at first it wasn't' quite noticeable but later o like on Iwo, the Japanese tried to interfere by cutting in on our radio frequency, so we had more than one radio, and this changed the frequencies that we were receiving and sending, and to confuse this, they through everything at us, tried to knock our communications center, but our communications set up was in different, a distance apart from each other so that if one was hit you could always move into another radio set.

Q: What awards or honors or medals have you won, and what did you do to receive them?

AS: Well, the only award that I received was from the General during my service with the 7th Fleet. It was a Commendation Letter from the commanding general of the 4th Marine division and also from the 5th Amphibious Corps.

Q: What was that for?

AS: That was for being on the radio continuously for 24 hours, and something that never got into the record was that they had to give me a shot, one of those sample shots by the medical to keep me going, because that's how much communication was going on - and the there was just two of us between the shore and the radio ship, the command ship.

Q: So they had to inject you with something?

AS: They had to five me a sample of whiskey.

Q: Ohh!

AS: Which was illegal, but then and under this condition they had to do it to keep me going. And then they had a guard by, almost constantly by us. Like when we were in one - there were two of us, so one was inside while the other was receiving in another area and if the person was busy and another call came in, both of would be busy and so there was a guard with us at all times.

Q: While you were in the military, did you perceive that there was any prejudice against you because you were an Indian?

AS: There were times it showed, but it didn't bother us. We had a duty to do and there was enough of us that if I was by myself it might have made a difference, but there were more than one. There were always two or four of us in a unit together, so that if somebody was using those tactics on us we didn't, it didn't bother us.

Q: I need you to tell me that again, including something about the prejudice in your answer.

AS: I mentioned there was some because sometimes there was slang remarks but we got used to it. Just like for example sometimes they would call us chiefs and we weren't chiefs but then it was just one of those glancing remarks. And sometimes as we pronounce a word, we'd get percussion on it, but then it didn't bother us.

Q: Whenever your service was over was there any kind of a homecoming celebration that your people gave for you?

AS: There was none. I just came home and spent one week at home. This was during Christmas. And I went back, if here was something, maybe if I had waited longer they might have given me something, yeah. But, I just went directly back to school and I didn't want to use my G.I. to finish high school so I asked if I could take an exam and try to go through, finish my high school as soon as possible without using my G.I. Bill and I was allowed to do that.

Q: So how long were you in the military?

AS: I was in a little over two and a half years.

Q: When you came back home did you have any kind of problem readjusting to civilian life?

AS: No, I didn't have any difficulty, because that was one of the reasons I left, because of the problems. I had the summer before I worked at eight different jobs, and there were some other social problems, but they were minor so it didn't bother me.

Q: Okay, so when you enlisted it was maybe because of social pressures. Did alcohol have anything to do with that?

AS: No, I didn't have any problem to go into that before. I wasn't involved in any drinking. I didn't like it.

Q: So then after your military experience, do you feel like maybe you matured a little bit more so you were able to adjust – did you have as many problems when you came out as you did when you went in - pressures?

AS: No, I didn't. It was the old - I wasn't in the community. I was away from the community. I was living out on the reservation about four or five miles out. And the only time I went into town was, oh, for groceries or for food or just to shop for minor things. Otherwise I didn't have anything much to do with the town.

Q: Were you wounded in any way?

AS: No, that's one thing about that "doing" I had. I had some close calls but I went through it without a scratch.

Q: Do you see that there's an interest in building a National Indian Veterans Memorial ? And if so, where do you think it should be located?

AS: Yes, I see that. There is an interest.

Q: In this last question, I am going to ask you to say something in your tribal language and then translate it back into English.

AS: We had, for example, was - we didn't' have a term for hand grenade so we developed that and called it potato (in Navajo). And in one of the other major items was, see the code was based on the basic military terms, the essential terms, and we used the - when we were talking about the planes, in our code we'd be talking about the birds. And if we were talking about the ships, we'd be talking about the fishes.

Q   Say that in Navajo.

AS: (He speaks a sentence in Navajo.) Amphibious tractor – (continues in Navajo) – carrier – (continues in Navajo) – submarine.

Q: So, submarine for instance, what did that really mean in Navajo?

AS: It means an iron fish.

Q:	Use a whole sentence using submarine as if it were in a message you would give, in Navajo and then translate it in English.

AS:	(He speaks a Navajo sentence.)

Q:	Tell me what you just said.

AS:	I said we were using the term the iron fish when we were using torpedoes to - for a landing or for a destroyer services to bombard the coastline.

Q:	I think that's all we need. Can you think of anything?

AS:	Oh, yes. And I don't know if this would help. One prisoner of war - the Japanese found out that they had a Navajo who was a prisoner of war, and he was a Navajo, they found that out. And they did everything to him to try to have him decode our messages, and the only thing that he got out of it was that the men were having eggs, and the only thing that he could arrive at was the pilots were having breakfast. (He laughs.)

Q:	Good. Can you tell us about your ribbons and medals.

AS:	(Pointing to the ribbons on his shirt) This is the medal. This is my Commendation for Iwo Jima. This one is a Navy unit citation from the Navy department. This one is a good conduct medal. This one is a presidential unit citation, one for Saipan and one for Iwo, with the stars. This one was defense. These are my battle stars for campaign ribbons. This is my service in Japan, and this is my overseas, overseas duty and my victory medal, and this one is for another overseas duty, only in a peacetime. And this patch I have here (pointing to his right sleeve) is our logo (Navajo Code Talker Association). It indicates the short rainbow with the eagle feathers at the end. This is signifying a good travel, a safe travel. This is a shield, which they used before in combat, and it was also used - what I am doing right, now communicating. And it was also used in the legend when the two twins (Navajo legend) - I don't know if you have read about it - the two twins were communicating trying to locate their father, and there was a spark that came to them just like the dove in your traditional (Christian) ways, and this is the staff showing the various stages of our tribal development. The bottom stages, these are usually the base, the bottom, is black signifying the dark ages. Then the next would be a blue bar, indicating the time when the waters came, like even in your biblical stories. Then the next bar is a yellow indicating that his was the time the development of electrical lights. And then the last bar, the last one would be white and that is where we are now, using cosmic rays.

Q: That's really interesting.

AS: (Indicating the yellow shirt all the Navajo Code Talkers wear.) The yellow color signifies a pollen, which Navajos use in their prayers. And our cap used to be blue signifying the sky, but it faded so we switched to the Marine Corps league, which is red, with the writing on the side.

Q: Can you take it off so we can see it up close?

AS: (Pointing to pins on his cap) Now, on this side, these are my honorable discharge button from the Marine Corp. And this is a congressional pin by Congressman Richardson, and this is the unit that I served with, the same as this one on the side. So this side the tribal seal and my forty-year pin from the government service and the youth from the Native Association. I help out and not only me, but most of the code takers, we contribute to the advancement of youth by being a promoter for scholars, promoter for good health - we have talks, we present talks, and we also help the youth to help them to attend, like this one youth that is going to be with the American Indian Science Society in Washington, DC, in November. So we are going to be sending one individual there, and I received it - this is thirty-year, and this is a pin from the Apaches, from the White Mountain Apaches.

Q: Very good. Thank you.

Interview with William Dean Wilson (Navajo)

Mr. William Dean Wilson (Navajo) – U.S. Marine Corps code talker

Q: Tell me your name, your tribe, where you're from…..

DW: My name is William Dean Wilson. They just call me Dean for short, and I come from Navajo country - Navajo land. They call it "Dineh" as that was what our people were called way back, according to my dad. But this, I don't know how far back now, he used to tell us there is no more of those people. They are all gone. So somewhere they were called Navajos, so there is a different story about that name. Some Spanish people say, "Oh, we call them that because they used to steal our horses, women, and stuff like that. (he laughs) Which is - I don't know how true that is - but it is a name that stuck with the people. But there are a good many of them now that they call themselves Dineh, like up in Alaska, and they talk like we do. So some of their singers come down for our powwow, and their songs have Navajo words in them. So that's neat.

Q: Tell us why you are here?

DW: Why we are here in this barn, big barn. We came to Norman by invitation. To meet some code talkers from this area, Oklahoma. So, here during this powwow, we are honoring these folks who did the same kind of work that we did, only over in Europe during the WWI and WWII. So that's a celebration that they're having here honoring those people. So we came to do our share, meet with them and talk with them and see what the situation is that they were in during that time.

Q: Can you tell me how you were chosen as a code talker - how they actually chose the Navajo code talkers?

Dean: After the first combat engagement, we understand, on Guadalcanal - that's down there in the Solomon islands - the enemy were catching, deciphering, many of their important messages that they were sending, so that they (*the enemy*) knew what the next move was going to be of these Marines. So word came back - what shall we do? Well, at the same time, this Philip Johnston, he claimed he was a son of a missionary, had some idea about using the Navajos to be brought - I understand a couple or maybe 4 Navajo boys - down to Camp Elliot. That is where the Marine headquarter was for the west coast. That is just about thirteen miles northeast of San Diego. And he introduced them to the brass there and gave them an assignment to transmit to one another, one over there (*pointing across the room*), and one over here, and wrote them a message. Sure enough they go it, just like that. So, that idea became a reality. So they send word back to the Marine Corp headquarters in Washington. So the Commandant gave an order to go ahead and recruit, instead of regular sixty men - that's a platoon - just recruit thirty and run them through the boot training, and see what they can do on making up this code. So that's how I came on. They recruited at Fort Wingate High School. And Fort Defiance High School (*both on the Navajo Reservation*). These were boarding schools, Indian boarding schools. That's was up north. I was up there. I always say the only reason I got in was my teacher kind of pushed me into it because I was the bad lot in the class, ninth grader. The rest were all tenth, eleventh, and twelfth graders. Anyway, I don't know how many - about fifty I guess - went through physical training or examination at Fort Defiance Beatrice Hospital. Quite a few of them couldn't make it because they either can't see too well or had something wrong - the eyes, and this and that. That's why you hear the ad, you know. What do they say in the Marines? (*the few, the proud, the brave*) So, only thirty came through. So we got on a bus. Incidentally, this year is our 50th anniversary – May, 1942 - they put us on a greyhound bus and headed out to San Diego.

Thirty of us. Somewhere, maybe in Phoenix, one of the thirty jumped off. So when we got to San Diego, there were only twenty nine of us. So we went through boot training, all that, rifle range shooting. These guys did pretty good. They got a lot of compliments on their training - rifle, pistol shooting and all that. And after that, of course, they sent you to what they call that advanced training, which at that time was at Camp Elliot, about thirteen to fourteen miles northeast of San Diego. That was where the marine base was. Before Camp Pendleton came about, that was a big ranch, you know. Margarito Ranch. So that became Marine Corps base later, and at this Camp Elliot, of course, we went through, they taught us all phases of communications. They taught some of us about telephone, how to lay telephone wire, climb poles, climb all that in the jungle, and radio - how to transmit by voice, how to transmit by Morse Code, and then how to use all these flags, you know, like the Navy use. You know, it's a long pole with a flag, one way, dit, and the other way is dash, you know. So this was another way. Then, of course, the Navy uses this on the ship, those blinkers. So they taught us all that, but during all that time we spend some hours trying to make up the code. We get together and went through the alphabet first. What shall we call letter A, letter B, and on down the line. We want to use the shortest Navajo words. So different ones made suggestions. So for A, we use the word aunt – olachi, and B –(Navajo word) and on down the line. Then we went into military personnel, officers, and then the various shops and equipment, all that - airplane, submarines, the whole bit, and some military terminologies. We all find some Navajo word for them, so that by the time we got down we all went through a course while we were making this. We knew what they were. So then after we finished it, of course, they ran us through what they called field exercises, right there. Some went out to ship at sea; some went into the air with the airplanes; some just right there in the area in tanks or, you know, boondocks, and sent messages one way or the other. And they must have come out pretty good, because they okayed everything. None of this ten day leave for us, they said. Boy, they shipped us out right now. That was about October, 1942. They sent two guys from this original "29" back to the reservation to recruit some more for the same operational signal course. Some more guys came right after us, and others, a little later. So, they all claim that they were one of the "29" when they really weren't, you know. See our "29," we made up the code real quick-like, and we went overseas and they spread us out into different combat units that were already out and did what we had to communicate. So then eventually when more of these people came about, they added

251

some more to the code. They made up some more - added words one at one time. I believe it was after Iwo Jima, they called us over to the Big Island of Hawaii, and there we went through all the new code that added to the ones we made up, so that we had to study that and then use it there before we went back to the units that these guys came from. So that was how the code was used. And, when it was unclassified in 1968 or 1969, all kinds of stories started up - that we even had bodyguards, which was a joke. We were just another jarhead out there, you know. We did mess duty. We did guard duty - just about anything that our fellow Marines did. The only thing that they used to identify us with was, we were radio communicators. That's all – voice - except that we "yak" in our language, which was coded. They taught us how to decipher and cipher a message. And there were other areas that they taught us, infantry duty. So we were just kind of oriented in all phases, in case.

Q: So you were highly trained outside.

Dean: We were not just code talkers, you know. That was just one of the duties we had to—in the event a general or someone wants to send a special message, maybe highly classified message, to aircraft out there or somewhere or in the area where they are fighting. That was the time that these guys would get together. We only used two radios. One was where you had to crank it out with a generator. The other one was operated by a battery. That was the one we carried in front of us. And the pack in the back, it was kind of like a burro – pack burros. So that was the way the whole thing came about.

Q: Okay. Thank you. That's all we need.

Interview with Harold Foster (Navajo)

Harold Foster (Navajo) Code Talker

(This interview was conducted in Window Rock, AZ)

Q: Where and when were you born?

HF: I was born in the hills of western New Mexico on the Navajo Reservation on May 15, 1925. And when I was 5 years old, I entered a school. They put me in school Toadlena, NM. I stayed there from kindergarten to 8th grade. After I finished, I went to Fort Wingate. This was a vocational school. It was from 9th to 12th grades. May 15, 1942 - that's when I graduated from high school. In March 1942, I enlisted into the Marines. And then it took me 3 months - March, April, May - to have my parents decide if they would let me go into the service, because when I was still at Wingate, one Sunday afternoon, it was Dec 7th 1941 – that's when the Japanese bombed Pearl Harbor – we were in the living room when it came over the radio that the Japanese bombed Pearl Harbor, and then the President of the United States Franklin Delano Roosevelt and the congress declared war on Japan. Since then I decided to go in the Marines because of the posters they had at Ft. Wingate. They had these posters that showed the uniform that ideal for me to wear if I had to go in the service.

Q: Recruiting posters?

HF: Yes, posters at Wingate. Because where I lived, there's nothing. It's way out on the reservation. So it struck me as the one I wanted to wear. I took me 3 months for them to say. The second month in April they decided, okay let him go, let him go in the service, and my mother said "No, we need him here." And my late father said, "No, there's nothing here. He's finished school, and he can work anywhere but there's no jobs."

Q: So that was when you went in?

HF: No it was still April - see March is when I enlisted – March, April, May, that's when I went in, right after I got my graduation. Finally we got the witnesses together. I did not register for selective services. I wasn't old enough. And if your sixtenn or seventeen - I was sixteen when I volunteered. Like I said, it took me 3 months to have my parents to say okay. And then on the rules and regulations they said, you need 3 witnesses - so we got the missionary, the trader to get them together for my parents to give their thumbprints. My parents are uneducated. They never went to school - they don't know how to write. Thumb prints was the only thing they could do.

Q: When you asked for your parents' permission to enlist, what did they say?

HF: They figured that since I graduated, they said, "Let him go ahead and defend the country." See I was a Catholic, so we'd have to have a priest to come and witness, and the priest was the interpreter - he explained certain things to them, to my parents, so it was important for him to come.

Q: So, are you still catholic? have you ever included traditional Navajo teachings in your life?

HF: Catholic, being Catholic is secondary, but my Navajo religion is part of who I am that I'll never forget, because they're the reason why – they have this certain protection ceremony which they have done for me and for other Marines. When I got back, they had another one to purify my soul.

Q: So who did that for you?

HF: This one medicine man from my area.

Q: Did your parents come to this ceremony?

HF: Well my parents went over there, and they brought me, and he did the ceremony.

Q: What is that ceremony called?

HF: That's the Enemy Way ceremony – what it used to be called.

Q: So when you left here, how did you get into the code talkers?

HF: Let's go back. After I graduated, after they signed me up - my parents signed the agreement allowed to go in, I went to Albuquerque. That's where I got my first physical. And then there was about six of us that went to Santa Fe. And then at Santa Fe High School, we went to the gym for another exam. There were thousands of kids same age. Some of them were inducted to go into the army, to go into the Navy, air force and the marines. They were all there getting their physicals.

Q: Was that Santa Fe Indian School?

HF: No, not the Indian school. Santa Fe High School. I got my physical there and then they told us they'd allow us a couple of days to go home, that's when I had my ceremony for the protection. And my parents dropped me off on Highway 666. I caught the bus there, and then I went over to the train depot in Gallup. That's where my package, which included the ticket, the meal ticket, to go into L.A.

Q: You went to Los Angeles?

HF   Yeah, we stopped on the way, Winslow, Flagstaff, Needles, Barstow. We got there in the morning, we drove all night, I mean we rode the train all night. Have you ever been to the L.A. train depot?

Q: Not to the train depot.

HF: That train depot waiting room is big. That thing was full of kids the same age as - I just turned seventeen - same age as me. Some were older. And then we waited for an hour or so. At 10 o'clock - we got in there around 7:30. We were waited until 10 o'clock in the morning, and they said all the kids there are going to San Diego Naval Base or the San Diego Marine Corps base. They called our names off, and we boarded the train. We waited there until the afternoon, and then we started.

Q: You were on the train waiting from 10 o'clock to 3 o'clock waiting?

HF: Yes. We finally moved and we didn't get there until 10 o'clock that night. Then they got us in these cattle cars, three deckers. We board the cattle cars and they took us to the Marine corps base in San Diego. It took us eight weeks for boot camp.

Q: What time was it when you finally got to the base?

HF: Two o'clock in the morning. It was 2 o'clock in the morning when they showed us how to make up our beds. This is how you make the Marine Corps bunk. We just got to sleep and got up around 3:30 and started again.

Q: Where along the process were you selected - ?

HF: I'm getting to that. The next day, we got our uniforms, and we sent our civilian clothes home. That same day, after we ship our clothes home, we got our "good" haircut. They kidded us: "How do you want your haircut, Chief?" See, I was the only Indian in that platoon, the rest were all white kids.

Q: o naturally they called you "chief."

HF: Yeah. So a little later, they gave us a rifle, and then we started off. At 4 o'clock is our revelry, 4:30 we're supposed to be out there for calisthenics, day in and day out for six weeks. In that six weeks we went to the classroom to learn our general orders, attend general orders, know how to swim, how to take our rifle apart, how to hold the rifles. Then we went to night class where we learned all about what we're supposed to do – how to defend ourselves. It really wasn't very different from my parents used to say when they were teaching me how to do things. You do this, and you do this, and you don't do that. What I did when I was civilian wasn't very different from this except being away from home. On the third or fourth day I, after long classwork, running, everything, I was laying there resting there thinking, "Why, why did I join? Then I thought to myself that I joined because I wanted to defend my people, my parents, my relatives, the reservation, the state and the United States of America. So if it wasn't for my parents I wouldn't be with you. So I have to start there. I kept that in my mind. Some of these kids, white kids couldn't take it. They were bawling like a calf calling for its mother.

Q: Did you have a sense that was the main reason why….

HF: That's the main reason why most of these code talkers, even these veterans, these Navajo veterans, signed up for the service.

Q: Defending the homeland. It's a different kind of patriotism.

HF: Well, it's not different. It's all in the same line - there's no difference. If you think about it that way. Its just like going to a church – the church and the ceremony, they pray to one. So this was like that.

Q: Did your father or grandfather or other part of the family serve in WW1 or serve in the military?

HF: Okay, let's go back. This Chief Manuelito is my great, great grandfather on my mother's side, great. And how he conducted himself was pretty much down to me how to conduct myself, how to take orders, how to give orders. I had an older brother, he was in Normandy, and my oldest brother was a code talker, too, and my brother-in-law was in the air force.

Q: So growing up, you heard stories about Manuelito?

HF: Yes.

Q: Okay, so back to your experiences.

HF: Okay, like within those six weeks, we had to learn how to do judo, how to defend ourselves, and after the graduation - the last two weeks, you spend at the rifle range. I knew how to shoot, anyway, when I was on the rez. And I knew how to take care of rifles. So the only bad part of it - I'm small. Some of those guys are taller than I am - 6'2", 6'3" and I'm only 5'7". When you go into the prone position, I almost broke my arm off, the way they wanted you to hold yourself. Because my body structure is shorter. Even in the standing position, I don't have any trouble. But sitting or kneeling, you have you have to sit down and rock back and forth. Especially when you get down on your belly, and he says, "Get down a little more, chief." So 340 is the possible score you can get on the shooting range. I missed two. I used to hunt prairie dogs, squirrels, everything that's on the reservation. That's because all those are good eating. Now all the prairie dogs have fleas with rabies.

Q: So let's go back to the training.

HF: When I was growing up, I was with the Boy Scouts. That's where I learned the dots and dashes. Morse Code. So in the service, everybody had to take that. So knowing I was going to be a Navajo code talker, that didn't phase me at all. But they did tell me, "You're going to be in the communication." So the scores I made were pretty good. Some of those boys were going into the SeeBees, to serve on aircraft carriers, or heavy cruisers, stuff like that. After we were assigned to go to extensive training, some were shipped over to Florida for their Navy Seal school there. Some of them went to Air

Force, Marine Corps, different branches. I got my order to report to Camp Elliot. It didn't state on there what kind of assignment.

Q: Where is that?

HF: It's about 30 miles from San Diego. And I report there, and that was dots and dashes communications school. Then later I was transferred to Camp Pendleton for more field and class work. That's where, when I report to Camp Elliot, they say, "Ok you going to be in the Navajo communication."

Q: When was that? How long had you been in?

HF: Let's see - May 20th - that's when we were at the boot camp - after eight weeks, that's when we start to get into the classroom. The instructor, the communications officer, which was a major, said, "Okay, this First Lieutenant's going to be in charge, but you'll have two other instructors. So when we got into a classroom, they give us a folder, which the first twenty nine had set up. Let's go back on the how that code was set up. When the first 29 - a man by the name of Phillip Johnston was on the reservation when his parents were missionaries. He was here when he was four years old – he played with the Indian kids, because there's no other white kids around. So he learned a little of the language. They said he was an interpreter, but when I saw him, he doesn't speak fluent Navajo. In 1919, he went to WWI, in Germany and France, and he seen and heard other Indians, like Choctaw, Comanches sending messages on the radio, on the telephone. Not coded, just talking their language. So, after he got discharged, his parents were already living here. So when he got discharged, he went to school in LA, graduated as a engineer. When he got back from work one evening, he was looking at a newspaper where he seen they were having maneuvers in Louisiana where some of those Indians were trying to send messages. And then he saw right away that he should demonstrate how to put a code in Navajo. And then the following day, he knew that that other Indians tried but it wasn't in code. And they sent Germans and Japanese here to study these other languages, but not the Navajo. So he went to Camp Elliot, to General Vogel and then he explained how wanted to demonstrate how to set up a code and then General Vogel said that this has been done before. It won't work. Anyway they gave him permission to do that, So he went, back to LA to the employment office where he picked up well-educated Navajos, about six of them. At least he got five from employment office. The sixth one was Navy person, we don't know who that Navy person was. He was a new recruit at San Diego Naval training station. So they gave him two weeks to try it, to send messages, use certain words to spell it out, so they made up a code. This wasn't in training - this was just a demonstration for the general and his staff to know how the code would work. So they give him eight messages. These were all spelled out and they came out okay. And then a couple weeks later, Gen Vogel gave permission to recruit at least 200 Navajos, but before that there were only thirty, as a special project for the test. So the this thirty - the recruiters here on the reservation - they got thirty recruits, and then this thirty, they took off from Gallup - between Window Rock and San Diego, they lost one. They still don't know who that thirtieth man was. They ended up with 29 down there. Somebody dropped off on the way.

Q: Somebody got lost along the way.

HF: None of the first twenty-nine knew who the 30th man was. Different persons, when you mention this, they will say, "I was the 30th man, I was the 30th man." Stuff like that.

Q: So we have several 30th man, right?

HF: After the project – they went through boot camp like the other recruits – six weeks at the San Diego doing their duties. After graduation there, they went to Camp Elliot. And then it was really closed in project. It was a top, top secret. They would have bars on the windows and doors. And on the outside they got guards. And then they go back to the barracks. The first twenty-nine are the ones - just like a round table discussion, they sat there and each one of them say what the alphabet should use – name of animals here on the reservation. Like for instance, an A. You go outside, you see an ant. That's the first letter of the animals that you use for alphabet.

Q: Then you use the Navajo word for ant?

HF: Yup. For instance when they say (Navajo word) - it's ant in Navajo – you put the letter A. So B you say "shush" - that means bear. And for C, (Navajo word) - that means cat. First letter of the animal. And then they went along and figure out, like "attack" – what do we do for "attack" or "charge?" Advance? And then "machine gun?" We don't have words in Navajo for that, but what do machine guns do? Rapid fire. So they said (Navajo word). So when you hear that, you put "machine gun." And then for tank. What does a tank do? Crawl. So tank and turtle are the same thing in the code. And "hand grenade." (Navajo word). Hand grenade is like a potato. And then for bomb (Navajo word), which means "blow up." The first twenty-nine set all that up. They give to you in the classroom. We had to check these things out, these files, and then check them back in. At 8 o'clock, we checked them out. We studied them until the break - we had a break, during the break you don't go outside. You stay around. You have your folder with you all the time. First thing that they said is that this is a confidential, top secret. Don't reveal this. After you go outside, don't say anything about this. If you're married, you don't say anything to your wife. If you're not married, if you have a girl friend, hell no. Your brother, your father, your mother, your sister - nobody. This is a top, top secret. See we didn't know that. When we'd go on liberty – most of the men would go to Los Angeles. On 4th Street, all the different tribes congregate there, come together there. Here on the Rez, they don't have bars, but there it's open, so they go there. After they leave, after they go back to camp, the FBI goes in there and pick up these girls or whoever they were with to see if anything was revealed. If you do, out you go – transfer you to infantry. And they stressed that your pronunciation has got to be perfect. Your writing – you got to print, you can't use script. Just like being in the 1st grade again, you learn how to print again. They want it fast and clear. So that's the eight weeks we were in there. The first six weeks were classroom, the last two weeks were out in the field.

Q: Practicing?

HF: Practicing, training. We were even sent down to San Diego aboard the submarine. It would take us out to Catalina Island, a couple miles out, the submarine pull up, and then we take the rubber raft and then we hit the island and send messages back to the mainland. Then we did the final code. At Camp Pendleton, there's a landing area there, so we'd land. So this is one of the field training that we had. The officer would give a person a message and then he'll sneak and go to another radio and see if that message comes out the same way. So that's the training we had.

Q: Pretty extensive.

HF: I never thought I was going to be as a code talker. I thought I'd be like any other Marine. And then after our eight weeks is up, then we shipped overseas – 284 was my draft number. We were aboard ship 14 days.

Q: Where did you land?

HF: At that time, Guadalcanal was secured. So we landed there. Then we were separated. Some when to 1st Marine division; I was sent to 2nd Marine division – headquarters signal company - third battalion, 28th Marines, second Marine division. And then second marine division had hit Tarowa already. So we just went to the next island. It's adjacent to the channel and other islands next to Tarowa.

Q: So when was the first time you had to apply all this training?

HF: When we landed, we were going so fast we didn't have to transmit anything. Until we secured the island. And then after that I was transferred to the 5th Marine division as it was forming, so they need the code talkers. See we're placed wherever we're needed.

Q: How many different units of code talkers were there?

HF: It's hard to say how many - like in 5th Marine division itself, we had thirty eight of us, up from the division all the way up to the Admiral Nimitz (ship) all the way down to command ship, all the way down to battalion. See I was with the battalion on front lines.

Q: How many…

HF: So, thirty-eight within the within the 5th Marine division. I think there more than that or less than that in the 4th Marine division. And then 3rd marine division was like that too, so in each division there's some. Something like a pool, whereever you're needed, they'll transfer you there.

Q: You say thirty-eight, you mean thirty eight different guys?

HF: Yeah, thirty-eight different personnel.

Q: When did you get out?

HF: After the war, after Iwo Jima, we went back to Hawaii, and then we were getting ready to go to Okinawa again, which was the last island. We were supposed to be - the 5th marine division was supposed to be in reserve, but they didn't use us so after that, Nagasaki was bombed with the atomic bomb, so right after that, after Okinawa, the war was over. Then I spent four months at Nagasaki and four months at (Japan location) - occupation force. And then after that, I had enough points to come home, but I decided to go there to see I want to come home, but I decided to go there to see what kind of a people, what kind of country it is.

Q: Japan?

HF: Yes, Japan.

Q: Did you fight any more?

HF: No, not after -for me, not after Iwo Jima, it was a nothing after.

Q: What did you discover about those people?

HF: It's, it's something like us, but the center part of it, it's not so good. It's so darn crowded, after the occupation. There were just the policeman, are the only ones that, at each street corner - there's no civilians, no nothing. Then after that, they started coming - migrating back from the mountains back to the city.

Q: So when you got back there, you still couldn't talk about it.

HF: No, I couldn't. It's so horrible to talk about it. It's after you go through your ceremony after the war - my parents told us not to talk about it anymore after that. So that was it, nobody talked about it.

Q: Did the military keep it…

HF: It's not a secret, see, our code was declassified in 1956. It was declassified. And here they said they had code talkers in Europe and elsewhere, not even the Philippines; they didn't have any in the Philippines and none in Europe. Only in the Marines in the Pacific.

Q: So after the purification ceremony, traditionally you didn't talk about your wartime experiences?

HF: That's the way it was with me.

Q: Some other tribes, they come back from battle and recount the deeds in battle, because that had something to do with becoming a chief or something. But that's not the tradition in Navajo?

HF: No, we don't. It's just like a rank. See, after I got discharged, I was in the active reserve for fifteen years. When I got discharged, I had the rank of a tech sergeant when I got discharged, fifteen years after the war.

Q: You kept that rank?

HF: Yeah, See active reserve.

Q: Do you feel like there's anything else about your experience or the code talker's experience in the military?

HF: Each code talkers got their own experience. Like, Iwo - we went forward, up to observation to set up the forward command post. And then they start shelling. All our officers, all our sergeants, it was bombed. So our sergeant, a day before asked me, he said, "Chief, since you're the senior on this squad of your original 5th marine division, something tells me I won't be around the next couple of days." This was a code that he made - he said, "Chief, I want you to be in charge. You're the person that can take orders and give orders. You're that type of person. So I took charge, that's the way I am. That's where I got my field stripes. It wasn't on my record until later, fifteen years later.

Q: How come it took so long?

HF: I don't know. It's like - see all the veterans here, especially the code talkers, if they're given the bronze star and a citation, any kind of citation, they weren't awarded that. It's all mostly on paper. It's been 50 years now.

Q: So what other citations were you supposed to get?

HF: Unit citation, presidential citation, national defense, Asiatic, with two stars, victory medal, two purple hearts with gold star, because I was wounded twice.

Q: You were wounded twice?

HF: Yeah, Iwo Jima - enough to be evacuated. So, totally I got thirteen citations, which I never got. None of these, 5th Marine division never gave out awards. The 2nd marine division never gave out awards either. It's on their discharge papers. That's on paper.

Q: You mentioned earlier, and I want to get it on tape, so I don't miss it. This September you're going to Oklahoma with a group of code talkers.

HF: There's a lady - she's a Navajo living in Norman, Oklahoma. She's working at the University of Oklahoma. Her name is Effie Tsosee Tee. Tee is her last name. And she's from Arizona, about thirty miles from here. She called me at my house and said that we'd like to have Navajo code talkers come to Oklahoma in September. I asked her why. She said that the month of September is American Indian month (in Oklahoma). And then they're having the code talkers of the Comanche, the Choctaw, and would like to invite Navajo code talkers. So on the 26th and 27th they're having a powwow. See, I dance at the pow wow. I dance the gourd dance in the powwow. So I'll be dancing with the Comanches.

Q: This will be a unique event.

HF: So after she gave me that I said, "How can we get the code talkers, that many?" She asked me how many code talkers there are. I said "Thirty-five." We got almost sixty, since 1971 that are registered with us, with the Navajo Code Talker Association, but only thirty-five paid their yearly dues, that come to the meetings. So I told her that we were having a meeting, and then I brought this up at that meeting and they said okay. So that part of it was the Association saying "okay, we'll go there." So we'll meet with the Comanche code talkers, and in the meantime I called the Navajo transit office, that is to make arrangements to get the tribal bus to take us.

Q: So you'll take a bus over there.

HF: Bus load, yeah, with their, with their spouses. I think there'll be about twenty three or twenty four code talkers go. I got her phone number at home. I can give you that so you can contact her. I'd like to meet those code talkers, even though they just talked in everyday language. It wasn't really a code. Ours was in code.

Q: Are you involved in the discussions about a national cemetery?

HF: The code talkers are involved because we're the only organization that's got officers, and we're chartered in New Mexico. The reason why we're in New Mexico because we don't have an office or facilities where we can meet here in Window Rock on the Navajo Reservation. We tried that. We asked for land or office space, but they never gave it to us, no. So Chamber of Commerce in Gallup good enough to say we can use their office, free. I'll make a contract. How many years you want to use that office? The room that we use used to be called Kiva, but they changed it to Navajo Code Talker Room.

Q: You meet in Gallup at the Chamber of Commerce. The Association had an address up in Shiprock.

HF: No, we never did have anything up there.

Q: o what's your title in the Association?

HF: I'm the vice president.

Q: Thank you for your time, Mr. Foster.

CHAPTER SEVEN

THE PRESERVATION OF AMERICAN INDIAN LANGUAGES AND CULTURES

J.P. Harrington (seated left) works with several American Indian "informants" to record the songs and speech patterns of California Indian peoples.

sack čɨlɨ, meš	savory, to be tuštom
x̌ɨkɨ	saw, to aqlɨlɨ-wɨy
sacrum ʔiko	say, to axutiwil, ʔip
sad, to be šaqnikulš,	scabby, to be puqpuqeč
šu-mišup, takululun	scale (of fish) yep
sage wewey	scar akučuwič
sage, thistle (chia sp.) pax	scarce, to be uqti-yɨw
salamander tiqweneqweń	scare, to saɬ-ulkuwin,
saliva uqčɨk	s-utaxtaxsɨn
salmon ʔokowoč ~ ʔokowoyoč	scattered, to be pilɨɨa-nań,
salt tip	util-pakaš, util-pamay,
saltgrass liton	wekey

This is a sample page of a linguist's dictionary notes demonstrating the use of phonetic spelling when indicating the pronunciation of a language.

And so the question must be asked: what might have been the ultimate cost to America and her freedom if the alternating federal policies of genocide and assimilation had been successful with regards to American Indians and their languages?

From the onset of the European invasion of the Americas that started in 1492, foreign Christian political powers consistently failed to recognize or value American Indian cultures, naming them the products of the minds of "savages" in official state policies and even the products of the devil in some church proclamations.

In more recent times, citizens of the United States, and the world for that matter, have begun to mature in their attitudes toward indigenous peoples, their languages and cultures. One could say there has been considerable progress.

The U.S. federal government, in the 1960s and 1970s, at long last arrived at the policy of "self-determination" with regards to American Indian tribes and began methodically transferring the responsibility for making decisions and operating programs that affected the lives of American Indian people to tribal governments.

In 1990 the United States Congress even passed the "Native American Languages Act," which recognized the unique status of American Indian languages and cultures and called for the means to ensure their survival. The law, also known as Public Law 101-477, declared that from that time forward, it was to be the policy of the United States to preserve, protect and promote the rights and freedoms of American Indians to use, practice and develop their languages. The entire text of the law is included here because it reflects the policy that should be in place in all nations regarding the treatment of indigenous languages and because it reflects such a stark reversal of the U.S. government's policies towards native languages.

PUBLIC LAW 101-477; NATIVE AMERICAN LANGUAGES ACT

SHORT TITLE

SEC. 101. This title may be cited as the "Native American Languages Act."

FINDINGS

SEC. 102. The Congress finds that-

(1) the status of the cultures and languages of Native Americans is unique and the United States has the responsibility to act together with Native Americans to ensure the survival of these unique cultures and languages;

(2) special status is accorded Native Americans in the United States, a status that recognizes distinct cultural and political rights, including the right to continue separate identities;

(3) the traditional languages of Native Americans are an integral part of their cultures and identities and form the basic medium for the transmission, and thus survival, of Native American cultures, literatures, histories, religions, political institutions, and values;

(4) there is a widespread practice of treating Native American languages as if they were anachronisms;

(5) there is a lack of clear, comprehensive, and consistent federal policy on treatment of Native American languages which has often resulted in acts of suppression and extermination of Native American languages and cultures;

(6) there is convincing evidence that student achievement and performance, community and school pride, and educational opportunity is clearly and directly tied to respect for, and support of, the first language of a child or student;

(7) it is clearly in the interests of the United States, individual states, and territories to encourage the full academic and human potential achievements of all students and citizens and to take steps to realize these ends;

(8) acts of suppression and extermination directed at Native American languages and cultures are in conflict with the United States policy of self-determination for Native Americans;

(9) languages are the means of communication for the full range of human experiences and are critical to the survival of cultural and political integrity of any people; and

(10) language provides a direct and powerful means of promoting international communication by people who share languages.

DEFINITIONS

SEC. 103. For purposes of this title-

(1) The term "Native American" means an Indian, Native Hawaiian, or Native American Pacific Islander.

(2) The term "Indian" has the meaning given to such term under section 5351(4) of the Indian Education Act of 1988 (25 U.S.C. 2651(4)).

(3) The term "Native Hawaiian" has the meaning given such term by section 4009 of Public Law 100-297 (20 U.S.C. 4909).

(4) The term "Native American Pacific Islander" means any descendent of the aboriginal people of any island of the Pacific Ocean that is a territory or possession of the United States.

(5) The terms "Indian tribe" and "tribal organization" have the respective meanings given each of such terms under section 4 of the Indian Self-Determination and Education Assistance Act (25 U.S.C. 450b).

(6) The term "Native American language" means the historical, traditional languages spoken by Native Americans.

(7) The term "traditional leaders" includes Native Americans who have special expertise in Native American cultures and Native American languages.

(8) The term "Indian reservation" has the same meaning given to the term "reservation" under section 3 of the Indian Financing Act of 1974 (25 U.S.C. 1452).

DECLARATION OF POLICY

SEC. 104. It is the policy of the United States to-

(1) preserve, protect, and promote the rights and freedom of Native Americans to use, practice, and develop Native American languages;

(2) allow exceptions to teacher certification requirements for federal programs, and programs funded in whole or in part by the federal government, for instruction in Native American languages when such teacher certification requirements hinder the employment of qualified teachers who teach in Native American languages, and to encourage state and territorial governments to make similar exceptions;

(3) encourage and support the use of Native American languages as a medium of instruction in order to encourage and support;

(A) Native American language survival,

(B) educational opportunity,

(C) increased student success and performance,

(D) increased student awareness and knowledge of their culture and history,

(E) increased student and community pride;

(4) encourage state and location education programs to work with Native American parents, educators, Indian tribes, and other Native American government bodies in the implementation of programs to put this policy into effect;

(5) recognize the right of Indian tribes and other Native American governing bodies to use the Native American languages as a medium of instruction in all schools funded by the Secretary of the Interior;

(6) fully recognize the inherent right of Indian tribes and other Native American governing bodies, states, territories, and possessions of the United States to take action on, and give official status to, their Native American languages for the purpose of conducting their own business;

(7) supporting the granting of comparable proficiency achieved through course work in a Native American language the same academic credit as comparable proficiency achieved through course work in a foreign language, with recognition of such Native American language proficiency by institutions of higher education as fulfilling foreign language entrance of degree requirements; and

(8) encourage all institutions of elementary, secondary and hirer education, where appropriate, to include Native American languages in the curriculum in the same manner as foreign languages and to grant proficiency in Native American languages the same full academic credits as proficiency in foreign languages.

NO RESTRICTIONS

SEC. 105. The right of Native Americans to express themselves through the use of Native American languages shall not be restricted in any public proceeding, including publicly supported education programs.

EVALUATIONS

SEC. 106. (a) The President shall direct the heads of various federal departments, agencies, and instrumentalities to-

(1) evaluate their policies and procedures in consultation with Indian tribes and other Native American governing bodies as well as traditional leaders and educators in order to determine and implement changes needed to bring the policies and procedures into compliance with the provisions of this title;

(2) give the greatest effect possible in making such evaluations, absent a clear specific federal statutory requirement to the contrary, to the policies and procedures which will give the broadest effect to the provisions of this title; and

(3) evaluate the laws which they administer and make recommendations to the President on amendments needed to bring such laws into compliance with the provisions of this title.

(b) by no later than the date that is 1 year after the date of enactment of this title, the President shall submit to Congress a report containing recommendations for amendments to federal laws that are needed to being such laws into compliance with the provisions of this title.

USE OF ENGLISH

SEC. 107. Nothing in this title shall be construed as precluding the use of federal funds to teach English to Native Americans.

End of Legislation; Approved October 30, 1990.

On an international scale, in the 1990s, the United Nations began developing an official international policy on the rights of indigenous peoples. For more than ten years, the international community debated this issue. Finally, in 2007, that declaration, known as the United Nations Declaration of the Rights of Indigenous Peoples, was finally ratified with 143 nations in favor and four against. The opposition votes were cast by Canada, Australia, New Zealand and, somewhat surprisingly, the United States. It wasn't until 2010 that the U.S. reversed its position on the issue and ratified the U.N. declaration, as did the other three hold-out nations.

Article XIII of the Declaration states: Indigenous peoples have the right to revitalize, use, develop and transmit to future generations their histories, languages, oral traditions, philosophies, writing systems and literatures, and to designate and retain their own names for communities, places and persons.

Article XIV of the Declaration states: Indigenous peoples have the right to establish and control their educational systems and institutions providing educational systems and institutions in their own languages, in a manner appropriate to their cultural methods of teaching and learning.

The changes in policies within the U.S. government and the United Nations reveal that hopefully, finally, majority populations realize that promotion of the languages and cultures of indigenous peoples isn't only healthy for those indigenous peoples, but for society as a whole. As declared in the Navajo Nation's Education department documents in 1994, "our work with the language has not been work just on language in isolation. It has been part of a far larger effort to restore personal and social wellness."

This is echoed in the language policy enacted by the tribal council of the Pascua Yaqui Tribe several years ago: "Our language is the foundation of our cultural and spiritual heritage."

So, together, may all Americans everywhere offer up our gratitude and appreciation to American Indians for tenaciously holding on to their indigenous languages and specifically to the American Indian soldiers of World War I and World War II who used their native words as weapons of war on our behalf in the ultimate language of victory.

The Language of Victory
Credits and Acknowledgments

The interviews conducted with code talkers in Norman, Oklahoma in September 1992:

Interviewer: Kathryn Bell
Videographer: Scott Swearingen
Segment Producer: Gary Robinson
Interview questions developed by: Gary Robinson

Interview with Navajo code talker Harold Foster conducted at Window Rock, AZ, 1992:

Interviewer: Gary Robinson

Special Thanks to:

Comanche Nation Museum

Comanche Nation Public Information Office

Comanche veteran Lanny Aseperme

Choctaw Nation Public Information Office

Choctaw Nation Office of the Principle Chief

Don Loudner, National Commander, National American Indian Veterans, Inc.

U.S. Mint

Navajo Code Talkers Association

Original Book Cover Art by Michael Horse

Photographs:

National Archives and Records Administration (public domain)

U.S. Army Center of Military History (public domain)

National Anthropology Archives (public domain)

Dr. Richard Applegate (used with permission)

Bibliography & Sources of Information
for Further Reading

Allen, Phillip; "Choctaw Indian Code Talkers of World War I." Choctaw Nation website.

Bloor, Colonel A.W. "Transmitting Messages in Choctaw." Memo to Captain Commanding General of the 36th Division, Washington, D.C.; U.S. Military archives 23 Jan.1919.

"Code Talkers Suggested by Choctaw Soldier." BISHINIK (Choctaw Nation newspaper), Sept. 1986: 2.

Flaherty, Thomas H. and Henry Woodhead, eds. The American Indians: The Way of the Warrior. Alexandria, Virginia: Time-Life Books: 117.

Imon, Frances. Smoke Signals from Indian Territory, volume II. Limited Edition. Wolfe City, Texas: Henington Publishing Company, 1977: 86-88.

Hirschfelder, Arlene and Kreipe de Montano, Martha. The Native American Almanac: A Portrait of Native Americans Today. Prentice Hall General Reference, New York, 1993.

Britten, Thomas A. American Indians in World War I. University of New Mexico Press, Albuquerque, NM, 1997.

Bernstein, Alison R. American Indians and World War II. University of Oklahoma Press, Norman, OK, 1991.

Daily, Robert. The Code Talkers: American Indians in World War II. Franklin Watts, New York, 1995.

Durrett, Deanne. Unsung Heroes of World War II: The Story of the Navajo Code Talkers. Facts on File, New York, 1998.

http://americanindians.si.edu/education/codetalkers/html/index.html.
Hunter, Sara Hoagland. The Unbreakable Code. Northland Publishing, Flagstaff, AZ, 1996.

Littlefield, Holly. <u>Children of the Indian Boarding Schools</u>. Lerner Publishing Group, Minneapolis, MN, 2001.

Meadows, William C. <u>The Comanche Code Talkers of World War II</u>. University of Texas Press, Austin, TX, 2002.

Plunkett, Barry. "Oklahoma's Greatest War hero Also Choctaw Code Talker." The Valliant Leader, 9 Sept. 1987: 1.

Pyle, Chief Gregory E. Official State of the Choctaw Nation Address, Sept. 6, 1999.

Rebecca Robbins Raines, <u>Getting the Message Through: A Branch History of the U.S. Army Signal Corps.</u> U.S. Army Center of Military History, Washington, D.C., 1996.

Seelinger, Matthew J.,"124th Signal Battalion." U.S. Army Center of Military History, Washington, D.C.

SECTION THREE

DOCUMENTARIES ON NATIVE
WARRIORS TO WATCH ONLINE

I Am the Warrior*

Spanning centuries and generations, this $3^{1/2}$-minute video reflects the feeling shared by many American Indian veterans who consider service in the U.S. military to be the continuation of the unbroken warrior tradition of defending their native homelands, regardless of who governs the land or by what name it is called.

*The prologue of this book is a transcript of this video.

Watch Online at
vimeo.com/652518173
(Go to the Internet and enter this web address
in the URL field at the top of the page)

The Language of Victory:
American Indian Code Talkers
of WWI & WWII

This 22-minute documentary explores how Native American soldiers used their own tribal languages to develop and send coded messages during WWI and WWI – messages that were never deciphered by enemy forces and helped win two world wars.

Watch Online at
vimeo.com/218085990
(Go to the Internet and enter this web address
in the URL field at the top of the page)

Healing the Warrior's Heart
PBS Documentary

A Production of the
Western Folklife Center and Tribal Eye Productions

This one-hour groundbreaking TV documentary examines how traditional Native American warrior traditions and healing ceremonies are being used to help both Native and non-Native veterans suffering from PTSD.

Watch Online at

www.westernfolklife.org/healing-the-warriors-heart

(Go to the Internet and enter this web address
in the URL field at the top of the page)

The Story Behind "Soldier Boy"

Many years ago, the Grammy-winning Black Lodge Singers created a simple song titled "Soldier Boy" in the traditional style of Powwow songs. One of the most requested songs at Native American Powwows, it became famous world-wide with active-duty military personnel and veterans. In this short video, Black Lodge founder Kenny Scabbyrobe explains the song's creation and, along with his sons, performs the song.

Produced in association with Taki Telonidis and the Western Folklife Center. Edited by Gary Robinson

Watch Online at
vimeo.com/205143457
(Go to the Internet and enter this web address
in the URL field at the top of the page)

The American Indian Veteran
(music video)

The lyrics of this original song point to the fact that not enough attention has been paid to American Indian service in the US military. The proposed memorial, to be located in California's Riverside National Cemetery will be the only such memorial located within national cemetery grounds.

Song composed by Jimmy Ray Sells, Bob Regan, Don Goodman, and Don Loudner.
Video produced and edited by Gary Robinson.

Watch Online at
vimeo.com/234226559
(Go to the Internet and enter this web address
in the URL field at the top of the page)

SECTION FOUR

NATIVE AMERICAN HONOR GUARDS

Service, Sacrifice,
Tradition & Honor

Pictured are members of the Chumash Community Color Guard,
headquartered in Santa Ynez, California.

Native American Honor Guards

Service, Sacrifice, Tradition, Honor. These are words that come to mind when we think of our nation's soldiers, sailors, and airmen. And these are the values that many of our nation's veterans continue to demonstrate throughout their lives, long after their military service has ended.

One of the ways the values of service, sacrifice, tradition, and honor are maintained and represented by veterans is through volunteer participation in Color Guards all across America. But what is the role of a color guard, and what meaning do they have for those who participate in them? One such unit, the Chumash Community Color Guard, can help us discover answers to those questions.

Historically, trained armies of every nation carried regimental and national flags into battle. These flags, also known as "the colors," were protected by a specially assigned group of soldiers--the color guard. As long as the flags were visibly standing, soldiers on the battlefield knew their brothers-in-arms were still standing.

In modern times, the colors are no longer used in battle, but continue to be carried and presented at formal community events. In addition to the flag bearers, who are positioned in the center of the color guard, there are usually at least two members of the guard who carry rifles or sabres. This is a symbol that our flag and our nation are always protected.

The display of the American Flag is governed by United States laws to ensure that it will be treated with the respect due to the symbol of our nation.

Members of the Chumash Community Color Guard, for example, donate their time for several kinds of events, including posting the colors for conferences and gatherings, leading the grand entry at area powwows, carrying the colors at the front of parades, and burial services for veterans that can include Native drumming and singing. All of these activities are meant to bring honor to the Chumash Tribe and to veterans and their families.

As with other Native American groups, the Chumash Community Color Guard sometimes also carries an Eagle Staff in the front their procession. This symbolizes the unique status Native Americans have within this country, recognizes the cultural sacredness of the Eagle, and acknowledges the Eagle staff as the original flag of many Native Nations.

Nowhere are veterans more revered than within Native American communities. Native peoples have often sacrificed and suffered for a longer period of time in defense of their homelands than anyone else in this land. Powwows are a time our own native communities honor that special status and pay tribute to our native veterans.

One of the most sacred duties a color guard can perform is to officiate burial ceremonies for one of their fellow veterans. Veterans and their families deserve our deepest respect for the service they provided this nation.

Serving in a color guard is a proud and highly appreciated activity. It is the way many veterans choose to continue their practice of Service, Sacrifice, Tradition and Honor.

Members of the Blackfeet Nation's Honor Guard take their turn presenting a wreath at Arlington National Cemetery's Tomb of the Unknown Soldier.

Tomb of the Unknown Soldier, Arlington National Cemetery

SECTION FIVE:
THE FINAL WORD

Remembering and Honoring
American Indian Service
In the US Armed Forces

"The Gift" by Thomas Schomberg *"Warriors' Circle of Honor" by Harvey Pratt*

Bicoastal Memorials

It is more than fitting that American Indian Veterans Memorials were planned for both the east and west coasts of America.

Thanks to legislation passed by Congress in 2013, visitors to the nation's capital can visit the *Warriors' Circle of Honor* memorial plaza located on the grounds of the National Museum of the American Indian in Washington, DC, which was dedicated in 2022.

And, thanks to the dedicated work of the American Indian Alaska Native Veterans Memorial Committee, a memorial to Indigenous military service is becoming a reality within the sacred grounds of the Riverside National Cemetery in California, known as the "Arlington of the West."

Photo by Michael Perrin provided courtesy of the Dept. of Defense

*National Native American Veterans Memorial
Washington, D.C.

The National Native American Veterans Memorial opened on November 11, 2020, on the grounds of the National Museum of the American Indian (NMAI) in Washington, D.C. This tribute to Native military heroes recognized for the first time on a national scale the enduring and distinguished service of Native Americans in every branch of the US military.

An elevated stainless-steel circle balanced on an intricately carved stone drum, the design of the memorial is simple and powerful, timeless, and inclusive. The design incorporates water for ceremonies, benches for gathering and reflection, and four lances where veterans, family members, tribal leaders, and others can tie cloths for prayers and healing.

According to the NMAI website, the memorial creates an interactive space for gathering, remembrance, reflection, and healing. It welcomes and honors Native American veterans and their families, and also educates the public about their extraordinary contributions.

A distinguished group of Native and non-Native jurors unanimously selected the design concept *Warriors' Circle of Honor* by Harvey Pratt (Cheyenne and Arapaho of Oklahoma) from among more than 120 submissions. Pratt is a self-taught artist whose works include themes of Native American history and tradition and the Cheyenne people. A veteran himself, Pratt served in Vietnam from 1962 to 1965 as a US Marine in Air Rescue and Security stationed at Da Nang Air Base.

Why did the National Museum of the American Indian build this memorial? In 2013, Congress passed legislation authorizing the NMAI to create such a memorial to give "all Americans the opportunity to learn of the proud and courageous tradition of service of Native Americans in the Armed Forces of the United States," according to the legislation.

The legislation from Congress did not allow for any federal funding to be used in the construction of the memorial. Funding for the memorial came from individuals, organizations, and American tribes.

People can visit the memorial every day, 24 hours a day, on the grounds of the National Museum of the American Indian, Washington, DC.

This information came from the website of the National Museum of the American Indian - https://americanindian.si.edu/visit/washington/nnavm

Rendering of the planned American Indian Veterans Memorial

*The American Indian Veterans Memorial
--Riverside National Cemetery / California

In every foreign war, including the present conflicts that face our nation today, Native Americans have enlisted in larger numbers than any other group. Currently, studies show that one out of every four American Indian adult males have served or are serving in the U.S. Military. To honor the sacrifice these men (and women) gave to this country is the proposed American Indian Veterans Memorial.

During World War I, American Indians volunteered to serve in the military even though they had not been granted citizenship in their own country. As a result of their sacrifice and extraordinary patriotism, the U.S. Congress granted returning American Indian Veterans citizenship. This action later assisted in promoting citizenship for all Native Americans in 1924.

The proposed American Indian Veterans Memorial has been years in the making, a journey that began in 2005. The American Indian Alaska Native Veterans Memorial Committee has spent years organizing and fundraising to bring this memorial to full realization. This memorial was approved nearly a decade ago with the committee raising over a million dollars to have it built.

This American Indian Veterans Memorial monument will be the first national memorial at any of the Veterans Administration / National Cemetery Administration's 155 National Cemeteries to specifically honor the American Indian and Alaska Native veterans.

American flags fly over veterans graves at Riverside National Cemetery

The American Indian Veterans Memorial, as a small token of our nation's gratitude to the Native Americans, represents gratitude for more than 250 years of service and their sacrifice throughout our nation's history. World-renowned sculptor, A. Thomas Schomberg, designed and sculpted the memorial's centerpiece statue and named it *The Gift*.

Also, of significance, the Riverside National Cemetery sits on Indian land that was once home to the Cahuilla tribes. Five Indian governments and reservations are located nearby with 19 reservations (more in one county than any state) in adjacent San Diego County. California is home to 109 federally recognized tribal governments. The nearby city of Los Angeles has the largest population of urban Indians, making the Riverside National Cemetery geographically centered for American Indian and Alaskan Native Veterans.

The future site of the Memorial was dedicated September 25, 2021. As of this writing (February 2024), the entire memorial plaza is expected to be completed by the end of 2024.

This tribute to Native American warriors and their service in defense of this country will end with an extensive quote from Nikki Symington, a member of the American Indian Alaska Native Veterans Memorial Committee:

Standing 12 feet tall, a proud Indian wrapped in the American flag, *The Gift* is much more than a monument. It contains the pride and spirit of the Native Warrior, and memories of the flesh and blood lives of more than 100,000 of America's indigenous patriots from Alaska to Hawaii that served the United States in every military engagement since 1770.

In contrast to the many public perceptions of indigenous people, the sculpture counters images of drunken Indians, rich casino owners, or old women in blankets, selling trinkets to tourists. It, instead, says, *"See me-- the forgotten Indian, lost to time's passage, shunned, demeaned, imprisoned, and murdered. I am the proud*

Warrior Spirit of my ancestors, who defended our lost lands, our reservations and all of America's people without hesitation or fear for their lives. I stand unconquered, the courageous warrior erased from America's history.

The Gift tells the story of the Warrior Spirit--the cultural and ancestral heritage that gives Indians the resilience to survive the horrors of removal from their lands and homes, genocide, racial oppression, and economic depression throughout American history. Beginning with the arrival of European colonists, the indigenous people have been traumatized, and struggling with the consequences of poverty and identity loss.

Much more than an icon or mascot of sports teams, Halloween costumes, or a Thanksgiving myth, the Warrior Spirit that runs through Indian blood flows with fierce love for the land and country, family, and community.

Another view of the American Indian Veterans Memorial
Riverside National Cemetery – California

*For more information go to: rncsc.org/index.php/American-indian-memorial

APPENDIX

Emblems of the U.S. Armed Forces' service branches

OVERVIEW OF THE AMERICAN ARMED FORCES

Overview of the US Armed Forces

The United States Armed Forces are the military forces of the United States. The armed forces consists of six service branches: the Army, Marine Corps, Navy, Air Force, Space Force, and Coast Guard. All six armed services are among the eight uniformed services of the United States.

Each of the different military services is assigned a role and domain. The Army conducts land operations, while the Navy and Marine Corps conduct maritime operations, with the Marine Corps specializing in amphibious and maritime littoral operations in support of the Navy. The Air Force conducts air operations, and the Space Force conducts space operations. The Coast Guard is unique in that it both specializes in maritime operations and is also a law enforcement agency.

From their inception during the American Revolutionary War, the U.S. Armed Forces have played a decisive role in the country's history. They helped forge a sense of national unity and identity through victories in the early-19th-century First and Second Barbary Wars. They played a critical role in the territorial evolution of the U.S., including the American Civil War. The National Security Act of 1947 created the modern U.S. military framework, creating the National Military Establishment (later the Department of Defense or DoD) headed by the Secretary of Defense and creating both the U.S. Air Force and National Security Council; in 1949, an amendment merged the cabinet-level departments of the Army, Navy, and Air Force into the DoD.

The president of the U.S. is the commander-in-chief of the armed forces and forms military policy with the DoD and Department of Homeland Security (DHS), both federal executive departments, altogether acting as the principal organs by which military policy is carried out.

The U.S. Armed Forces are one of the largest military forces in terms of personnel. They draw their personnel from a large pool of professional volunteers. The U.S. has used military conscription, but not since 1973. The Selective Service System retains the power to conscript males, requiring the registration of all male citizens and residents living in the U.S. between the ages of 18 and 25.

The U.S. Armed Forces are considered the world's most powerful military. The military expenditure of the U.S. was US$877 billion in 2022, the highest in the world, accounting for 39% of the world's defense expenditures. The U.S. Armed Forces has significant capabilities in both defense and power projection due to its large budget, resulting in advanced and powerful technologies which enables a widespread deployment of the force around the world, including around 800 military bases outside the U.S. The U.S. Air Force is the world's largest air force, followed by the U.S. Army Aviation Branch. The U.S. Naval Air Forces is the fourth-largest air arm in the world and is the largest naval aviation service, while U.S. Marine Corps Aviation is the world's seventh-largest air arm. The U.S. Navy is the world's largest navy by tonnage. The U.S. Coast Guard is the world's 12th-largest maritime force. The U.S. Space Force is the world's only active independent space force.

History

The history of the U.S. Armed Forces dates back to 1775, with the creation of the Continental Army, even before the Declaration of Independence marked the establishment of the United States. The Continental Navy, established on 13 October 1775, and Continental Marines, established on 10 November 1775, were created in close succession by the Second Continental Congress in order to defend the new nation against the British Empire in the Revolutionary War.

These forces demobilized in 1784 after the Treaty of Paris ended the Revolutionary War. The Congress of the Confederation created the current United States Army on 3 June 1784. The United States Congress created the current United States Navy on 27 March 1794 and the current United States Marine Corps on 11 July 1798. All three services trace their origins to their respective Continental predecessors. The 1787 adoption of the Constitution gave Congress the power to "raise and support armies", to "provide and maintain a navy" and to "make rules for the government and regulation of the land and naval forces", as well as the power to declare war. The President of the United States is the U.S. Armed Forces' commander-in-chief.

The <u>United States Coast Guard</u> traces its origin to the formation of the <u>Revenue Cutter Service</u> on 4 August 1790, which merged with the <u>United States Life-Saving Service</u> on 28 January 1915 to establish the Coast Guard. The <u>United States Air Force</u> was established as an independent service on 18 September 1947; it traces its origin to the formation of the <u>Aeronautical Division, U.S. Signal Corps</u>, which was formed 1 August 1907 and was part of the <u>Army Air Forces</u> before being recognized as an independent service in the National Security Act of 1947. The <u>United States Public Health Service Commissioned Corps</u> was formerly considered to be a branch of the United States Armed Forces from 29 July 1945 until 3 July 1952, and is now one of the eight uniformed services of the United States.

The <u>United States Space Force</u> was established as an independent service on 20 December 2019. It is the sixth branch of the U.S. military and the first new branch in 72 years. The origin of the Space Force can be traced back to the <u>Air Force Space Command</u>, which was formed in September 1982 and was a <u>major command</u> of the United States Air Force.

Appendix A: Military Rank

Military rank is fairly confusing to most civilians, but this "pecking order" is all important to everyone in the armed forces. Although there are variations in each branch, all American military services use the same general command structure. The lowest category of rank is <u>enlisted personnel</u>, followed by <u>noncommissioned officers</u>, and finally <u>commissioned officers</u>. A branch-by-branch summary of the ranks is listed here, starting from the top down to help you better understand the role veterans played during military service. The name of each rank, its abbreviation and pay grade is included. In the pay grade column, "O" stands for Officer, "W" stands for Warrant Officer, and "E" stands for Enlisted.

Army		
<u>Commissioned Officers:</u>		
General of the Army (5 Star)	GOA	wartime only
General (4 Star)	GEN	O-10
Lieutenant General (3 Star)	LTG	O-9
Major General (2 Star)	MG	O-8
Brigadier General (1 Star)	BG	O-7
Colonel	COL	O-6
Lieutenant Colonel	LTC	O-5
Major	MAJ	O-4
Captain	PT	O-3
First Lieutenant	1LT	O-2
Second Lieutenant	2LT	O-1
<u>Warrant Officers:</u>		
Chief Warrant Officer 5	CW5	W-5
Chief Warrant Officer 4	CW4	W-4
Chief Warrant Officer 3	CW3	W-3
Chief Warrant Officer 2	CW2	W-2
Warrant Officer 1	CW1	W-1
<u>Enlisted:</u>		
Sgnt Major of the Army	SMA	E-9
Commander Sgnt Major	CSM	E-9
Sergeant Major	SGM	E-9
First Sergeant	1SG	E-8

Master Sergeant	MSG	E-8
Sergeant First Class	SFC	E-7
Staff Sergeant	SSG	E-6
Sergeant	SGT	E-5
Corporal	CPL	E-4
Specialist	SPC	E-4
Private First Class	PFC	E-3
Private	PV2	E-2
Private	PVT	E-1

Navy

Commissioned Officers:

Fleet Admiral (5 Star)	FADM	wartime only
Admiral (4 Star)	ADM	O-10
Vice Admiral (3 Star)	VADM	O-9
Rear Admiral (2 Star)	RADM(UH)	O-8
Rear Admiral (1 Star)	RADM(LH)	O-7
Captain	CAPT	O-6
Commander	CDR	O-5
Lieutenant Commander	LCDR	O-4
Lieutenant	LT	O-3
Lieutenant Junior Grade	LTJG	O-2
Ensign	ENS	O-1

Warrant Officers:

Chief Warrant Officer 5	CW05	W-5
Chief Warrant Officer 4	CW04	W-4
Chief Warrant Officer 3	CW03	W-3
Chief Warrant Officer 2	CW02	W-2
Warrant Officer 1	CW01	W-1

Enlisted:

Master Chief Petty Officer of the Navy	MCPON	E-9
Fleet/Command Master Chief Petty Officer	CMCPO	E-9
Master Chief Petty Officer	MCPO	E-9
Senior Chief Petty Officer	SCPO	E-8

Chief Petty Officer	CPO	E-7
Petty Officer First Class	PO1	E-6
Petty Officer Second Class	PO2	E-5
Petty Officer Third Class	PO3	E-4
Seaman	SN	E-3
Seaman Apprentice	SA	E-2
Seaman Recruit	SR	E-1

Marine Corps

Commissioned Officers:

General, Commandant of the Marine Corps (4 Star)	Gen.	O-10
Lieutenant General (3 Star)	Lt. Gen.	O-9
Major General (2 Star)	Maj. Gen.	O-8
Brigadier General (1 Star)	Brig. Gen.	O-7
Colonel	Col.	O-6
Lieutenant Colonel	Lt. Col.	O-5
Major	Maj.	O-4
Captain	Capt.	O-3
First Lieutenant	1st Lt.	O-2
Second Lieutenant	2nd Lt.	O-1

Warrant Officers:

Chief Warrant Officer 5	CW05	W-5
Chief Warrant Officer 4	CW04	W-4
Chief Warrant Officer 3	CW03	W-3
Chief Warrant Officer 2	CW02	W-2
Warrant Officer 1	CW01	W-1

Enlisted:

Sergeant Major of the Marine Corp	SgtMajMC	E-9
Sergeant Major	SgtMaj	E-9
Master Gunnery Sergeant	MGySgt	E-9
First Sergeant	1stSgt	E-8
Master Sergeant	MSgt	E-8
Gunnery Sergeant	GySgt	E-7

Staff Sergeant	SSgt	E-6
Sergeant	Sgt	E-5
Corporal	Cpl	E-4
Lance Corporal	LCpl	E-3
Private First Class	PFC	E-2
Private	PVT	E-1

Air Force

Commissioned Officers:

General of the Air Force (5 Star)	GOAF	wartime only
General (4 Star)	Gen.	O-10
Lieutenant General (3 Star)	Lt. Gen.	O-9
Major General (2 Star)	Maj. Gen.	O-8
Brigadier General (1 Star)	Brig. Gen.	O-7
Colonel	Col.	O-6
Lieutenant Colonel	Lt. Col.	O-5
Major	Maj.	O-4
Captain	Capt.	O-3
First Lieutenant	1st Lt.	O-2
Second Lieutenant	2nd Lt.	O-1

Enlisted:

Chief Master Sergeant AF	CMSAF	E-9
Command Chief Master Sergeant	CCM	E-9
First Sergeant	1st Sgt	E-9
Chief Master Sergeant	CMSgt	E-9
First Sergeant	1st SgtT	E-8
Senior Master Sergeant	SMSgt	E-8
First Sergeant	1st Sgt	E-7
Master Sergeant	MSgt.	E-7
Technical Sergeant	TSgt.	E-6
Staff Sergeant	SSgt.	E-5
Senior Airman	SrA	E-4
Airman First Class	A1C	E-3
Airman Basic	Amn	E-2
Airman Basic	AB	E-1

Coast Guard

Commissioned Officers:

Admiral, Commandant of the Coast Guard (4 Star)	ADM	O-10
Vice Admiral (3 Star)	VADM	O-9
Rear Admiral (2 Star)	RADM(UH)	O-8
Rear Admiral (1 Star)	RADM(LH)	O-7
Captain	CAPT	O-6
Commander	CDR	O-5
Lieutenant Commander	LCDR	O-4
Lieutenant	LT	O-3
Lieutenant (Junior Grade)	LTJG	O-2
Ensign	ENS	O-1

Warrant Officers:

Chief Warrant Officer 4	CW04	W-4
Chief Warrant Officer 3	CW03	W-3
Chief Warrant Officer 2	CW02	W-2

Enlisted:

Master Chief Petty Officer of the Coast Guard	MCPOCG	E-9
Fleet/Command Master Chief Petty Officer	CMCPO	E-9
Master Chief Petty Officer	MCPO	E-9
Senior Chief Petty Officer	SCPO	E-8
Chief Petty Officer	CPO	E-7
Petty Officer First Class	PO1	E-6
Petty Officer Second Class	PO2	E-5
Petty Officer Third Class	PO3	E-4
Airman, Fireman or Seaman	SN	E-3
Airman, Fireman or Seaman Apprentice	SA	E-2
Airman, Fireman or Seaman Recruit	SR	E-1

*Source: <u>A Civilian's Guide to the U.S. Military</u>

Appendix B: Medals, Decorations and Ribbons

There are several medals and awards given by the military for bravery, service, or skill. Awards called *decorations* are given for valor or meritorious service. They are traditionally in the shape of a circle, star, cross, hexagon or some heraldic design. Each campaign or war has a unique *ribbon* to denote service in that event. They are worn individually or in a bar formed of several. There are other devices worn on the ribbon bar to indicate additional awards, campaigns or special service. The term *badge* is often used when indicating a learned skill. Individuals may also wear small *devices* on the ribbon bar to indicate additional awards, campaigns or special service. As noted in the pages of this book, many Chumash veterans have earned decorations and ribbons for their service, skills and various individual deeds. Beginning with the highest medal offered, here are the military's most important decorations.

Medal of Honor – Only the <u>President</u> can award this medal, which was initially created in 1861. Since then, the requirements for awarding this medal have gone through a series of increasingly stringent revisions. Since 1963, it is only given for an act of bravery or self-sacrifice so conspicuous as to clearly distinguish the individual above his comrades, representing gallantry well beyond the call of duty. At least two eye witnesses must verify the action. Unlike all other medals, the Medal of Honor is worn around the neck on a ribbon.

Distinguished Service Cross (Army), **Navy Cross**, and **Air Force Cross** – These are presented to individuals who <u>display extraordinary heroism</u> while engaged in a conflict with an enemy. The act of heroism must clearly set the person apart from comrades under similar circumstances.

Distinguished Service Medal – This is awarded to any person who has distinguished himself by exceptionally meritorious service to the United States government in a duty of great responsibility during <u>war or peace</u> times.

Silver Star – This, the <u>third highest award</u> designated for heroism in combat, was created in 1918. The first Silver Star was awarded to General Douglas MacArthur in 1932.

Legion of Merit – Established by Congress in 1942, this medal is awarded for exceptionally meritorious conduct <u>above</u> the normal performance of duties and may accrues through a succession of important positions.

Distinguished Flying Cross – Created in 1927, this award is presented to those who distinguish themselves during aerial combat. Heroic acts must include voluntary action in the face of danger, well above the actions of others at the same time.

Bronze Star – This medal is given to individuals who distinguish themselves by heroism, outstanding achievement, or meritorious service in any arena except aerial flight. It was established in 1944.

Soldier's Medal for Valor - The Soldier's Medal is awarded to any person of the Armed Forces of the United States or of a friendly foreign nation who, while serving in any capacity with the Army of the United States, has distinguished himself or herself by heroism not involving actual conflict with an enemy.

Purple Heart – George Washington created the "Badge of Military Merit" in 1782, and this award was revived by the War Department in 1932 as the Purple Heart. It differs from all other decorations in that an individual is not recommended for the decoration, but becomes entitled to receive it upon being wounded or killed under certain circumstances.

Meritorious Service Medal – This is awarded to any member of the U.S. Armed Forces or member of the Armed Forces of a friendly nation who, while serving in a noncombat area, has distinguished himself or herself by outstanding achievement or service.

The Air Medal – Ranked just below the Distinguished Flying Cross, the Air Medal is given to individuals who display heroism while engaged in aerial flight.

Other Medals – Each branch of service has a medal that may be awarded to members for heroism not involving actual conflict with the enemy. They rank above the Bronze Star and include the Army's "Soldiers Medal," the Navy Medal, the Marine Corps Medal and the Air Force "Airman's Medal."

Source: A Civilian's Guide to the U.S. Military